CRC Press
Computer Engineering Series

Series Editor
Udo W. Pooch
Texas A&M University

Algorithms and Data Structure in C++
Alan Parker, Georgia Institute of Technology

Computer System and Network Security
Gregory B. White, United States Air Force Academy
Eric A. Fisch, Texas A&M University
Udo W. Pooch, Texas A&M University

Discrete Event Simulation: A Practical Approach
Udo W. Pooch, Texas A&M University
James A. Wall, Simulation Consultant

Handbook of Software Engineering
Udo W. Pooch, Texas A&M University

Microprocessor-Based Parallel Architecture
for Reliable Digital Signal Processing Systems
Alan D. George, Florida State University
Lois Wright Hawkes, Florida State University

Spicey Circuits: Elements of Computer-Aided
Circuit Analysis
Rahul Chattergy, University of Hawaii

Telecommunications and Networking
Udo W. Pooch, Texas A&M University
Denis P. Machuel, Telecommunications Consultant
John T. McCahn, Networking Consultant

Computer System
and Network Security

Gregory B. White
United States Air Force Academy[†]
Eric A. Fisch
Texas A&M University
Udo W. Pooch
Texas A&M University

[†]The views expressed in this book are those of the authors and not necessarily those of the United States Air Force or the Department of Defense.

SunOS and Solaris are trademarks of Sun Microsystems Incorporated
UNIX® is a registered trademark of UNIX System Laboratories
VAX and VMS is a trademark of Digital Equipment Corporation

CRC Press
Boca Raton   New York   London   Tokyo

Library of Congress Cataloging-in-Publication Data

White, Gregory B.
  Computer system and network security / Gregory B. White, Eric A. Fisch, Udo W. Pooch
      p. cm.
  Includes bibliographical references and index.
  ISBN 0-8493-7179-1 (hardcover : alk. paper)
  1. Computer security. 2. Computer networks—Security measures.
  I. Fisch, Eric A.   II. Pooch, Udo W., 1944-   . III. Title.
  QA76.9.A25W45 1995
  005.8—dc20   95-4905
                                                                                                  CIP

PREFACE

The objective of this text is to provide a source suitable not only for a college course on computer security but one useful for security professionals in the field as well. Computer security, which was once considered synonymous with "unnecessary overhead", is now recognized as an important aspect of operating systems and networks. The public perception of a computer intrusion has also changed. What was once seen as just a nuisance perpetuated by high school students and targeted at government agencies, is now slowly being seen as the actions of "road bandits" along the information superhighway. No longer does one have to go to technical or trade journals to read about computer security incidents; their impact is now considered so widespread and general that all major newspapers and periodicals have featured articles on various aspects of computer security. Terms such as *encryption, viruses, worms,* and *hacking* are no longer confined to discussions between computer professionals but are now heard in everyday conversations.

While the specter of security has made itself visible to the general public, there is still much misconception about what computer security entails, how much is needed, what is appropriate, and when to apply it. While the danger of threats such as viruses or hackers is indeed real, the picture is not as bleak as some may perceive from press reports. There are a number of basic actions that can be performed to protect computer systems and networks from all but the most talented and persistent of intruders. While some may claim this is not enough—that we need to be able to fully protect our systems (which, in fact can be done by completely limiting access)—this is neither realistic nor needed. As we accept a certain amount of latitude in our physical environment, the same should be true for our "cyber-environment". For example, one locks his front door to keep intruders out of his home, but a determined thief could still drive a car through the walls to gain access. We accept this level of risk because the likelihood it will occur is low. The same should be true of our computer systems. The problem today involves understanding the threats to our computer systems and knowing what we can do to protect the systems. It is these problems that are addressed in this text.

This book is suitable as a general reference on computer security for the security practitioner or as a general text for a course on system security at the senior undergraduate or graduate level. This book is designed to offer a basic understanding of the issues and elements involved in securing computer systems and networks. A basic understanding of computer operating systems is required as background. An understanding of or experience with the UNIX operating system would also be useful as a number of the examples cited involve this widely used system.

Chapter 1 provides an introduction to the field of computer security and some of the relevant issues. This general introduction continues in Chapter 2 with a discussion of the threats to computer systems, the risks that are posed by these threats, and the use of risk analysis for determining the appropriate protections to employ.

Chapter 3 provides a background to what is required to have a secure computer system and how such a system is designed. Chapters 4 through 7 discuss, in detail, several of these components: Security Models, User Authentication, Access and Information Flow Controls, and Auditing and Intrusion Detection.

Chapter 8 introduces a topic for which relatively little has been written (in terms of automated approaches to the problem and its solution) but which is concerned with one of the most important aspects of an organization's security policy, Damage Control and Assessment.

Chapter 9 addresses the topic of Network Security and how it differs from single host security. Securing networks is not just a matter of extending the practices used for one machine to many but also entails additional elements that are not a concern at the single host level.

Chapter 10 discusses one method in wide use to secure computer systems and networks that are connected to large, wide area networks and internetworks such as the Internet. This method involves the construction of a Firewall that will filter the traffic allowed to access a network or individual host.

Chapter 11 discusses Database Security and its unique requirements. While many of the basic security concepts are the same for both databases and operating systems, the goal of most databases, to provide easily accessible information, introduces additional security concerns which must be addressed.

Chapter 12 provides a background to cryptography. It begins with a discussion of general purpose cryptographic techniques and then discusses the application of cryptography to digital communications.

Various types of Malicious Software are discussed at several points in the text. Chapter 13, however, goes into more depth in this area of concern. Viruses, Worms, and Trojan Horses are examined as well as methods to address each of these threats.

Chapter 14 provides a brief explanation of the various governmental security standards found in use today. Their history, application, and probable future are also addressed.

Chapter 15 presents studies of several incidents that have occurred which illustrate the problems and potential for harm when security fails. They also serve to illustrate the difficulty in protecting against concerted attacks and in discovering the culprits behind such attacks.

Finally, we close the text with an appendix on *Information Warfare*, a term that refers to what many believe to be the newest form of combat and which some believe will be the warfare of choice for terrorists in the future.

In preparing this text, we have attempted to provide a broad coverage of the topics associated with computer and network security. We have not gone into detail on any single subject found in this text. Indeed, each chapter could be extended to become a textbook in itself. Instead, we have included the detail necessary to provide the readers with an understanding of the problems associated with the many aspects of security which will then, hopefully, allow them to better secure the networks and computer systems they are, or will be, responsible for. We include at the end of each chapter not only a list of the references cited in the chapter but an extended bibliography as well. We chose not to place all citations in a section at the end of the book as we wanted to provide the readers the ability to easily find useful references for a specific topic they might find of interest.

We close this Preface with an acknowledgment of those who have helped make this book possible. Many individuals have contributed to this text and we would be remiss if we were to not take the time to recognize some of them. We offer a special thanks to Ellen Mitchell, David Hess, and Doug Schales for the time they spent in reviewing the manuscript and for the helpful comments they offered. We also acknowledge the Department of Computer Science at Texas A&M University for its support and stimulating environment in which to write this book. Our final acknowledgments go to the many researchers, practitioners, and colleagues who have contributed to the development of this fast growing field. As always we thank all contributors, named or otherwise, while acknowledging our responsibility for the accuracy of that which has been included in this text.

Gregory B. White
Eric A. Fisch
Udo W. Pooch
College Station, Texas

TABLE OF CONTENTS

Chapter 1	**Fundamentals of Computer Security** 1

1.1	Objectives of Computer Security................................2
1.2	Issues Involved in Computer Security 3
1.3	Privacy and Ethics...5
1.4	Exercises...6
1.5	References...7
1.6	Extended Bibliography...7

Chapter 2	**Risk Analysis** 9

2.1	Theory 10
2.1.1	Possible Loss (L) 11
2.1.2	Probability of Loss Occurrence (P) 12
2.1.3	Burden of Preventing Loss (B)................................13
2.1.4	Applying the Risk Analysis Equation 13
2.2	Risk Analysis in Computer Security..........................15
2.2.1	Terminology 15
2.2.2	Application..18
2.3	Summary...21
2.4	Exercises...21
2.5	References...22
2.6	Extended Bibliography...23

Chapter 3	**Developing Secure Computer Systems**...................... 25

3.1	External Security Measures.....................................25
3.2	Structure of a Computer System...............................27
3.3	Secure Computer System Issues...............................29
3.4	Summary...33
3.5	Exercises...34
3.6	References...34
3.7	Extended Bibliography...35

Chapter 4	**Security Models** 37

4.1	Specification and Verification..................................37
4.2	Security Models...38
4.2.1	Bell and LaPadula 39
4.2.2	Clark-Wilson...41
4.2.3	Goguen-Meseguer 44
4.3	TCSEC 45

4.3.1	Discretionary Access Requirements	46
4.3.2	Mandatory Access Requirements	47
4.4	Summary	48
4.5	Exercises	49
4.6	References	49
4.7	Extended Bibliography	50

Chapter 5   User Authentication **53**

5.1	Authentication Objectives	53
5.2	Authentication Methods	54
5.2.1	Informational Keys	54
5.2.1.1	Passwords	54
5.2.1.2	Questionnaires	55
5.2.2	Physical Keys	56
5.2.2.1	Magnetic Cards	56
5.2.2.2	Smartcards	58
5.2.2.3	Calculators	59
5.2.3	Biometric Keys	60
5.2.3.1	Voice Prints	60
5.2.3.2	Fingerprint	62
5.2.3.3	Retinal Prints	65
5.2.3.4	Facial Profiles	66
5.2.3.5	Hand Geometry	67
5.2.3.6	Signature Analysis	69
5.3	Summary	70
5.4	Exercises	71
5.5	References	71
5.6	Extended Bibliography	74

Chapter 6   Access and Information Flow Controls **75**

6.1	File Passwords	77
6.2	Capabilities Based	78
6.3	Access Control Lists	79
6.4	Protection Bits	82
6.5	Controls for Mandatory Access	83
6.6	Trojan Horses	84
6.7	Summary	86
6.8	Exercises	87
6.9	References	88
6.10	Extended Bibliography	88

Chapter 7   Auditing and Intrusion Detection **91**

7.1	Audit Trail Features	91
7.2	Intrusion Detection Systems	93
7.2.1	User Profiling	95

7.2.2	Intruder Profiling	96
7.2.3	Signature Analysis	96
7.2.4	Action Based	97
7.2.5	IDES	97
7.2.6	MIDAS	100
7.2.7	Haystack	101
7.3	Network Intrusion Detection	103
7.3.1	Network Attack Characteristics	103
7.3.2	NSM	104
7.3.3	DIDS	105
7.3.4	NADIR	107
7.3.5	CSM	107
7.4	Monitoring and the Law	109
7.5	Summary	110
7.6	Exercises	110
7.7	References	111
7.8	Extended Bibliography	113

Chapter 8   Damage Control and Assessment   117

8.1	Damage Control	118
8.1.1	Inform the Authorities	118
8.1.2	Backup System Data	119
8.1.3	Remove the Intruder	120
8.1.4	Contain and Monitor the Intruder	121
8.1.5	Lock Stolen User Accounts	122
8.1.6	Require Additional Authentication	122
8.2	Damage Assessment	123
8.2.1	Attack Recovery	124
8.2.1.1	Examine Audit Trails	124
8.2.1.2	Identify Stolen Accounts and Data	126
8.2.1.3	Locate System Modifications	127
8.2.1.4	System Restoration	129
8.2.2	Damage Prevention	129
8.2.2.1	Patch Security Holes	129
8.2.2.2	Lock Stolen User Accounts	130
8.2.2.3	Change Passwords	131
8.2.2.4	Employ Shadow Password Files	132
8.2.2.5	Backup Information	133
8.2.2.6	Reduce Network Services	134
8.3	Summary	135
8.4	Exercises	136
8.5	References	136
8.6	Extended Bibliography	137

Chapter 9   Network Security   139

| 9.1 | Network Fundamentals | 139 |

9.2	Network Security Issues	143
9.2.1	Basic Network Security Objectives and Threats	144
9.2.2	Security Services	145
9.3	The Trusted Network Interpretation	149
9.3.1	TNI Security Service	150
9.3.2	AIS Interconnection Issues	153
9.4	Distributed Systems Security	155
9.5	Summary	157
9.6	Exercises	158
9.7	References	159
9.8	Extended Bibliography	159

Chapter 10   Firewalls   163

10.1	Simple Damage Limiting Approaches	163
10.2	Network Firewalls	164
10.2.1	Packet Filtering Gateways	165
10.2.2	Circuit Level Gateways	169
10.2.3	Application-Level Gateways	170
10.3	Firewall Costs and Effectiveness	170
10.4	Sample Security Packages	172
10.5	Summary	174
10.6	Exercises	175
10.7	References	175
10.8	Extended Bibliography	176

Chapter 11   Database Security   179

11.1	Database Management System Primer	179
11.2	DBMS Vulnerabilities and Responses	181
11.2.1	Inference	181
11.2.2	Aggregation	182
11.2.2.1	Inference Aggregation	182
11.2.2.2	Cardinal Aggregation	183
11.2.3	Data Integrity	184
11.2.4	Trojan Horses	186
11.3	Summary	187
11.4	Exercises	188
11.5	References	188
11.6	Extended Bibliography	191

Chapter 12   Cryptography   193

12.1	Substitution Ciphers	194
12.1.1	Caesar Cipher	194
12.1.2	ROT13	195
12.1.3	Substitution Cipher Variations	195
12.1.4	Vigenere Ciphers	197

12.1.5	One Time Pads	200
12.2	Transposition Ciphers	201
12.3	Encrypting Digital Communication	202
12.3.1	DES	203
12.3.2	IDEA	206
12.3.3	Key Escrow	208
12.3.4	Public Key Cryptography	210
12.3.4.1	Diffie-Hellman Algorithm	210
12.3.4.2	Knapsack Algorithms	211
12.3.4.3	RSA	213
12.3.5	Digital Signatures	215
12.3.5.1	The Digital Signature Standard (DSS)	216
12.3.5.2	ESIGN	216
12.4	Summary	217
12.5	Exercises	218
12.6	References	219
12.7	Extended Bibliography	220

Chapter 13 **Malicious Code** **225**

13.1	Viruses	225
13.1.1	Infection	226
13.1.2	Theory behind Viruses	227
13.1.3	Prevention, Detection, and Removal	231
13.1.3.1	Prevention and Detection	232
13.1.3.2	Disinfection	234
13.2	Worms	235
13.2.1	Infection	235
13.2.2	Theory of Worms	236
13.2.3	Prevention and Removal	240
13.2.3.1	Preventing Worm Attacks	240
13.2.3.2	Worm Removal and System Recovery	240
13.3	Trojan Horses	241
13.3.1	Receiving Trojan Horses	242
13.3.2	Theory of Trojan Horses	243
13.3.3	Prevention, Detection, and Removal	244
13.3.3.1	Trojan Horse Prevention and Detection	245
13.3.3.2	Trojan Horse Removal	246
13.4	Summary	247
13.5	Exercises	247
13.6	References	248
13.7	Extended Bibliography	249

Chapter 14 **Government-Based Security Standards** **251**

14.1	The History of Security Standards	252
14.2	The Trusted Computer System Evaluation Criteria	253

14.3   The Information Technology Security
Evaluation Criteria 255
14.4   The Canadian Trusted Computer Product
Evaluation Criteria 257
14.5   The Federal Criteria..259
14.6   The Common Criteria 261
14.7   Summary..263
14.8   Exercises..263
14.9   References..263
14.10   Extended Bibliography..265

Chapter 15   Case Studies 267

15.1   The Hannover Hackers...267
15.2   An Evening With Berferd 271
15.3   The Internet Worm 275
15.4   Summary..277
15.5   Exercises..278
15.6   References..278
15.7   Extended Bibliography..279

Appendix A   Information Warfare 281

A.1   Levels of Information Warfare.................................283
A.2   Weapons of Information Warfare 285
A.3   Summary..287
A.4   Exercises..288
A.5   References..288
A.6   Extended Bibliography..290

Index 291

1

FUNDAMENTALS OF COMPUTER SECURITY

"**Undetected Theft of Credit-Card Data Raises Concern About On-Line Security**" *The Wall Street Journal,* Friday, February 17, 1995.

"**Computer Experts See Hackers Gaining An Upper Hand in Fight Over Security**" *The Wall Street Journal,* Tuesday, January 24, 1995.

"**Internet Web Found to Have Security Lapse**" *The Wall Street Journal,* Tuesday, February 21, 1995.

Computers have become commonplace in today's society. They are used in banking for everyday actions such as Electronic Funds Transfer (EFT) and Automated Teller Machine (ATM) transactions. They are used to store a wide range of information about us such as medical, credit, and financial data. They are used to help fly the commercial aircrafts we travel in and to operate the cars we drive. They store trade secrets for corporations and military and diplomatic secrets for governments. They are used to help control our telephone communication networks and to process our paychecks. It can be truly said that everyone's life has somehow been touched by a computer.

With this tremendous amount of interaction comes a comparable level of responsibility for those who control these computers. It is of the utmost importance that the records computers contain paint an accurate picture of who we are. We have probably all heard stories about individuals who have had their credit rating inadvertently affected by a mistake in one of these systems. Mistakes of this kind can affect our ability to buy a home or car, or can even lead to legal actions against us until the mistake has been corrected. Even more important than the computers that control our financial well-being are those that are used in critical applications that can affect our physical well-being. The modern hospital is filled with advanced medical equipment run by or with the aid of computers. Should one of these machines malfunction, it could result in a loss of life.

The unintentional error in a program or entry in a database are not the only problems that we must worry about; we must also be concerned with the intentional misuse of these computer systems. Dishonest employees may try to modify account information in order to funnel funds or goods to themselves. Companies may attempt to access marketing plans and trade secrets of rivals in order to gain a sales advantage. Individuals who feel they have been treated unfairly or have been offended in some way may attempt to seek revenge by attacking another person's financial or credit records. It is these and similar problems that **Computer System and Network Security** is concerned with.

1.1   Objectives of Computer Security

When computers were first developed, computer security was simply a matter of providing the physical protection mechanisms to limit access to all but a few authorized individuals. With today's worldwide networks, however, computer security involves much more. Despite its expanded nature and increased importance, computer security today has the same basic objectives as forty years ago. The three fundamental objectives of computer security are:

- **Confidentiality**
- **Integrity**
- **Availability**

Confidentiality requires that the data in a computer system, as well as the data transmitted between computer systems, be revealed only to authorized individuals. This may not only include protection from unauthorized disclosure of the actual data, but the fact that certain data even exists. The fact that an individual has a criminal record, for example, is often just as important as the details of the crime committed.

Integrity stipulates that the data in a computer system, as well as the data transmitted between computer systems, be free from unauthorized modification or deletion. It also includes the unauthorized creation of data. The unauthorized insertion of false credit records, for example, could jeopardize an individual's ability to obtain credit. It is important that records such as these are only created, modified, or deleted by authorized individuals and that this occurs in a prescribed manner.

The objective of availability requires that the authorized users of the computer systems and communications media not be denied access when access is desired. This objective is also associated with the concept of *denial of service* which is manifested by a reduction in system performance. This does not include normal degradation of the system performance during peak operating periods but rather specific acts taken by attackers to influence the ability of authorized users to access the system.

Most research in computer security has been in the area of confidentiality. The historical reason for this is that the majority of funding for computer security has been supplied by the federal government whose chief concern has always been maintaining the secrecy of its classified documents. The problems caused by the destruction or modification of data have always taken a back seat to the one of disclosure. Fortunately for proponents of integrity issues, the safeguards and techniques used to implement confidentiality are closely related to that of integrity. If a person can't see the data, it will generally also be hard to destroy or modify.

In addition to the three fundamental objectives already mentioned, several other secondary objectives are frequently listed including *authorized use*, *message authentication*, and *nonrepudiation*. Authorized use simply means that only authorized individuals may use the computer system or its peripherals and then only in a prescribed manner. Message authentication and nonrepudiation are both associated with the widespread use of computer networks. Often when a message is received we want to be sure that the individual who the system claims sent the message did indeed transmit it. This is message authentication. At other times we want to know that an individual did receive a message that was transmitted. This is nonrepudiation. Taken together, all of these objectives serve to provide the needed foundation for computer and network security.

1.2   Issues Involved in Computer Security

The objectives of computer security seem simple enough yet a foolproof implementation still eludes us. The reason for this is that, fundamentally, securing a computer system is a complex task. There are several factors which make securing a computer system or network hard. These include:

- Secure operating systems involve a tremendous amount of software and large software projects have historically proven to be nearly impossible to implement error-free.
- Security is often not included in the originally designed or implemented system but is added later in the project.
- Security costs and often "gets in the way".
- Very often the problem lies with the people who use the system and not in the technology.

The first issue is a common one in computer science. Anyone who has ever written software knows how hard it is to create a program that is error-free. The larger the program the more this is true. For a "normal" program, the existence of a few bugs can generally be tolerated as the users simply learn to live with the problem or to somehow work around them. In security, however, the existence of a single error can result in a hole through which intruders can gain access to the system. This is clearly not acceptable. For security then, the existence of a single error is often fatal. In addition, an intruder does not have to find all holes that exist in an operating system in order to break in, only one hole is required. The programmer responsible for the operating system, however, needs to worry about all holes in order to plug them.

The second issue is a financial one. Most projects in the government and industry operate under very tight budgetary constraints. When the purchase or development of a computer system is contemplated, the chief concern will be whether the system will be able to accomplish the task it was intended to perform. Secondary concerns generally are centered around issues such as how much will the system cost and how fast will it accomplish the required task. Seldom is security considered. In fact, security is often not considered until later when the occurrence of a security incident forces the issue. Attempting to retrofit security is an expensive process, both in terms of money and labor.

Another issue in implementing security is that it is often viewed as "getting in the way" of the user. For example, many computer operating systems provide the capability to record the actions of all users on the system. The resulting *audit trail* may occupy a tremendous amount of disk space and recording the actions, especially if any analysis of the data is performed, takes valuable CPU time away from other processes. This security feature is thus often viewed as an expensive overhead that can be done without. Another example of a security feature that is often viewed by users as bothersome is passwords. Passwords are used to control access to the computer system and its data. They are analogous in many respects to a combination for a safe and just like the combination, they are often hard to remember. Often users are allowed to select their own password to use. This leads to an interesting dilemma. If a user picks a password that is easy to remember, then it is probably also easy for an intruder to guess. This defeats the purpose of the password in the first place. If, on the other hand, a totally random sequence of characters is chosen for the password, then it is hard to guess but also hard for the authorized user to remember. If we make it easy for the authorized users, then we make it easier for the intruders. If we make it hard for the intruders, then we also make it hard for the authorized users. Thus security, in terms of passwords, is often viewed as either worthless or cumbersome.

One final issue that must be considered in any discussion on computer security is that often the problem is not technology, but people. The majority of computer crimes committed by "insiders" (i.e., authorized users) do not involve any violation of the system's security rules. Instead they involve an abuse of the individual's authority which has been granted to them in order that they may perform their assigned job. This can be illustrated by examining what occurred in one office of an agency of the Federal Government. An employee discovered that the computer system she worked with would allow an individual who had been receiving benefits to be "resurrected" should the individual inadvertently be listed as deceased (through some clerical error). This individual could then be issued a special check to retroactively provide for the benefits that should have been received while the individual was listed as deceased. The employee decided to take advantage of this system and collected a series of names of people who had been dead for at least five years. She then used the resurrection feature to generate a check for each, which she had sent to her own post office box. After the check was issued, she changed the individual's records back to show them as deceased [1.1]. This was not a case of an unauthorized intruder gaining access to a system to perpetrate a crime but rather an authorized individual abusing her authorized permissions. To prevent this sort of crime involves a different approach to computer security than does protecting a computer system or network from an unauthorized individual attempting to gain access.

1.3 Privacy and Ethics

An issue related to computer security provides an interesting paradox involving the joint concerns of privacy and ethics. One of the reasons we are so concerned with the security of computer systems is to maintain the privacy of the individuals whose records the computers maintain. This is a reasonable desire which few, if any, would argue with. If we lived in a society where everyone acted in an ethical manner we would not have a problem. Unfortunately, we live in a society where the actions of a few require certain precautions. This is really no different than the fact that we must lock our homes because a small percentage in our society would take advantage of a more trusting environment. The paradox in computer security occurs when we try to enforce what individual ethics have failed to do. To illustrate this point, consider a common technique used by administrators. One way suggested to ensure the confidentiality and integrity of individual records is to monitor the actions of those who have access to the system. The extent of this monitoring for security purposes has sometimes extended so far as to include the reading of an individual's electronic mail to ensure that no unauthorized activity is occurring. The action of looking through an individual's U.S. Postal Service mail is strictly regulated by law and can only be done under very specific circumstances. Many, however, see no problem with the monitoring of an individual's electronic mail. We must be sure that we are not enforcing the privacy of the records maintained on the system at the cost of the privacy of the users. It should be noted that this is a drastic simplification of a very complex issue. Nevertheless, as we consider the various techniques discussed in this text, we should also consider our actions and how, in the name of security, these actions affect the rights and privacy of all individuals involved.

1.4   Exercises

1.1   Try to create a list of jobs in today's society that do not somehow involve the use of a computer. Don't forget modern telephone switching is controlled by computers or the more mundane but commonplace applications such as word processors which have all but eliminated the use of typewriters in today's business world.

1.2   What are the privacy implications of local merchants maintaining a database of customers and their purchases? What if the business is a grocery store that sells alcoholic beverages or a bookstore that sells pornographic magazines? What if the business rents video tapes? Does it matter if this type of information about an individual becomes public knowledge?

1.3   Many of the individuals who break into computer systems never cause any damage but claim to do it only because of the intellectual challenge involved. In addition, a number claim that they actually are helping computer and network security professionals by revealing holes or weaknesses in security packages. Comment on these assertions.

1.4   Computer networks have been used for a variety of illegal activities including the transmission of child pornography. Individuals who send and receive these files often encrypt (disguise) them so it isn't obvious what they contain. Some law enforcement agencies want to restrict the use of encryption schemes so that they can uncover these (and other) criminal activities and to be able to obtain the evidence necessary to convict the individuals involved. Is this a valid request by our law enforcement agencies or is this an infringement on our right to privacy? How is it helpful to consider the rules that govern U.S. Postal Service mail when considering this problem? What about laws governing wiretaps and electronic surveillance?

1.5   References

1.1   Martin, L., "Unethical 'Computer' Behavior: Who is Responsible?",
         Proceedings of the 12th National Computer Security Conference,
         Baltimore, Maryland, October 1989, pp. 531-541.

1.6   Extended Bibliography

1.2   Campbell, M., "Security and Privacy: Issues of Professional Ethics",
         Proceedings of the 10th National Computer Security Conference,
         Gaithersburg, Maryland, September 1987, pp. 326-333.

1.3   DeMaio, H., "Information Ethics, A Practical Approach", *Proceedings of the
         12th National Computer Security Conference*, Baltimore, Maryland, October
         1989, pp. 630-633.

1.4   Gasser, M., *Building a Secure Computer System*, Van Nostrand Reinhold,
         New York, New York, 1988.

1.5   Perry, T. and Wallich, P., "Can Computer Crime Be Stopped?", *IEEE
         Spectrum*, Vol. 21, No. 5, May 1984, pp. 34-45.

1.6   Schou, C. D. and Kilpatrick, J.A., "Information Security: Can Ethics Make
         a Difference?", *Proceedings of the 14th National Computer Security
         Conference*, Washington, DC, October 1991, pp. 305-312.

1.7   Shankar, K.S., "The Total Computer Security Problem", *Computer*, Vol.
         10, No. 6, June 1977, pp. 50-73.

1.8   Turn, R. and Ware, W.H., "Privacy and Security Issues in Information
         Systems", *IEEE Transactions on Computers*, Vol. C-25, No. 12, December
         1976, pp. 1353-1361.

2

RISK ANALYSIS

Computer security risk analysis is the process of identifying and evaluating the risk of being successfully attacked and suffering a loss of data, time, and person-hours versus the cost of preventing such a loss. The goals of performing this process are to determine the strength of a computer system's security and make a rational decision as to how the security of the system can and should be improved. The benefits of performing a security risk analysis are not just the end results of improving the security of a system. The benefits also include a better understanding of a system and its flaws. Table 2.1 provides a list of the information gained by performing a risk analysis. Note that much of the terminology in the table requires definition, if not clarification. This is done in the sections that follow.

Table 2.1 Information gained by performing a computer security risk analysis

```
• Precise determination of an organization's
  sensitive assets
• Identification of system threats
• Identification of specific system
  vulnerabilities
• Identification of possible losses
• Identification of probability of a loss
  occurrence
• Derivation of effective losses countermeasures
• Identification of possible security safeguards
• Implementation of the cost effective
  security system
```

Risk analysis is not unique to computer science, let alone computer security. As will be demonstrated, applying risk analysis to the computer security field is a matter of associating, or relating, the ideas used in computer security to the general concepts of risk analysis. This association includes the terminology, risk standards, and risk tolerances.

2.1 Theory

Risk analysis is a byproduct of the many decisions a person makes each and every day. The analysis occurs in such mundane decisions as crossing the street or driving to the supermarket, and in more significant decisions such as purchasing a new car or home. Whether a rational decision maker is aware of the specific mental balancing performed in making a decision, the concept remains the same: weigh the benefit of performing an action to the possible risks involved. In each of the actions mentioned earlier, a decision is made whether the time and effort expended to perform the action is warranted by the possible danger that could ensue. The theory and thought process behind these decisions can be reduced, however, to the basic theories and formula of risk analysis.

The risk analysis process compares the cost of preventing a loss or damage to the cost resulting from the loss. The cost of preventing a loss, however, must also take into account the probability of the occurrence of any loss. That is, the chances that the loss will or will not occur must be considered in the analysis. The formula in Figure 2.1, borrowed from another discipline, provides the basic means of making a risk analysis.

$$B > P \cdot L$$

Figure 2.1. The BPL, or risk analysis, formula.

The formula in Figure 2.1, further referred to as simply BPL, demonstrates the relationship of the factors involved in risk analysis. In a nutshell, the three elements of this formula are: B, the burden of preventing a specific loss; P, the probability of a specific loss occurring; and L, the total impact of a specific loss. Using the formula then, when the product of the probability of the loss occurring and the loss itself exceed the burden of avoiding the loss, then the loss avoidance measure should be implemented. When the burden of avoiding the loss is greater than the product of the probability of the loss occurring and the loss itself, the loss avoidance measure should not be implemented.

While the concept embodied by this formula is straight forward, it is the abstract valuation that causes rational minds to disagree over implementing risk avoidance activities.

In some cases, specifically at the extremes, the formula valuation process is simple and results in little disagreement among rational minds. For example, the burden of locking one's house door is so small and the possible loss from a robbery by not locking the door so great, namely the loss of everything one may own, that evaluating the probability is almost insignificant, because the other two formula components are at such extremes.

When not dealing with extremes, the most likely situation in risk analysis, the more informed the rational decision maker is to the aspects of each element, the wiser the total decision will result. As the reader may have already intuitively determined, because the formula need not have specific quantities to be effective, the trends of specific elements is acceptable. That is, the exact valuation of a loss is not required as long as a trend can provide a reasonable approximation or estimation of the formula component in question.

In seeking to further explore the means of evaluating each element, this chapter first starts with a discussion of L, the potential loss. Next, this chapter addresses P, the probability of the loss occurring. Finally, the chapter addresses B, the burdens imposed on avoiding the loss. Once presented with these elements, the remaining sections of this chapter increase the reader's awareness of the elements that go into the valuation of BPL with respect to the computer science field.

2.1.1   Possible Loss (L)

The L component of the BPL equation is the valuation of that which can be lost. This includes loss due to damage to information and equipment, loss of system repair and restoration costs, and loss of usage time. Other factors that are included in the valuation of L are intangibles such as the loss of life and the loss of perceived safety and security, both by those inflicting damage as well as those affected by the damage. The greatest problem in objectively evaluating these factors is determining a comprehensive loss for any event. For example, different people may value the cost of loss of a life differently. Some people may place a value on life that is commensurate to a person's age and experience; others may value a life at an amount commensurate of a person's potential future earnings. Regardless of how it is calculated, there is no precise or easy assessment. This uncertainty is not limited to life. Secretarial time, for example, can also bring great debate in terms of loss valuation. That is, one can precisely calculate the loss of one hour of secretarial data entry time; however, the final valuation must also include such aspects as loss of a contract as a direct result of the lost data entry time. The easy valuation of such a task has now become more difficult because of the difficulty in assessing an appropriate cost of both direct and cascading loss. This presents a problem when the valuation results in an inaccurate risk assessment and course of action.

To prevent an inaccurate valuation of the loss component, an organization must select a knowledgeable assessment team and assessment evaluation process. The assessment team should consist of persons knowledgeable in the cost of various losses that can and will ensue. In addition to being knowledgeable in the cost assessment of a loss, the persons responsible for determining the value of the L component should also be able to accurately determine the probability of a loss occurring. This is important as evaluating the cost of a loss may not be a part of an event's risk assessment equation. Clearly, this would be useful information in determining any associated risk.

2.1.2   Probability of Loss Occurrence (P)

The second component of the BPL equation is P, the probability of a loss. This concerns the possibility of any specific loss actually occurring. For example, for any given event, one possible loss may be that of human life. The probability of a loss of human life actually occurring, however, is not constant with each event. That is, the probability of human life being lost when jumping out of an airplane without a parachute is very high. The probability of a loss of human life from not going to a shopping mall is much smaller. There may still be some chance of this happening, but it is minimal when compared to that of other events. This variance in risk probability must be accounted for in any risk analysis.

Risk probability valuation, like loss valuation, is an imprecise art. Attempting to ascertain the possibility that any given event will occur is very difficult. A specific valuation is not always necessary. Again, like loss valuation, a trend in the possibility of an occurrence is sufficient to determine a reasonable probability of a loss occurring. This is not necessarily the best solution or means of determining the possibility of a loss occurring. This is understandable, however, as the valuation process is an attempt to qualify an abstract, unquantifiable object which cannot otherwise be evaluated. Regardless of how a probability is determined, it should accurately reflect the possibility of an event.

Once the P component of the BPL equation has been evaluated for a given L component, they may be combined to determine half of the risk analysis. The resulting value indicates the relative cost-probability of the loss occurring. This value, when compared to the B component, will provide a risk analysis that indicates what actions, if any, should be taken. Further discussion of this analysis is provided after discussion of the B component of the risk analysis equation.

2.1.3 Burden of Preventing Loss (B)

The B component of the risk analysis equation concerns what is required to prevent the loss from occurring. For example, the burden of preventing a vehicle from "running out of gasoline" is the cost of the gasoline. Burden is not limited to only money. The burden involved with running out of gasoline must also include the time involved in filling the gas tank, as well as the cost of the gasoline. Burden should be further expanded to include solution design time and costs, installation time and costs, maintenance time and costs, and testing time and costs. Clearly, the burden involved with many risk prevention techniques is not just a one time plug and play process. Every aspect of implementing a prevention technique will have to be included in the risk assessment. This is not always an extravagant amount, however. For example, locking one's house front door is a minor burden in the prevention against the possible risk of robbery and possible personal harm.

In addition, complexity is added to the calculation of the burden component of BPL when the issue of the amount of prevention is mentioned. That is, how much protection is needed for any given loss? Referring back to the gasoline example, the question of how much gasoline is required must be asked. The answer will depend largely upon the needs of the persons taking the risk. It may be that, in this case, the decision maker (the driver) needs only enough gasoline to get home. Clearly, this answer is situation dependent and would greatly differ if the driver needed to travel a great distance.

Another question that must be addressed concerns the form of the burden. That is, there are often many means by which a given risk can be prevented or reduced, but the decision maker must decide the solution that will be implemented. If the situation allows, many risk assessments and techniques can be explored. Using the example of locking a front door to prevent a robbery — there are easily many opinions such as locking the front door or barring the windows or installing an alarm system. A decision must be made, however, as to the amount of burden the decision maker is willing to accept. While this decision will be primarily based upon the associated risk, the decision maker will have some amount of flexibility in selecting a more involved and possibly expensive burden.

2.1.4 Applying the Risk Analysis Equation

To apply the risk analysis equation to a particular event, the three components of BPL must be evaluated [2.4]. As mentioned, this may be difficult as the valuations are often subject to and based upon trends as opposed to well-defined values. Nonetheless, the analysis is still a valuable and executable process.

Many analyses are often instigated with a loss or potential loss. To illustrate the process, an example of studying for a final exam is given. The question a student must answer is whether she should study for a final exam or go dancing. The loss involved in not studying would be failing the exam and thus failing the class. The effective loss, L, would be the cost of taking the class over, and possibly the loss of salary for a delayed graduation, and any embarrassment associated with failing and retaking a course. The probability, P, of the student failing her test will depend on how well she knows the material and how difficult the test will be. This, in turn, will depend upon her knowledge of past tests and her ability; a trend in the events and her past performance will determine the appropriate valuation of the probability. The final value in the risk analysis equation is the burden, B, of studying for a few hours as opposed to enjoying herself dancing. This burden will also depend upon the previous experience of the student. It is safe to assume, however, that in this case the burden of studying as opposed to going out is very low. Thus, the value of B is low. The student, with or without realizing it, will perform a risk analysis and compare the burden of studying against the probability that she will fail and have to retake the class. If she believes that the probability of failure is very low and the burden is great, she will go dancing. If, however, she feels that the burden of missing the study time is relatively small to the loss of failing her test, no matter how great or small the probability, she will study. Thus, a risk analysis has been made and used to determine an appropriate course of action.

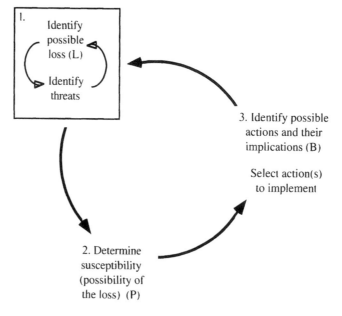

Figure 2.2. The steps of performing a risk analysis.

The steps that the student followed in performing her risk analysis mirror the risk analysis process performed by other individuals, business, and governments. The first step in the student's analysis was determining the possible loss from her actions. Once these were identified, the student examined the probability of the losses occurring. The next step of the analysis process was determining the burden that her actions would place upon her. The process of acting upon the analysis that she has made is not directly involved in the risk analysis process. It is included in this step, however, as it is the logical conclusion to this step. This process is shown in Figure 2.2. Note that while the student's risk analysis began with an evaluation of the possible loss, many risk analyses begin with the identification of an existing threat, thus the grouping of these two actions as the first step of the process.

While the above example is rather trivial, nonetheless, the risk analysis methods can be applied to computer security issues as well as study patterns. The rest of this chapter re-examines the risk analysis methodology in terms of computer security.

2.2 Risk Analysis in Computer Security

Risk analysis is used by numerous companies and organizations to provide the foundation for determining the security needs of their computer systems [2.1, 2.2]. This process must therefore be accurately performed so that the results provide a reasonable and appropriate solution to any security shortcoming. An incorrect risk analysis could lead to expensive, inappropriate security measures, misdirected efforts, and possibly a loss of information or other assets. To prevent this from occurring, the risk assessment process must be clearly defined. This includes both the application of the terms and criteria used to gather and prepare the data for this process.

2.2.1 Terminology

The terms associated with both the risk analysis process and computer security must be related and defined in order to learn how to perform a computer security risk analysis. Terms that must be defined in both meaning and usage include risk, vulnerability, threat, susceptibility, loss, burden, and safeguard. Once defined, the process of computer security risk analysis will be better understood.

To understand how to perform a proper computer security risk analysis, one must first know how computer security risk assessment is defined. Recall that the general goals of computer security are to prevent three actions: (1) the unauthorized access of information contained on a computer system; (2) the unauthorized use of computing resources; and (3) the unauthorized destruction of a computer and the contained information. To accomplish this task, administrators must understand how the system is at risk. They must ask and answer the question of how their system can be compromised; how is the system threatened? Risk, however, is not just a measure of some undefined, unknown threat. It also takes into account the probability of the threat occurring. It is, as Haimes [2.6] puts it, "a measure of the probability and severity of adverse effects". In terms of the BPL equation previously introduced, risk, be it computer security related or not, can be defined as $P \cdot L$; the probability times the loss.

Threat is an integral part of computer security risk and risk analysis, and it needs to be defined in these terms. Again, recall that in the general risk analysis model, loss or the possibility of a loss was mentioned as often being the catalyst to performing a risk analysis. While this loss is often considered the threat to a system, it is actually the source of this loss that is defined as the threat [2.3, 2.4]. This subtle difference, however, can cause great confusion — and often does. It should not be surprising that the definition of a threat differs from risk model to risk model. Some models, for example, consider the threat to be the undesirable outcome such as the threat of a power failure. In this model, however, threat is defined as the damage causing agent; for example, the infamous "insider threat" in which the threat of an attack or damage comes from someone inside the organization. This raises another concern about threat; that is, what threats exist and should be included in the computer security risk model.

Threats to a computer's safety and security are not only limited to the insider threat. Other types of threats include natural disasters, structural failure, sabotage, human error, and indirect aggressive behavior (such as the nuclear threat) [2.3, 2.7]. Not all of these threats, however, are of concern to a given system. This is clear by looking at an organization's computer system or the BPL equation. Few organizations, for example, protect their computer systems from earthquakes and fewer protect against a nuclear attack. This can be attributed to their own risk analysis and application of the BPL equation. The equation itself lends credence to the fact that each threat is of differing concern by its inclusion of a loss probability component. This component does not directly measure any threat's probability, but it does measure the probability of a threat-causing loss occurring.

As the possible threats to any given organization will be unique, the concept of identifying the threats that are of concern must be addressed. Because no complete list of threats exists, those people involved with the analysis will have to create a site specific list. Places to begin looking for information on threats are local installation records, discussions with the security officers at similar installations, and organizations specializing in computer security, such as the Computer Emergency Response Team (CERT). A more complete list is provided in Table 2.2.

Table 2.2 Useful locations of threat identification information

```
• Local installation security records
• Local computer logs
• Software vendors
• Professional computer security organizations
• Similar computer installations
• Security newsletters and other publications
• Electronic news groups and lists
• Local system users
```

In discussing risk analysis, probability refers to the possibility of any given loss occurring. It does not reflect the possibility of a threat being present. For example, the threat of an intruder is only indirectly relevant to a risk analysis as there may be no loss resulting from the threat. The possibility of a loss as a result of the intruder, however, is of concern. The probability of any loss occurring will depend on many variables. Some of these variables include the responsibility and knowledge of the system administrator, the presence of existing loss countermeasures, the environment of the system, and the public knowledge of the system's existence. Each of these, in some manner, affect the probability of various losses differently. For example, the known existence of a computer system increases the possibility that an intruder will attack. It does not, however, affect the possibility that an earthquake will destroy the system or its data. When a system is susceptible to a loss, that is, there is an opportunity for a loss to occur, the system is said to have a vulnerability [2.3]. For example, the probability that an intruder will attack a computer that is not attached to a network is non-existent. Thus, it is not susceptible to a network attack and therefore not vulnerable to the threat of a networked intruder. Vulnerability can be further refined; a system can be vulnerable to a remote intruder that is guessing passwords, but not to a remote user that is attempting to exploit an operating system hole. The exact level of granularity will have to be defined by the individuals involved in the risk analysis.

The final terms that must be defined with respect to computer security are burden and safeguards. Burden, the B component of the BPL equation, concerns the costs involved in preventing a loss (implementing a countermeasure). These costs are not limited to just financial expenses, but include time, resources, and education. These are further broken down into the burdens listed in Table 2.3. It should be noted that this list is both environment and site specific. It is not expected that governments, businesses, and educational organizations have either the same priorities or needs.

Table 2.3 A partial list of known risk analysis burdens

```
• Time and cost involved with the design,
  installation, testing, and maintenance of
  countermeasures
• Time and cost of loss removing outdated or
  ineffective countermeasures
• Time and cost of lost computation during
  countermeasure installation
• Purchasing cost of countermeasures
• Time involved with user education
```

Closely related to burden is the concept of safeguards. Safeguards are the items or actions that remove a specific vulnerability from a system [2.3]. For example, a backup disk drive safeguard protects a system, to some degree, from data loss. Likewise, the UNIX shadow password safeguard protects a system, again only to a certain degree, from theft of passwords. Safeguards such as these are rarely encompassing enough to guarantee the complete safety of a system. That is, even with the use of any given safeguard, a vulnerability is not removed; rather, only the possibility of its exploitation is reduced. This is evident with the shadow password safeguard; it does not remove the opportunity for an intruder to steal accounts, it only reduces the likelihood. This is a key concept in risk analysis and burden evaluation. Not every safeguard will resolve the same problems, nor will it do a complete job in protecting the system. Furthermore, each safeguard will have its own burdens. In most instances the amount of burden placed upon the system, the administration, and the users is directly proportional to the strength of the safeguard. It is often preferred that the amount of burden be minimized while the strength of the safeguard is maximized. Clearly, the people involved with performing a risk analysis will have to determine the most advantageous burden-safeguard trade-off for their respective system.

2.2.2 Application

The application of risk analysis to computer security is little different than when applied to other fields. The process still requires cost and probability trends for the B, P, and L components of the risk analysis equation. This does present a problem, however, as trends are often derived from information that does not have a strong empirical basis [2.3]. An incorrect analysis could result if too much faith is placed on this data; available data is often not realistic or outdated. As computer security incidents are often difficult to analyze, the availability of more accurate data is limited [2.5]. Furthermore, each computing system's unique operating environment will add to any inaccuracy from the available data. While this method has its drawbacks, it does reduce the vagueness otherwise associated with a more qualitative risk assessment such as "we have a big security hole".

Once the cost and probability trends of a computer system are identified and evaluated, the BPL equation can be applied. These valuations will take the form of various components of BPL. L, the loss component of BPL, will be substituted with the cumulative cost of a specific loss. The probability component of BPL, P, will be replaced with the probability of a loss occurring. B, the burden component, will be replaced with the complete cost of preventing such a loss from occurring. Once the values are identified, the equation can be evaluated. In the event that the cost of the burden (B) is greater than the product of the probability of a loss and the comprehensive cost of the loss ($P \cdot L$), the associated safeguard is excessive. If, however, the cost of the burden is less than the product of the probability of a loss and the comprehensive cost of the loss, the analysis would indicate that the cost of the associated safeguard is justified. Application of this type of analysis is demonstrated with the following two examples.

The first example concerns an organization's desire to modify their existing computer system in response to the growing size of the attached network and the inexplicable rise in failed login attempts. The security administrator is interested in removing some of the more vulnerable network services from the system. As each of their 300 computers are directly connected to the network, he will have to modify files on all 300 systems. Another administrator has determined that, should they proceed with this plan, he will write a program to automatically make the necessary changes to every computer. They have also decided that after the modifications have been made, they will reboot each system to ensure the changes are applied. Before they begin making the changes, they first attempt to determine if the changes are necessary. As the services in question are well known for being employed by intruders, coupled with the increase in failed login attempts, the administrators believe their site to have a very high probability of losing sensitive information to a successful attack. After gathering information about the threat of an intruder from similar organizations and professional security groups, they have evaluated their probability of a loss at 1:10. Discussions with the research and development group have informed the administrators that the proprietary information and research contained on the system is alone valued at $850,000. The destruction of this research, however, would result in negligible loss as the information is backed up on a nightly basis. The hours involved in recovering from such an attack, as well as the lost time, would cost the department approximately $35,000. While the psychological effect of knowing that the systems were attacked is a concern to the administrators, they choose not to include it in their loss assessment (it would be negligible). Thus, the final cost of a loss to the research and development group would be $885,000. The administrators include an estimated $30,000 for the time and cost placed upon them for system recovery. In calculating the cost of imposing the network restrictions, the administrators calculate that the time to write and execute the necessary program, the time to restart the machines, and the lost computing time during the restart would cost approximately $7,000. The burden of losing the network services is estimated as $2,000 for modification of software and assisting and educating the users in alternative methods. Using the BPL equation above, they calculate the adjusted cost of the loss at $91,500 ($915,000 * .10) and the burden cost at $9,000. As the cost of the burden was much less than the cost of the adjusted loss, the network services were removed and the users were provided alternate means of continuing their work.

The second example concerns a less obvious situation. The computer administrator of a 50-computer company is concerned about remote access to the system. She is concerned that remote access may be too vulnerable to an intruder. Like the administrators in the previous example, she speaks with system users to determine the extent of the damage that could result from an intruder breaking in and stealing information. While the system does not contain any confidential information, and the information is backed up on a weekly basis, the users' primary concern is loss of time. Approximations of the cost of system restoration, which appear to be based solely on labor, are $360,000. After speaking with other administrators in similar positions, computer security professionals, and informal electronic discussions, she estimates the probability of a remote attack at 5%, or 1:20. She has considered the possibility of removing remote system access. While she cannot estimate the burden this would place upon the users, she does believe it to be too drastic and result in too many irate users. More reasonable countermeasures under consideration are security calculators and additional software authentication mechanisms such as Kerberos. Calls to her software vendor and others familiar with the software mechanisms reveal that the cost of the software is minimal and that the costs of such an alternative will be labor related. These costs are estimated at approximately $5,000. Further calls to calculator vendors indicate that an authentication system suitable for the organization's needs would range between $18,000-$20,000, including the cost of labor for installation and testing. In an attempt to complete the risk analysis, the adjusted cost of the loss is estimated at $18,000 ($360,000 * .05). As this is less than (or relatively equal to) the burden of implementing both countermeasures, implementing either will provide a cost effective solution.

Not included in either of these burden estimations, however, is the burden placed upon a user. That is, additional software authentication schemes will require the user to provide a second password — more of a nuisance than anything else. The calculator authentication scheme, however, will require each user to carry with them an additional device for authentication. Furthermore, loss, theft, or damage to the device will result in a denial of system access and replacement of the calculator. As the additional burden on the user is rather large for an already expensive countermeasure, it may sway the administrator's decision of which countermeasure to implement.

2.3   Summary

Risk analysis assists a rational decision maker in determining the most appropriate action in any given situation. In terms of computer security, risk analysis assists in identifying cost effective security countermeasures in an attempt to prevent data loss. This process requires the analyst to identify any possible loss or threats, determine the system's susceptibility to the loss, and identify and implement countermeasures to prevent the loss. If the data collection and analysis is properly performed, the result will be a cost effective means of preventing data loss. Properly collecting and analyzing data, however, is a difficult task. Accurate data is not only difficult to obtain, but difficult to evaluate. To reduce the problems that may arise in obtaining loss costs and probabilities, loss trends and history are often used. Trends in the cost of specific losses and the probability of a loss occurring provide a strong foundation for accurate data. The data resulting from a trend analysis will have to be modified to account for any different or unusual site specific circumstances. Once the data has been appropriately adjusted, it can be used in selecting a cost effect means of providing additional system security.

2.4   Exercises

2.1   Can a risk analysis be guaranteed to produce accurate results? Why, or why not? If not, how can the accuracy of the results be improved?

2.2   (a) Can identical risk analyses performed by two different organizations be expected to provide the same results? Why, or why not?

           (b) Can the same risk analyses, individually performed by two people at the same organization, be expected to provide identical results? Why, or why not?

2.3   How are threats, losses, susceptibilities, and vulnerabilities related to each other?

2.4   Table 2.3 contains a partial list of known risk analysis burdens. This list is
            not complete as it will vary from site to site, organization to organization.
            What would be added in this list if the site is a research organization? What
            will be added if the site is a government military installation?

2.5   Identify the threats for an isolated thirty computer network that contains
            proprietary data. What are the possible losses to this environment?

2.6   Identify the threats to a computer system that contains proprietary
            information and is attached to a world-wide network. How will these threats
            differ if the data is not proprietary? How would the cost of possible losses
            change?

2.7   How does the increased user burden resulting from new countermeasures effect
            system use? At what point is the user burden too great?

2.5   References

2.1   Badenhurst, K. and Eloff, J., "Computer Security Methodology: Risk
            Analysis and Project Definition", *Computers & Security*, Elsevier Press,
            New York, Vol. 9, 1990.

2.2   Banks, S., "Security Policy", *Computers & Security*, Elsevier Press, New
            York, Vol. 9, 1990.

2.3   Bennett, S. P. and Kailay, M. P., "An Application of Qualitative Risk
            Analysis to Computer Security for the Commercial Sector", *The 8th Annual
            Computer Security Applications Conference*, IEEE Computer Society
            Press, New York, New York, 1992, pp. 64-73.

2.4   Bodeau, D. J., "A Conceptual Model for Computer Security Risk Analysis",
            The 8th Annual Computer Security Applications Conference, IEEE
            Computer Society Press, New York, New York, 1992, pp. 56-63.

2.5   Fisch, E. A., White, G. B., and Pooch, U. W., "The Design of an Audit Trail
            Analysis Tool", *Proceedings of the 10th Annual Computer Security
            Applications Conference*, IEEE Computer Society Press, New York, New
            York, 1994, pp. 126-133.

2.6   Haimes, Y. Y., "Total Risk Management", *Risk Analysis*, Vol. 11, No. 2, June 1991.

2.7   Palmer, I. C. and Potter, G. A., *Computer Security Risk Management*, Van Nostrand Reinhold, New York, New York, 1989.

2.6   Extended Bibliography

2.8   Bilbao, A., "TUAR: A Model of Risk Analysis in the Security Field", *The Carnahan Conference on Security Technology*, IEEE Press, New York, New York, 1992, pp. 65-71.

2.9   Drake, D. L. and Morse, K. L., "The Security-Specific Eight Stage Risk Assessment Methodology", *Proceedings of the 17th National Computer Security Conference*, Baltimore, Maryland, October 1994, pp. 441-450.

2.10   Garrabrants, W. M., Ellis III, A. W., Hoffman, L. J., and Kamel, M., "CERTS: A Comparative Evaluation Method for Risk Management Methodologies and Tools", *The 6th Annual Computer Security Applications Conference*, IEEE Computer Society Press, New York, New York, 1990, pp. 251-257.

2.11   Lavine, C. H., Lindell, A. M., and Guarro, S. B., "The Aerospace Risk Evaluation System (ARiES) Implementation of a Qualitative Risk Analysis Methodology for Critical Systems", *Proceedings of the 17th National Computer Security Conference*, Baltimore, Maryland, October 1994, pp. 431-440.

2.12   Orlandi, E., "The Cost of Security", *The Carnahan Conference on Security Technology*, IEEE Press, New York, New York, 1991, pp. 192-196.

3

DEVELOPING SECURE COMPUTER SYSTEMS

Having come to the realization that a computer system requires security measures to protect the data it stores and processes, the next logical step is to determine how to implement them. Early computer systems were made secure through external security means such as maintaining the computer system in a locked room. As computer systems added remote users and eventually became connected to networks of other computers, external security measures were no longer sufficient to maintain security. Internal measures implemented within the hardware and software of the computer system were also needed, though external security measures could not be ignored entirely. Both internal and external measures need to be considered together in order to establish a security policy for a computer system or network.

3.1   External Security Measures

Typical External Security measures include those portions of the total security package for the computer system that do not include the hardware or software of the actual system itself. These measures include:

- Physical Security
- Personnel Security
- Administrative Security

Physical Security measures consist of those techniques used to secure any high-value item including locks, guards, remote surveillance cameras, and alarm systems. These measures are used to not only protect the information that is stored on the computer but to prevent the theft of the computer system and its peripherals. Obviously, the more important the data or the more expensive the equipment, the more physical controls we will want to employ. If denial of service is of concern, you may also need to consider how an individual bent on denying you the use of your computer system could attack the source of your power or attempt to start a fire at your site in order to activate a fire suppression system. Either attack would bring processing to a halt. While measures to protect against these threats are no different then measures for other high-value pieces of equipment, it is something that we must at least be cognizant of from a security standpoint.

As has been shown on a number of occasions, a system is only as secure as the people who use and operate it. Personnel security is concerned with the procedures used to determine the amount of trust the organization can place in any particular individual. In the military this roughly equates to the security clearance (e.g., Secret, Top Secret, etc.) the individual is granted. In a business it can equate to the number of functions an employee is allowed to run (e.g., payroll, shipping, etc.). In either case, it involves the level of access that the organization has given the individual based on the individual's background, previous experience, and current job requirements. The large percentage of computer crime cases involving insiders illustrates how important it is to pay attention to this aspect of security. There have been numerous cases in which the crime occurred as a result of employee's violating the trust placed in him in order to take advantage of the system for personal gain.

Administrative Security describes the methods to be used to implement the chosen security policies. These statements detail such things as how printouts are to be disposed of, how magnetic media will be stored, erased, and destroyed, what procedures to follow when an employee is fired, and the procedures used for temporary employees or when visitors are in the area. Intruders have often taken advantage of the lack of administrative security (or the poor enforcement of it) to gain access to computer systems and networks. A common trick used by intruders is to call the organization who owns the targeted system posing as an employee of the vendor for the computer system. The intruder will, for example, weave a story involving maintenance problems with the computer system or network, and describe the dire consequences if a certain patch is not installed. To install the patch, however, the intruder will need to be given access for a short while to the system and will request that the individual set up a temporary account granting access. It is amazing how often this simple ploy works. Another common trick is for the intruder to call up posing as somebody else who does have permission to access the system and claiming to have forgotten their password. Often there are policies governing these types of events which are simply ignored or forgotten.

There are many other examples of the types of policies and procedures that should be described by an organization's administrative security mechanism. Consider, for example, the security procedures to be followed when an employee is fired. If an individual is given a two-week termination notice, that individual should immediately have access to the company's computer system revoked. A considerable amount of damage can be done by a disgruntled employee during a two-week period. An example of another policy might entail the use of multi-user accounts. Often several employees will be working on the same project and the temptation is to assign a single account to be used by all members of the project. This cuts down on the overhead involved in granting them access to the system and often simplifies their handling of jointly accessible files. The problem with this is that it makes it hard to provide a level of accountability since there would be no way of telling which individual made a change or deleted a file. In addition, should an employee switch jobs, a new password will have to be issued which must then be passed along to all those who still remain with the project. One final example of an administrative policy is the procedures in place to track the installation of updates or patches to operating system or application software. Often a vendor feature will exist in software that may violate certain local policies. An employee responsible for the operation of the computer system may remove or disable this feature but may not make any note of this. Later, when an update or new version of the software is installed, the same feature will need to be disabled. If no record of the previous actions taken to disable or remove the feature exists, the feature will remain in violation of local security policies. This is especially true if the original employee who initiated the action has transferred to a different job. These examples provide just a glimpse of the large number of factors outside of the actual computer system itself that must be considered.

3.2 Structure of a Computer System

Before we examine the components of a secure computer system it is useful to review the structure of a standard computer system. The parts of a computer system can be divided into two basic types of components, hardware and software (for purposes of discussing security issues, the combination of hardware and software resulting in firmware can be thought of as falling under both categories and will therefore need to be considered in the discussions for both). The hardware can be roughly divided into Input/Output (I/O) Devices, Secondary Storage, Main Memory, and the Central Processing Unit (CPU) as shown in Figure 3.1. For our purposes, software will be divided into two categories, the Operating System (OS) or just system software, and Application software.

A single-processor computer executes one program at any given moment. It must fetch an instruction to be executed from memory, decode it, execute it, store any results, and then repeat this cycle. The operating system is a set of special programs that manages the resources and controls the operation of the computer. In many respects, the

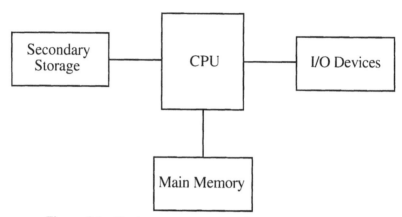

Figure 3.1. Hardware components of a computer system.

operating system serves as a buffer between the application programs and the hardware. The relationship between each of these elements is often represented by a series of concentric rings as depicted in Figure 3.2. Application software consists of those programs designed to perform a task using the resources of the computer system. Examples of application programs include data base management systems, word processors, spreadsheets, project management software, and communications packages. It will also include any programs written, compiled, and executed by the users themselves.

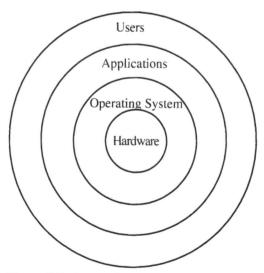

Figure 3.2. Layers in a computer system.

Since much of the time an application spends may be waiting for interaction with the user or some I/O device, it is useful to have several programs running concurrently. While a single processor can only execute one program at any instant, it is possible to make it appear as if several users have sole control of the machine by slicing the CPU time up and providing each user with a share of it. This is known as timesharing. A program that has used up its allotted time will be swapped out by the operating system for another program that is waiting to execute. Since the program being swapped out has not completed its processing, the current state of the program must be saved so that it can restart at the point it was interrupted. After the current state is saved, the next program is loaded, having been restored to the spot at which it had previously been interrupted, and then continues to process until its time slice has also expired and another program is swapped in. The time any single process gets before being swapped out is generally a small fraction of a second.

Another characteristic of most programs is they tend to execute instructions in blocks of code as opposed to individual instructions located great distances from each other. This means the entire program generally doesn't need to be kept in main memory in order for it to run. Instead, blocks of code can be brought in as needed. The implication is that we can actually have several programs in main memory at the same time with the operating system tasked with the responsibility of keeping track of each program and its various parts. This greatly speeds the process of swapping between programs since they do not need to actually be swapped out to secondary storage. This also, however, makes the operating system's task harder as it maintains control of the various parts of many different programs. One of the concerns of the operating system is that programs should not interfere with other programs by accessing memory outside of the space allocated to them. As it turns out, this is not only important for the smooth operation of the various programs in memory, but it also has security implications and is one of the issues that needs to be addressed when designing a secure computer system.

3.3   Secure Computer System Issues

The hardware structure of a secure computer system is conceptually no different than the one depicted in Figure 3.1. There are, however, a few additional concerns that must be addressed either by the hardware or software. One of these concerns is what is known as *object reuse*. The term object reuse is used to describe the actions that occur whenever one subject gives up an object so it can be reused by another subject. For example, when an individual deletes a file the memory, that had been used to store that file can now be used by somebody else to store another file. The security concern revolves around the method the computer system uses to release the memory so that it may be used by another. A good example of this is a PC using the MS-DOS operating system. If an individual uses the *del* command to delete a file, the file isn't actually destroyed, instead the pointer to it in the directory table is altered so that the file doesn't appear to be present. This allows another user to come along and use the space that was allocated to the original file. If someone were to actually examine the individual bits on the disk, however, they would still contain the information that had been stored there before. This is why the *undelete* command is able to function. It simply goes to the directory table and changes the entries so that the files once again appear to exist. The security implications of this should be obvious. If a file which was classified Top Secret is deleted and then the space allocated to a user who is only cleared for access to Secret information, the user, by simply reading the sectors on the disk, could obtain access to the Top Secret information. A secure computer system will need to insure that whenever an object is released, all information that had been contained on it is cleared so that no trace of it remains for another user to access.

Object reuse applies not only to files but to any object released for use by another subject. Main memory, for example, must also be cleared before it is assigned to another subject and, as was previously mentioned, part of the operating system's task is to insure that the various processes currently executing don't interfere with each other. Consider what would happen if, for example, the operating system allowed a process to access portions of memory not currently assigned to it and to write to them. Suppose the section of code the process overwrites contains the password file. This type of problem has actually occurred in systems, most recently in server software used to interact with the World Wide Web (WWW). The specific vulnerability allowed instructions to be pushed onto the program stack by overflowing an internal buffer [3.2]. An intruder could then, by careful selection of the instructions pushed onto the stack, gain unauthorized access to the WWW server.

One way to interject some security control over a computer system is to create what is known as *security* or *execution domains*. Similar to the concentric rings depicted in Figure 3.2, security domains provide a hierarchical structure to the application of security on the computer system. At the center still sits the hardware. Immediately surrounding the hardware is the operating system. The application programs will be split into several different categories. Each category corresponds to another ring in the diagram and allows access to the functions provided by the next most inner ring only. An example of this is a database management system which controls and limits access to data from programs that run at higher levels in the hierarchy. Some users might be allowed to read and manipulate data, others only to read data.

This concept of isolating various functions and restricting their access to specific systems can also be applied to the operating system itself. Various designs of secure computer systems have been created which employ this idea. Known as a *security kernel* [3.1, 3.3], this method provides a way to develop a secure computing base. The security kernel concept recognizes that modern operating systems are large, complex programs which can be extremely difficult to debug and even harder to ensure that they contain no security holes. The security kernel addresses this by limiting the protection mechanisms to a few routines which all other routines must use. Thus, instead of attempting to provide security mechanisms in each portion of the operating system, making each portion responsible for maintaining security over the files it manipulates, the security kernel concept defines just a few special programs which will be responsible for security. All other programs must interact with the kernel in order to gain access to the files it protects.

Key to the concept of the security kernel is the abstract notion of a *reference monitor*. The reference monitor enforces security by forcing all subjects (e.g., processes and users) who wish to access an object (e.g., files or portions of memory) to do so only through the monitor itself. Thus, it *monitors* all *references* to objects by subjects. The reference monitor is depicted in Figure 3.3.

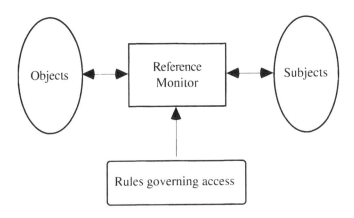

Figure 3.3. The reference monitor.

The reference monitor bases its access control decisions on a set of rules which explain what subjects can access which objects. These rules may explicitly specify certain files and objects or, as is more commonly the case, will represent a synopsis of the security policy and model chosen for the system. To be complete, a reference monitor will have to follow three design principles:

- Absolute Control — all access to the objects must be made through the reference monitor.
- Isolation — the kernel must be separated from the other routines and protected from modification or tampering.

• Verifiability — the kernel must be shown to implement some chosen
  security policy [3.1].

The actual implementation of a security kernel will include both hardware and software
concerns. A number of systems have been developed using a security kernel as the basis
for their security. The first, and possibly the best, example of this was accomplished by
MITRE in 1974 [3.1]. The kernel they developed was designed to operate on a Digital
Equipment Corporation PDP-11/45 computer system. The kernel consisted of fewer than
20 primitive routines with less than 1000 lines of high-level language code. Despite its
small size, the kernel was responsible for the physical resources of the system and
enforced protection of the system's objects. This kernel successfully demonstrated both
the feasibility of a kernelized design as well as epitomizing the goal of a minimal number
of routines responsible for security of the system's objects.

Simply implementing a security kernel does not guarantee that the system will be
secure. There are many issues that still need to be addressed, such as Security Models,
Authentication, Access Control, Auditing, and Cryptography. Security models are
chosen to express the security requirements of the system. Authentication involves the
determination that an individual is authorized access to the computer system. This
involves methods, such as the use of passwords, to verify that the individual is indeed
who he claims to be. Authentication is generally thought of as restricting access to the
system itself. Restricting access to the objects on the system is the responsibility of
access control techniques. Access control techniques determine what objects an individual
may access, and what type of access the user has been granted (e.g., read and/or write
permissions). Auditing, for security purposes, is a method used to monitor the actions of
users in order to determine when intrusive or abnormal system activities occur.
Cryptography, which is used to obscure data by encoding it, is a technique commonly
used to protect data. Each of these other issues are subjects of later chapters in this book.

An interesting problem that we must also be concerned with when designing a
secure computer system is the existence of possible *covert channels*. There exist many
definitions for a covert channel but for our purposes we will define them as the
transmission of information along a channel which is not allowed according to the
security policies established for the system. This transmission may either be intentional
or unintentional. There are two basic types of covert channels: *covert storage channels*
and *covert timing channels*.

A covert storage channel involves the use of a resource that is shared between
subjects in two different security domains. The resource (such as a storage location on a
disk) will be written to by one subject and read by the other. Normally the sharing of
resources between subjects in different security domains is not allowed, so in order to
communicate the two subjects will need to utilize methods not normally considered for
transmission of information. To illustrate, file names may be readable to everybody on a

system while the contents of the file are not. A subject functioning in one security domain (e.g., a user or process operating in a Top Secret environment) might change a file name to send certain information about the file to another subject operating in a different security domain (e.g., a Secret environment). Given sufficient time, a series of name changes could be accomplished which could be used to actually transfer the entire contents of the file. This transmission of information via the file name was not intended as a normal means of communication between processes and is thus a covert channel.

A covert timing channel consists of a method of communicating information between subjects by altering the use of system resources in order to affect the system response time. One process attempting to communicate with another process, for example, could either initiate CPU intensive jobs or not at certain predetermined intervals. The initiation of a CPU intensive job might then represent a 1 while the lack of the job might represent a 0. The process that is to receive the message checks the CPU utilization at the specified intervals to detect whether the other has initiated the job or not. In this manner, the two processes could communicate a message one bit at a time. Since there are many other processes that can also affect the CPU utilization, this type of covert channel is often considered less of a threat than the covert storage channels.

3.4 Summary

Many factors go into making a computer system secure. Some of the most basic and important don't involve technology but rather the physical side of the computer. Locks, guards, and surveillance cameras to discourage individuals from gaining unauthorized access to computer facilities are probably the first line of defense. Established policies and procedures to let people know how to do things such as properly discarding files, printouts and manuals, or to instruct them on how to handle visitors or maintenance personnel also help in this first line of defense. Eventually, especially in today's heavily networked environments, we must turn to the computers themselves to provide security.

A technique often employed for a secure system is the establishment of a security kernel and reference monitor. These should consist of a small subset of the operating system designed to control all subject's access to objects. While access control is one element of a secure computer system, there are many others that also need to be addressed, such as Security Models, Authentication, Access Control, Cryptography, and Auditing. Each of these are addressed individually in later chapters. Even after these are considered, other concerns still remain. One such remaining concern is the possible existence of covert channels. These covert means to transmit information between subjects in violation of the system's established security policy may consist of covert storage or timing channels and are often difficult to detect.

3.5 Exercises

3.1   A common practice among computer system vendors is to include a
maintenance userid and password on delivered systems. These userid/password
pairs are then used to allow vendor service personnel quick, remote access in
case a problem occurs. These userid/password pairs often consist of
combinations such as *guest/guest* or *system/maint*. What are the dangers in
allowing this type of maintenance or service userid and password to exist on
your system?

3.2   If the DOS *del* command doesn't actually delete the file, how can you be sure
that all remnants of the file you wanted destroyed actually have been? What
procedure is necessary to ensure this occurs?

3.3   One solution proposed to make systems more secure is to place the operating
system functions on a chip (in firmware). What are the advantages and
disadvantages to this proposal?

3.4   Two examples of covert channels were given in the text. What other
techniques could be used to provide covert channels?

3.5   How would you test for covert storage channels? What about covert timing
channels? Why is testing for them so difficult?

3.6 References

3.1   Ames. S., Jr., Gasser, M., and Schell, R., "Security Kernel Design and
Implementation: An Introduction", *Computer*, Vol. 16, No. 7, July 1983,
pp. 41-49.

3.2   Department Of Energy, "Unix NCSA httpd Vulnerability", *Computer
Incident Advisory Capability Advisory Notice*, F-11, February 14, 1995.

3.3   Popek, C.J. and Kline, C.S., "Issues in Kernel Design", *AFIPS Conference
Proceedings*, Vol. 47, 1978, pp. 1079-1086.

3.7   Extended Bibliography

3.4   Berson, T.A. and Barksdale, G.L. Jr., "KSOS – Development Methodology
           for a Secure Operating System", *AFIPS Conference Proceedings*, Vol. 48,
           1979, pp. 365-371.

3.5   Gasser, M., *Building a Secure Computer System*, Van Nostrand Reinhold,
           New York, New York, 1988.

3.6   Hardy, B., "An Overview of the Kernelized Secure Operating System
           (KSOS)", *Proceedings of the 7th DOD/NBS Computer Security Conference*,
           Gaithersburg, Maryland, September 1984, pp. 146-160.

3.7   National Computer Security Center, *A Guide to Understanding Covert
           Channel Analysis of Trusted Systems*, NCSC-TG-030, Version 1, November
           1993.

3.8   Saltzer, J.D. and Schroeder, M.D., "The Protection of Information in
           Computer Systems", *Proceedings of the IEEE*, Vol. 63, No. 9, March 1975,
           pp. 1278-1308.

3.9   Schell, R., Tao, T., and Heckman, H., "Designing the GEMSOS Security
           Kernal for Security and Performance", *Proceedings of the 8th National
           Computer Security Conference*, Gaithersburg, Maryland, September 1985,
           pp. 108-119.

3.10   Schell, R., "A Security Kernel for a Multiprocessor Microcomputer",
           Computer, Vol. 16. No. 7, July 1983, pp. 14-22.

4

SECURITY MODELS

Simply stated, the goal in computer security is to protect the computer system and the data it processes. How successful we are in reaching this goal depends a large part on the amount of care we put into implementing the security controls designed for the system. Before we can implement the controls, we need to understand the specific security requirements for our system. The purpose of a *Security Model* is to precisely express these security requirements. The model chosen to satisfy the specified requirements should be unambiguous, easy to comprehend, possible to implement, and should reflect the policies of the organization. This chapter discusses several security models as well as the Department of Defense's well-established criteria for what constitutes a secure computer system.

4.1 Specification and Verification

If the security controls implemented fail, it is usually a result of one of two general types of error: 1) there are errors in the software that control system security, or 2) the definition of what is required for the system to be secure was inaccurate or incomplete. With the exception of certain specific threats such as Trojan Horses and Trap Doors, the first of these two types of errors is addressed through the use of standard Software Engineering practices. The second type of error requires the selection of a security model that meets the requirements of the system and the correct application of this model to the system's development process. If the system has already been built, the job of adding security requires a less formal modeling approach. The formal models addressed in this chapter are intended for use in the design and specification of systems to be built.

For systems requiring the highest degree of security, a formal specification and verification is essential in addition to the formal security model. The goal of the specification is to describe the proposed behavior of the system in an unambiguous manner that lends itself to verification methods. The purpose of the security verification is to initially prove that the specifications conform to the formal security model. Later, the actual implementation will be tested to verify that it adheres to the specifications. Being able to develop specifications that lend themselves to verification generally requires the use of a special specification language and automated tools to aid in the process. The most popular tools used in security specifications are [4.3]:

- Gypsy Verification Environment (GVE) from the University of Texas.
- Formal Development Methodology (FDM) from the System Development Group of Unisys.
- Hierarchical Development Methodology (HDM) from SRI International.
- AFFIRM developed at the University of Southern California Information Sciences Institute.

These packages not only provide a specification language and their respective tools, they also prescribe an approach to actually designing the system itself. Each of these packages is large and complex and the field of formal specification is far from being mature.

4.2 Security Models

To develop a secure system, a formal model for the security should be included as part of the top-level definition of the system. The purpose of this model is to precisely define the desired behavior of the security-relevant portions of the target system. This desired behavior is strongly influenced by the expected threats to the system and the data it processes. An example can be seen in the differences between the broad security goals found in the military and commercial environments. Military security policy has long been chiefly concerned with disclosure of information to unauthorized individuals. While this is still of concern in the commercial sector, often the disclosure of information is not as important as preventing unauthorized modification of information. It is precisely this sort of detail that is addressed when selecting the security model to implement. There have actually been very few security models developed which have received widespread exposure. This is not due to problems in modeling but actually due to the broad applicability of the models that have already been developed.

4.2.1 Bell and LaPadula

Probably the best known security model is the Bell and LaPadula Model (BLP) [4.1]. This model is one of a group of *finite-state machine* models. A finite-state machine views the computer as a finite series of states. A transition function determines the next state of the system based on the current state and the value of any inputs which may cause a change in the system. The state is, in essence, defined by the current value of the *state variables* such as the value of the system registers and main memory. The *transition functions* are the various ways that the system can be changed. These functions also form the rules that govern the allowable ways in which the system can change. The security model will consist of a definition of the state variables and transition functions and will start at some provably secure state. Then, if all transitions can be proven to be secure and shown to result in a secure state, the model can, by induction, be shown to be secure.

The BLP model uses the concept of a finite-state machine to formalize its approach. It defines what it takes to be secure, what the allowable transitions are so that an insecure state cannot be reached from a secure state, and the various components of the finite-state machine itself. The model is designed to meet the requirements of what is known as the *Military Security Structure* which is concerned more with the disclosure of information rather than the unauthorized destruction or modification of information. The components defined in the BLP model are:

- *Subjects*: the system entities, which includes the users and processes.
- *Objects*: the data structures, which store the system's information.
- *Modes of Access*: how a subject interacts with an object.
- *Security Levels*: follows the military security system in which each object has a classification and each subject a clearance.

The modes of access specified in the model consist of operations such as read, write, and execute, as well as combinations of these basic operations. A state is considered secure if for each triplet consisting of a subject, object, and mode of access, the following properties are satisfied:

1) The level of the subject must be at least the level of the object if the mode of access allows the object to be read.
2) The level of the object must be at least the level of the subject if the mode of access allows the subject to write.
3) The operation may not change the classification of the object.

The first of these properties is commonly referred to as the *simple security property*. It describes what is known as the "no read up" policy. This means that no subject is allowed to read information which is of a higher classification than the subject is cleared for. For example, a user cleared for Secret information may not read information that is classified as Top Secret. The second property is the *confinement property* [4.2, 4.3] but is usually referred to as the **-property* (pronounced "star property"). This property dictates that a subject may not write to an object with a lower classification than the subject has clearance for. This is also known as the "no write down" policy. An example of this second property is a user cleared for Top Secret is not allowed to update a file with a classification of Secret. These first two principles are illustrated in Figure 4.1. In this figure, we show a user cleared for Secret information. The simple security property states this user is not allowed to read information from the Top Secret Domain. The *-property states this user may not write to the Unclassified domain. The user can both read and write to files in the Secret domain. The user may also read files that are unclassified and (based on this property alone) may write to files in the Top Secret Domain.

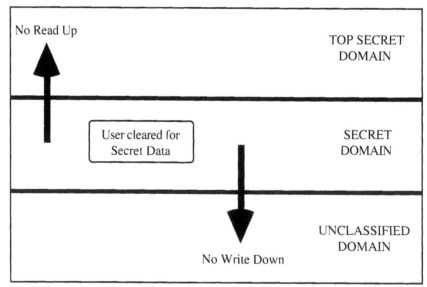

Figure 4.1. Bell and LaPadula properties.

The third property specified in the BLP model is known as the *tranquillity principle*. Though this last property, which keeps active objects from having their classification modified by an operation, is not strictly required for military security structures, Bell and LaPadula adopted it as an additional security measure. Essentially, this last property states that in terms of classification or clearance the subjects and objects found in each of the domains illustrated in Figure 4.1 will not change. The only way the domains will change is with the creation or deletion of subjects or objects.

The rigid adherence to the *-property was recognized by Bell and LaPadula as more strict than military security requires. Consequently, the idea of *trusted subjects* was developed. A trusted subject is one that can be relied on to not compromise information even if some of its invoked operations violate the *-property. Strict adherence to the *-property is only required of untrusted subjects. A criticism of the BLP model as described is the "flat" way it handles security levels.

The BLP model, or the BLP model along with some modifications, has been used in the design and implementation of several systems including MULTICS for the Air Force Data Services Center, the Kernelized Secure Operating System (KSOS), and the Honeywell Secure Communications Processor (SCOMP) [4.5]. The principal problem with the model has not been with what it allowed, but with what it disallows. The model has been criticized most often for being too restrictive and too concerned with the military security policy which may not be applicable in all environments. Other models have been developed to address these other environments.

4.2.2   Clark-Wilson

The BLP model addresses the military security policy's goal of unauthorized disclosure and declassification of information. In many environments, however, disclosure is less important than preventing the unauthorized modification of data. An example of this is the majority of commercial data processing that deals with management and accounting of financial assets. In this environment, preventing fraud is often more important than disclosure of information. This switches the emphasis from that of a privacy issue to one of enforcing integrity. The Clark-Wilson model was developed to address this commercial environment [4.7].

Besides stating that integrity policies are often of more importance than disclosure policies, Clark and Wilson also assert that there is a distinct set of policies that can be used to address the integrity issue and that separate mechanisms are required to do so. Clark and Wilson state the goal of a commercial system concerned with integrity of data is to insure that no user can modify data in a manner that would result in the loss or corruption of assets or accounting records for the company. This is true not only for unauthorized individuals but also individuals normally authorized access to the information. The model uses two categories of mechanisms to realize this goal. The first is called *well-formed transactions* and the second is *separation of duty* among employees.

The purpose of a well-formed transaction is to ensure that a user can't alter data arbitrarily. Instead, data can only be altered in specified ways that severely constrain the possible changes in order to preserve its internal consistency. An example of a well-formed transaction mechanism is an audit log, which records all data transactions. This provides system managers the ability to later recreate not only the sequence of events that may have led to an unauthorized modification but the original data as well. Auditing, as a well-formed transaction mechanism, is analogous to bookkeepers who, before the advent of computers, were once instructed to maintain their books in ink. When an error occurred, the bookkeeper also made the correction in ink. If an erasure was ever encountered, it was an indication of fraud. This method served as a deterrent to fraud, not as a mechanism that made it impossible to perform. The same is true of audit logs. They don't make it impossible to perform unauthorized modifications of data but instead simply deter it by making it easier to detect when fraud occurs.

Another example of a well-formed transaction mechanism is found in accounting systems that base their transactions on a double-entry bookkeeping principle. This principle requires that any modification to accounting information must be accomplished in two parts. If a withdrawal from a cash account is made, for example, an appropriate entry must also appear in another location such as an accounts payable account. If the transaction does not appear in both locations, it will be detected when the books are balanced. Once again, this does not make it impossible for an unauthorized action to occur but rather deters it from happening.

Applied to computer systems, well-formed transaction mechanisms result in the identification of only certain programs taht may modify data. These programs will thus perform very specific, and often limited, transactions. The programs themselves must be inspected and tested to ensure they have been written correctly and perform only their intended purpose. Their installation and modification must also be tightly controlled to ensure the integrity of the programs themselves.

The second category of mechanism used to reach the goal of commercial security is the separation of duty. This category attempts to maintain consistency of data objects by separating all operations into several parts and requiring that each part be performed by a different subject (e.g., a user). Basically this means that any user who is allowed to initiate a well-formed transaction is not allowed to execute it. For example, the process of purchasing some product might involve several steps. The first step might be the authorizing of the purchase. The second the ordering of the item. The third step might entail receiving and signing for the item and the last step could be the authorization of payment for the item. If each step in this process is performed by a different individual, the chance of collusion among employees for the purpose of fraud is reduced. To implement this mechanism on a computer system would entail permitting users to run only certain, specific programs. One individual, for example, would not be allowed to run the programs that governed the authorization, ordering, recording of reception, and accounting programs for the purchase of products as illustrated in our previous example.

There are several differences between the controls used for military security found in models such as that described by the Bell and LaPadula model and the controls for commercial security described in the Clark-Wilson model. The first is in the way in which data is treated. In military security models, data are assigned a security level and the mode of access granted depends on this level and the level of the subject. In the Clark-Wilson model data are associated not with a security level but rather with a set of programs which are allowed to access and manipulate it. Second, the subjects, or users, are not given authority to access certain data or classification of data but instead are given permission to access, or execute certain programs which in turn access specific data. Put simply, in military security users are constrained by the data they can access while in the Clark-Wilson model they are constrained by the programs they can execute. While military security policies use the triplet *subject/object/mode of access* to determine access restrictions, the Clark-Wilson model uses *subject/object/program* where the mode of access, and thus the operation to be performed on the data, is implied by the program being executed.

The Clark-Wilson model defines four elements to describe the operation of the model. Constrained Data Items (CDIs) are those data items in the system for which the integrity model must be applied. Unconstrained Data Items (UDIs) are those items which are not covered by the integrity model and may be manipulated freely. Transformation Procedures (TPs) change a set of CDIs which may also include new information in the form of a UDI from one valid state to another. Integrity Verification Procedures (IVPs) are used to confirm the internal data consistency of CDIs. Figure 4.2 illustrates the operation of these elements.

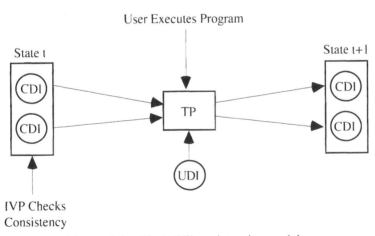

Figure 4.2. Clark-Wilson integrity model.

In this example, a user executes a program which will, based on the TP, transform two CDIs at State *t* and a UDI into the two CDIs found at State *t+1*. The IVP verified the consistency of the CDIs at State *t* before the transformation took place. Before this transformation took place, the user's authorization to execute this program (and transformation) would have been authenticated. In this example, the UDI is also supplied as input from the user. Implementations of the Clark-Wilson model have been developed independently by both Lee [4.6] and Shockley [4.7]. These implementations have shown that strong data typing is important and a transaction-oriented approach works well with the integrity-based approach of the Clark-Wilson model.

4.2.3 Goguen-Meseguer

The Goguen-Meseguer model introduces the concept of noninterference between users [4.4]. In essence this model prevents a higher-level user from interfering with a lower-level user. Simply stated, a subject, user, or group of users is said to be noninterfering with another subject, user, or group of users if what the first does has no effect on what the second can see. The elements of this model are:

- The set of all possible states for the system.
- The set of users.
- The set of commands which the users can execute.
- The set of outputs.
- The next state.
- The set of security levels.

In addition, there are two basic definitions:

1) A user is said to be **noninterfering** with a second user if, for any two strings consisting of a sequence of commands in which the commands issued by the second user are the same, the outputs for the second user are the same.
2) Given an initial secure state, the system is **multi-level secure** if the first user is noninterfering with the second user, unless the level of the first is less than or equal to the second user.

To illustrate this point, consider the following multi-level secure example. Suppose we have a user cleared for Top Secret information who wants to use an object classified at the Unclassified level to modify an object at the Secret level. In the BLP model this would not be allowed since the Top Secret user is sending information to the Unclassified level, in this case to modify some other data. The Unclassified level changing data at a higher level is allowed, just not the Top Secret user communicating with an Unclassified object. This violates the "no write down" *-property. While there is a possibility of a covert channel if we allow this operation, the essence of this change is nothing more than an upward information flow which is allowed in the BLP model. This operation would not, however, necessarily violate the rules associated with the Goguen-Meseguer model because, according to the definitions, the system could still be multi-level secure as long as the higher-level users' actions did not interfere with lower-level users.

Implementations of the Goguen-Meseguer model have focused on the idea of separating users based on their protection domains to avoid interference between groups. A version of this model was used by Honeywell in the Secure Ada Target research project. This implementation followed an object oriented, capability-based approach which restricted performance of actions on objects to subjects that had access to the domain in which the object resided.

4.3 TCSEC

As has been discussed, security models can aid in the development of security requirements for computer systems. Other documents have also been developed which aid in this process. The Department of Defense's (DoD) *Trusted Computer System Evaluation Criteria* (TCSEC), commonly referred to as the *Orange Book* because of the color of its cover, provides the DoD a basis for specifying security requirements in a computer system [4.2]. It also serves as an example of an approach to define specific security criteria for a chosen security model. Though officially only a standard for the DoD, this document has served as a basis from which to evaluate various computer security features for a number of years. It is not uncommon to see products developed for the commercial sector proclaim adherence to specific Orange Book requirements in their advertisements because of the widespread understanding of the basic requirements found in the book. The book thus provides a standard to manufacturers for what is required to satisfy basic requirements for a trusted system.

The criteria divide systems into four divisions based on the requirements they satisfy. The divisions are subdivided into classes to further categorize the evaluated systems. At the bottom is Division D, which has only one class. This division is reserved for those systems that have been evaluated but have been found to not meet the requirements for any of the higher classes. The next level up is Division C, which has two classes. This level introduces discretionary access controls. The next level is Division B, which consists of three classes and introduces the concept of mandatory access controls. Finally at the top is Division A, which also has only one class. Systems assigned this topmost rating are functionally equivalent to the highest class in the previous Division. B, but have had much more extensive formal design specification and verification techniques applied.

Each of the classes, except Class D, specify requirements in four broad areas: Security Policy, Accountability, Assurance, and Documentation. The **Security Policy** describes the set of rules that govern whether a given subject can access a specific object. **Accountability** includes such functions as identification, authentication, and auditing.

Assurance requirements provide criteria from which to evaluate the system's adherence to the other requirements. It includes concerns such as covert channel analysis, trusted recovery, security testing, and continuous protection (the mechanisms that enforce security must be protected themselves). Finally, **Documentation** requirements specify the documents required for each class and the basic contents of each document. The types of documents that may be required include Security Features User's Guide, Trusted Facility Manual, Test Documentation, and Design Documentation. All of these requirements together make up what the Orange Book refers to as the **Trusted Computing Base** (TCB). The TCB includes all hardware, software, and firmware which are used to enforce the systems security policy.

While the Orange Book describes four different divisions of trusted computer systems, it really splits them into only two categories. The first are those systems that enforce only **Discretionary Access Controls,** which limits processing to a single level of security. The second is **Mandatory Access Controls,** which allows processing of information from several different security levels on the same machine. This is known as *multi-level security.*

4.3.1   Discretionary Access Requirements

Discretionary Access Control requirements can be thought of as separating users from information on a need-to-know basis. This means that all individuals who use the system are cleared for the security level of the data with the highest classification processed on the system. Even though they are cleared at that level, they may not actually have a need to know what the data is. This is in keeping with the military's general rule of thumb, which keeps access to classified data to as few people as possible. If a problem occurs and access is granted to a user for a document the user does not have a need to know, the security breach is considered minimal since the user was still cleared for that level of information.

The requirements for providing discretionary security include a protected mechanism such as passwords to authenticate the identity of the user. In addition, the authentication data must itself be protected. An example of this would be encrypting the password file so that, should an individual obtain a copy of it, the users and their passwords would not be readable. Discretionary security also requires that access between subjects (users) and objects (files and programs) be controlled in a manner that allows sharing of the objects among subjects in specified groups while preventing access to subjects outside of the group.

At the C2 level, *object reuse* is introduced as a requirement of discretionary security. Object reuse entails the clearing of any portion of a storage device or memory location that has been previously used before access to it is granted. This ensures that a previous subject's information, which was once stored on the device or in memory, cannot be obtained by a subject. This even includes encrypted representations of information.

The C2 level also introduces the idea of *audit data*. The purpose of audit data is to provide a recorded trail of accesses to the objects protected by the system. This audit trail should include events such as the use of identification and authentication mechanisms, the access of objects, deletion of objects, and actions taken by computer operators and system and security administrators [4.2]. For each of these events the date and time of the event, user, type of event, and whether the event was successful or not should be recorded. The Orange Book also requires that the system administrator be able to selectively audit the actions of any specific individual or groups of users based on individual user identity. In addition to these requirements, the audit trail itself should be protected so that access to it is restricted not only to prevent unauthorized deletion but to limit read access as well. Other requirements for discretionary security include varying levels of assurance and documentation, depending on the specific class.

4.3.2 Mandatory Access Requirements

Mandatory access controls are required to implement multi-level security. In this division, Division B of the Orange Book, the requirements are designed to maintain the separation between different security levels of subjects and objects. Since unauthorized disclosure of information to individuals can result in prosecution, the controls for these systems can be said to be "mandated". For mandatory access, none of the requirements levied at the lower discretionary access level are eliminated. Instead, additional requirements are added.

For the system to be able to maintain the separation between the different levels of subjects and objects, a method needs to be implemented which identifies the respective clearance and classification levels. The Orange Book introduces the concept of *Sensitivity Labels* at the B1 Class in order to satisfy this requirement. Sensitivity labels are associated with each subject and object under control of the system. Whenever new data or new users are added to the system, the TCB is required to request and assign a security level for them. Additional requirements associated with labels include the maintenance of the label when objects are exported to other devices, and the need to include the sensitivity label as part of each page of hardcopy output. The labels mandated by the Orange Book are required to handle not only a minimum of two different hierarchical security levels but also any number of non-hierarchical categories. At the higher classes in this division additional requirements include the assignment of minimum and maximum security levels to actual physical devices (such as printers and terminals) to match constraints imposed by the physical environment.

The security model used by the Orange Book to specify its mandatory access control requirements is a version of the Bell and LaPadula model. The controls required by the

Orange book for this multi-level security system state that a subject can read an object only if the hierarchical sensitivity level of the subject is greater than or equal to that of the hierarchical level of the object to be read. In addition, the subject's non-hierarchical sensitivity categories must include all of the non-hierarchical categories of the object. A subject that wishes to write to an object can do so only if the subject's hierarchical sensitivity level is less than or equal to the hierarchical sensitivity level of the object and the subject's non-hierarchical sensitivity categories include all of the non-hierarchical categories of the object.

For obvious reasons, the integrity of the labels used by the system is of utmost importance. Consequently other requirements levied on systems starting at Class B1 include the addition of the object's sensitivity level on audit records and the auditing of any attempt to override security labels. At Class B2, covert channel analysis is also added to determine if any communication channel exists which might allow the transfer of information in a manner that would violate the security policies set.

4.4 Summary

How successful our security measures for a computer system are depends a great deal on how much care is used in implementing the chosen security controls. Prior to implementing the security controls, we need to select a security model that precisely expresses the system's security requirements. This model should have four characteristics. It should be (1) unambiguous, (2) possible to implement, (3) easy to comprehend, and (4) should be in keeping with the security policies of the organization.

The most widely known model in use today is the Bell and LaPadula model. This model implements military security policy, which is chiefly concerned with disclosure of information. The Clark-Wilson model, in contrast, addresses a major commercial concern of protecting the integrity of data. A third model, the Goguen-Meseguer model, introduces the concept of noninterference between users.

The Department of Defense's *Trusted Computer System Evaluation Criteria* (TCSEC) provides requirements and specific criteria to develop a system that implements a chosen security model. The model chosen for the TCSEC is a version of the Bell and LaPadula model. While it uses four divisions to classify the level of security implemented in a system, the TCSEC chiefly describes requirements for two specific types of controls: discretionary access controls and mandatory access controls. Discretionary controls separate users and information on a "need-to-know" basis while mandatory access controls separate them based on different security classifications.

4.5   Exercises

4.1   The Clark-Wilson model describes the auditing of transactions as a well-
        formed transaction mechanism. How does recording details relating to the
        modification of data ensure data integrity and internal consistency?

4.2   Recall the example given for the Goguen-Meseguer Model where a Top Secret
        user accesses an object at the Unclassified level to modify an object at the
        Secret level. Describe how this situation can lead to a possible covert
        channel.

4.3   Why does the TCSEC not require Security Labels for discretionary access
        controls? What other measures might be used to separate information of this
        type?

4.4   The Bell and LaPadula model allows users to write to information at a higher
        level of classification than they are cleared for. Besides the obvious
        possibility of data integrity problems, what concerns are there with allowing
        this type of transaction to occur?

4.5   Since Trojan Horses and Trap Doors are not "bugs" in the security software
        that can be discovered using normal testing procedures, what methods could
        be used to detect these types of malicious software? Is prevention or detection
        easier? Explain.

4.6   References

4.1   Bell, D.E. and LaPadula, J., *Secure Computer Systems: Mathematical
        Foundations and Model*, Technical Report, M74-244, MITRE Corp.,
        Bedford, Massachusetts, October 1974.

4.2   DoD 5200.28.STD, *Department of Defense Trusted Computer System
        Evaluation Criteria*, December 1985.

4.3   Gasser, M., *Building a Secure Computer System*, Van Nostrand Reinhold,
        New York, New York, 1988.

4.4   Haigh, J.T., "A Comparison of Formal Security Policy Models",
            Proceedings of the 7th DOD/NBS Computer Security Conference,
            Gaithersburg, Maryland, September 1984, pp. 88-111.

4.5   Landwehr, C. E., "Formal Models for Computer Security", *ACM Computing
            Surveys*, Vol. 13, No. 3, September 1981, pp. 247-278.

4.6   Lee, T.M.P., "Using Mandatory Integrity to Enforce 'Commercial' Security",
            Proceedings of the 1988 IEEE Symposium on Security and Privacy, Oakland,
            California, April 1988, pp. 140-146.

4.7   Shockley, W. R., "Implementing the Clark/Wilson Integrity Policy Using
            Current Technology", *Proceedings of the 11th National Computer Security
            Conference*, Baltimore, Maryland, October 1988, pp. 29-37.

4.7   Extended Bibliography

4.8   Bell, D.E., and LaPadula, J., *Secure Computer Systems: Unified Exposition
            and Multics Interpretation*, Technical Report, MTR-2997, MITRE Corp.,
            Bedford, Massachusetts, July 1975.

4.9   Biba, K. J., *Integrity Considerations for Secure Computer Systems*,
            Technical Report, MTR-3153, MITRE Corp., Bedford, Massachusetts, April
            1977.

4.10   Clark, D. D., and Wilson, D. R., "A Comparison of Commercial and
            Military Computer Security Policies", *Proceedings of the 1987 IEEE
            Symposium on Security and Privacy*, Oakland, California, April 1987,
            pp. 184-194.

4.11   Gove, R. A., "Extending the Bell & LaPadula Security Models",
            Proceedings of the 7th DOD/NBS Computer Security Conference,
            Gaithersburg, Maryland, September 1984, pp. 112-119.

4.12   Keefe, T.F., Tsai, W.T., and Thuraisingham, M.B., "A Multilevel Security
            Model for Object-Oriented Systems", *Proceedings of the 11th National
            Computer Security Conference*, Baltimore, Maryland, October 1988, pp.1-9.

4.13   Korelsky, T., Dean, B., Eichenlaub, C., Hook, J., Klapper, C., Lam, M., McCullough, D., Brooke-McFarland, C., Pottinger, G., Rambow, O., Rosenthal, D., Seldin, J., and Weber, D.G., "ULYSSES: A Computer-Security Modeling Environment", *Proceedings of the 11th National Computer Security Conference*, Baltimore, Maryland, October 1988, pp. 20-28.

4.14   McLean, J., "Reasoning About Security Models", *Proceedings of the 1987 Symposium on Security and Privacy*, Oakland, California, April 1987, pp. 123-131.

4.15   Page, J., Heaney, J., Adkins, M., and Dolsen, G., "Evaluation of Security Model Rule Bases", *Proceedings of the 12th National Computer Security Conference*, Baltimore, Maryland, October 1989, pp. 98-111.

4.16   Pittelli, P. A., "The Bell-LaPadula Computer Security Model Represented as a Special Case of the Harrison-Ruzzo-Ullman Model", *Proceedings of the 10th National Computer Security Conference*, Gaithersburg, Maryland, September 1987, pp. 118-121.

4.17   Roskos, J. E., Welke, S., Boone, J., and Mayfield, T., "A Taxonomy of Integrity Models, Implementations and Mechanisms", *Proceedings of the 13th National Computer Security Conference*, Washington, DC, October 1990, pp. 541-551.

4.18   Saydjari, S., "A Standard Notation, in Computer Security Models", *Proceedings of the 9th National Conference on Computer Security*, Gaithersburg, Maryland, September 1986, pp. 194-203.

4.19   Taylor, T., "Formal Models, Bell and LaPadula, and Gypsy", *Proceedings of the 10th National Conference on Computer Security*, Washington, DC, September 1987, pp. 193-200.

5

USER AUTHENTICATION

The first line of defense a computer system has against intruders is the user authentication system. The user authentication system attempts to prevent unauthorized users from gaining access by requiring users to validate their authorization to use the system. This validation is often accomplished with the use of a password that must be presented to the system. Other authentication schemes require the user to present a physical key or take advantage of the uniqueness of a user's physical characteristics such as fingerprints. This chapter discusses various authentication schemes and examines their implementations, advantages, and drawbacks.

5.1 Authentication Objectives

The primary objective of an authentication system is to prevent unauthorized users from gaining access to a computer system [5.8, 5.15]. By providing only authorized users with a key to access the system, unauthorized users have no means of access. This does not mean, however, that unauthorized users are unable to gain access to the system. It has become quite common for authorized users to be lax in the protection of their access key. That is, unauthorized users are able to access the system by appearing to the system as an authorized user. This is possible because the system does not authenticate the identity of a user, rather only who the user claims to be [5.15]. Since the authentication system cannot verify the user's true identity, methods must be in place to reduce the opportunity for an unauthorized user to access the system.

5.2   Authentication Methods

A computer system may employ three different types of authentication methods to prevent unauthorized users from gaining access |5.9, 5.19|. The first, and most common, method is through the use of informational keys. A system that uses informational keys requires the user to provide specific information to access the system. Examples of informational keys are passwords, pass phrases, and questionnaires. The second type of key is a physical key. Physical keys are objects that a user must have to access the system. Examples of physical keys include magnetic cards, smartcards, and security calculators. The third type of key is a biometric key. Biometric authentication systems rely on a user's physical characteristics to grant or deny access. Examples of biometric keys are fingerprints, voice prints, retinal prints, hand geometry, and facial profiles. Each of these types of keys is discussed below.

5.2.1   Informational Keys

Informational keys are predetermined words, phrases, or questions that an authorized user knows and can provide to the system when queried. The passwords and phrases may either be user selected or assigned by the system. The questions used in questionnaire authentication, however, are selected by the system and depend upon information collected by the system.

5.2.1.1   Passwords

One of the most commonly used authentication schemes employs passwords |5.19|. Along with a user name, a password must be presented to the authentication system to gain access. The system grants access to a user only when the password for the specified user matches the password on file for the user. This guarantees that only those users that have the correct passwords can access the computer.

Many systems allow the user to create his own password so that it is more memorable. User selected passwords, however, are often easily guessed |5.9, 5.15|. Accordingly, systems test passwords before they are accepted [5.7]. Examples of passwords not accepted are names and words found in dictionaries [5.7, 5.9]. Passwords that are generally accepted have more than five characters, at least one of which is a number, symbol or punctuation mark |5.15|. In general, a user's password should be both easy to remember but difficult to guess.

Even though users may select a password that is difficult to guess, their actions may lead to its compromise. A user can severely reduce the chance of their password becoming public knowledge by following three rules: (1) never write a password down, (2) never tell anyone the password, and (3) change the password on a regular basis. A large number of people write their password down because it is difficult to remember [5.7]. This may seem like a reasonable means of remembering a password. In practice, however, this has proven to be risky. Writing a password down allows both the casual observer and co-workers easy access to what would normally be considered a secure computer account. Just as risky as writing a password down is revealing a password to another person. Neither the actions of another person nor an unknown observer can be guaranteed beneficial to the user. To prevent unauthorized users from accessing a computer account, authorized users should change their password on a regular basis. This will reduce the possibility of intruders, both known and unknown, from unauthorized access.

An extension of the concept of changing a password on a regular basis is the single use password. A single use password is one that changes with each use [5.8]. That is, every time a user correctly presents their password to the authentication system, it changes. This requires an unauthorized user to obtain the current password to gain access. In the event an unauthorized user does obtain and use the current password, their presence is noticed when the authorized user cannot use what has become an old password.

To implement the single use password scheme two issues must be addressed: (1) distribution of the password list and (2) protecting the password list from theft. Distribution of the password list may either occur all at once or as each new password is needed [5.7]. The disadvantages of distributing the next password with each use are witnessed when an unauthorized user gains access. In this case, the unauthorized user would not only have the proper password for the one time it was valid, but will be provided the new password as well. Distribution of the entire list at one time prevents this from occurring but requires the authorized user to protect against theft, duplication, and loss. In the event that the list is stolen, copied, or lost, the computer system becomes vulnerable and a new list must be generated, installed and distributed.

5.2.1.2 Questionnaires

Questionnaire authentication attempts to validate a user with questions that an intruder is unlikely to know [5.7]. The system asks questions such as the name of the user's first pet, the color of the user's parent's home, or the name of the user's favorite teacher. For this system to function properly the user must prepare the questionnaire when the account is established and periodically update it to incorporate new information. Questionnaire authentication, however, is not likely to be used in a high security environment [5.7]. Since much of the information used in this process can be researched by an intruder, questionnaire protection is often insufficient and thus rarely used.

5.2.2   Physical Keys

Physical keys are items that a user must have in their possession to access the system [5.19]. Much like a key is required to enter a locked room, a special key may be required to access a computer system. Along with a user name or password, the user must present, or insert, their personal key to gain access. In the event that the key and identification number do not match or are invalid, the user is denied access to the system.

Three commonly used physical keys are magnetic cards, smartcards, and specialized calculators. These keys are widely used because they provide a higher level of security than passwords alone and are simple to use.

5.2.2.1   Magnetic Cards

Most people recognize the common credit card to be a magnetic card. A magnetic card is a piece of non-conductive material with an additional piece of magnetic recording material attached to it [5.1, 5.19]. Physical standards for magnetic cards have been

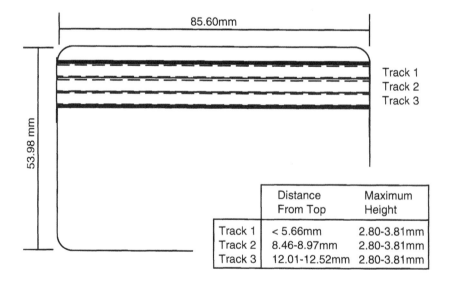

	Distance From Top	Maximum Height
Track 1	< 5.66mm	2.80-3.81mm
Track 2	8.46-8.97mm	2.80-3.81mm
Track 3	12.01-12.52mm	2.80-3.81mm

developed by The American National Standards Institute (ANSI) and the International Standards Organization (ISO) |5.1|. These standards allow multiple industries to take advantage of the technology.

The specific design of the magnetic card as described in ANSI/ISO standard 7810-1985 is shown in Figure 5.1 |5.1|. These standards indicate that the card must measure 85.60 mm wide by 53.98 mm high with a thickness of .76 mm. The magnetic strip on the backside of the card covers the full width of the card. The exact height and placement of the magnetic strip are not as important as that of the three data tracks within the strip. Each of the three tracks in the strip must measure between 2.80 mm and 3.81 mm high. The first track cannot be more than 5.66 mm from the top of the card. The second track should lay between 8.46 mm and 8.97 mm from the top and the third track should lay between 12.01 mm and 12.52 mm from the top.

To take advantage of the magnetic card technology, the system must have card readers attached to each terminal or physical access path such as a door. A user inserts his magnetic card into the reader and enters a personal access number. When the access number and magnetic card have been verified to be a valid matching pair, the user is authenticated and may access the system. The validation process occurs in four stages: (1) information input, (2) encryption, (3) comparison, and (4) logging. The process begins when a user enters both a card and access number. Depending on the authentication system either an encrypted copy of the password resides on the card or is obtained from the system by information on the card. In either case, an encrypted password is obtained for comparison. The authentication system then encrypts the access number entered by the user and compares it to the expected value obtained from the system. If the expected value matches the value entered by the user, the authentication system grants the user access. No matter the outcome of the comparison, the attempt to access the system is logged. These logs are used to locate unusual behavior such as excessive amounts of failed access attempts and concurrent accesses at different locations. Problems such as these must be considered as some magnetic cards are easily duplicated.

The problems associated with magnetic cards for user authentication are not limited to forgery. Other common problems include lost or forgotten cards and remote system access. In the event a user loses his card it should be immediately voided as to prevent unauthorized users from possibly accessing the system. The policy for handling users who have forgotten their magnetic card, however, will vary with each organization. Two possible policies are to provide the user with a temporary card or require the user to retrieve his own card. Each organization will not only have to determine whether temporary cards will be available but whether the users may remotely access the system. For a user to remotely access a system, either a portable card reader must be attached to the terminal or information written on the card must be manually entered into the computer. Providing card readers to all users that wish to remotely access a system will increase the risk to the system as there is little control over the performance and use of the reader. However, manually entering information that is written on a magnetic card, such as is done with many telephone access cards, reduces the level of system security to that of an information-based system.

5.2.2.2   Smartcards

In 1990 ANSI and the ISO approved a standard for identification cards that contain integrated circuits, or smartcards (ANSI/ISO standard 7816/1&2) [5.2]. Like magnetic cards, smartcards may contain information about the identity of the card holder and are used in a similar manner. A smartcard, however, has the ability to perform computations that may improve the security of the card and impede its unauthorized alteration or duplication [5.15, 5.21]. For example, the card may be programmed with the capability to apply its own encryption to the data, validate the integrity of the data, or verify the authenticity of the card [5.7, 5.15]. The issuing organization must decide what calculations a card will perform when used.

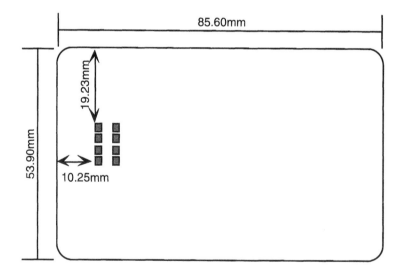

Figure 5.2. The layout and design of a smartcard.

Smartcards not only share much of the functionality of magnetic cards, but many of their physical characteristics as well. Figure 5.2 shows the dimensions of a smartcard as well as the layout of the circuit contained within the card. The card measures 85.60 mm wide by 53.98 mm high with a thickness of .76 mm. Eight circuit contacts are in the upper left corner; two rows of four contacts each. The contacts measure 2 mm by 1.7 mm each and are separated within a row by a gap of .84 mm and between rows with a gap of 2.62 mm. The upper left-most contact measures 19.23 mm from the top of the card and 10.25 from the left edge of the card.

With the two types of cards being so similar in design and use, the issuing organization must determine whether the additional security and functionality of using smartcards is worth their additional cost. The typical cost of a 100 card smartcard authentication system for one year is approximately two times that of an equivalent magnetic card system [5.21]. This value will change with time and the inevitable improvement in technology.

5.2.2.3 Calculators

Another type of physical security key is the security calculator. A security calculator is a small device that looks very much like a simple calculator with the addition of a few specialized functions [5.7, 5.15]. When used properly, the unidentified functions perform the computations necessary to authenticate a user for access to a computer system. To correctly grant access to authorized users, this scheme requires the user to remember his user name and a personal access number in addition to possessing a personalized calculator.

One common authentication process begins when a user presents his user name in an attempt to access the computer system. The authentication system responds with a challenge value. The user must enter his personal access number along with the challenge into his calculator. The calculator performs a series of mathematical computations on the challenge value and returns a response value to the user. The user must present the response value to the authentication system. The authentication system will grant the user access if the number presented matches the value expected by the authentication system. The response value from the calculator will be incorrect if the personal access number is incorrect, the user does not use his personalized calculator, or the challenge number is incorrectly entered.

Other authentication schemes that employ a calculator exist. These schemes work in a similar fashion — they present a challenge value to the user and require a specific response that only a calculator with the proper access code can correctly produce. These schemes, like the one presented above, provide numerous advantages over common password schemes while only incurring minimal drawbacks.

The benefits of using calculator authentication are immediately experienced upon its incorporation to existing systems. Calculator authentication requires no additional hardware be attached to the computer system. Thus, changing from a password-based system to a calculator-based system requires only minor software modifications. The only new hardware introduced during the installation process is the calculators. Their involvement, however, is minimal as they only require personalization and distribution. The benefits of calculator authentication are also noticeable after the installation process. Unlike other physical key authentication systems, users will retain their ability to remotely access the system. Furthermore, these users will not need to use additional authentication hardware.

5.2.3   Biometric Keys

Recent advancements in technology have made it possible for biometrics to be used in the user authorization process. Biometrics are measurements of personal characteristics such as a voice or fingerprint [5.15]. Biometric keys provide many advantages over informational or physical keys [5.15]. The three primary advantages of biometric keys are: (1) they are unique, (2) they are difficult to duplicate or forge, and (3) they are always with their authorized user. These characteristics make biometrics an excellent method for user authorization. Commonly used biometric keys include voice prints, fingerprints, retinal prints, facial profiles, hand geometry, and signature analysis [5.15, 5.19].

5.2.3.1   Voice Prints

Voice prints are mathematical representations of a person's speech patterns [5.3, 5.14]. These representations are often used by computer and telephone voice navigation systems. These systems, for example, respond to a user's audible request to speak with an operator or open a file. User authentication systems function in a similar manner; however, they also attempt to determine the identity of the speaker. This is accomplished by obtaining an unverified identity and speech sample from a user and comparing it to a previously authenticated speech sample. Before the voice print authentication process can occur, however, the system must be installed. This involves the installation of the proper hardware (e.g., microphones), creation of the authentication speech, and the creation of the authentic user speech samples.

During the hardware installation process, the information each user will be required to speak should be created. The information may consist of either complete phrases or single, unrelated words. While single word identification has been shown to be slightly more accurate than phrase identification, it has also been shown to be more susceptible to impersonation [5.3]. That is, the authentication system has a greater chance of identifying which words were spoken. It also has a greater chance of incorrectly identifying the user speaking [5.23]. Once the format of the speech has been determined, the actual words must be chosen [5.3]. Words should be chosen so that they emphasize the variability found in the speech patterns of different people [5.3, 5.14]. The words that

provide the greatest variability contain nasal or vowel phonemes [5.14].   A list of
suggested phonemes and words is provided in Figure 5.3 [5.14].

/i/	mean	/u/	moon
/I/	mint	/m/	man
/e/	men	/n/	nest
/æ/	mat		

Figure 5.3. Suggested voice print phonemes and words.

Once the installation process has been completed and the authentication text has
been determined, each user must prime the system with examples of his voice print.
Each user must record two or more versions of the speech to account for any variability.
To more realistically represent the expected authentication conditions, the recording
should be uncoached and take place in an environment with a moderate level of
background noise.   After a user makes a speech sample, he will use the voice
authentication system to gain access.

The complete voice print authentication process is accomplished in four stages: (1)
pre-processing, (2) sampling, (3) testing, and (4) system response [5.22].

In the first stage, pre-processing, a user wishing system access presents an
unverified identity to the system. This indicates to the system whom the user claims to
be and which authentic sample the system should use for comparison.

In the second stage, sampling, the user speaks a predetermined statement into a
microphone connected to the system. The system attempts to identify the key phonemes
of the new sample. In the event the system cannot identify the necessary phonemes, the
system informs the user that they must speak again.   Besides poor annunciation, two
problems that may require the user to speak again are background noise and unusually fast
or slow speech.   Most background noise, however, can be filtered out electronically or
with physical devices such as barriers or microphone padding. Like background noise,
most timing problems are also easily resolved electronically.   When there are no
significant problems and the system can accurately identify the phonemes, the testing
process begins.

The third stage, testing, uses the unverified identity and the voice sample to
determine whether the user is authorized to use the computer system. The authentication
system uses the unverified identity information to select the voice print that will be the
basis for identification of the user. Characteristics of the phonemes in the two samples,

such as the acoustic strength and frequency, are compared and weighted according to their importance in matching between the samples. These values are totaled and the result used to determine whether the user should be granted or denied access.

The final stage of the process occurs after the comparison of the two voice prints when the authentication system either grants or denies the user access to the system. In either case, the authentication system should log the time and date that access was attempted. This log will assist in determining the users that should create a more accurate authentic sample and the users whose voice print may be compromised.

The log files produced by the authentication system are useful in locating and resolving potential problems such as inaccurate authentic samples and voice print forgeries. The logs will reveal when a user continuously has a difficult time authenticating himself. This may indicate that either a user's voice has changed or that someone is attempting to subvert the system. System attacks, as well as voice print forgery, will also stand out when a user has been simultaneously authenticated at different locations. While voice prints are unique, advancements in digital recording technology make it possible to record a near perfect voice print. This may be of little concern on site where users are watched as they log in. Remote system attacks, however, present a greater problem.

Remote system access, while useful, presents numerous problems to the voice print authentication system. The first problem concerns how a user accesses the system. That is, how does a remote user present his voice print for authorization. Creative solutions involving multiple phone lines or authorization before a connect signal can be developed. These solutions, however, are often cumbersome and complicated. The second problem with remote access concerns the authenticity of the live voice print. It is difficult to determine whether the authentication comes from the authorized user or from an unauthorized user with a high quality or digitally generated recording. For these reasons, remote access is often limited to those who expressly request it or is not available. As will be seen, these remote access problems are not limited to voice print authentication, but are common to most biometric authentication methods.

5.2.3.2   Fingerprint

Fingerprint authentication is the processes of granting or denying access to a user based on his fingerprint [5.6, 5.15, 5.17]. This is accomplished by obtaining an unverified fingerprint from a user and comparing it to a previously authenticated fingerprint. Before the fingerprint authentication process can occur, however, the system must be installed. This includes installation of fingerprint readers and the recording of each user's authentic fingerprint.

Installation begins with the placement of fingerprint readers at each terminal or restricted lab entrance. During this installation process, each user must have a series of fingerprints recorded as a basis for future system access. Multiple prints of multiple fingers should be recorded so that personal injury does not affect a user's ability to access the system.

Once the authentic prints are recorded and the hardware has been installed, a user will be required to claim an identity and present his finger for comparison. The complete fingerprint authentication process can be separated into five distinct steps: (1) obtain information, (2) fingerprint cleaning, (3) feature extraction, (4) fingerprint comparison, and (5) system response [5.6, 5.18]. Each of these steps is discussed in detail below.

The first step in fingerprint identification is obtaining input from a user. This input includes an unverified identity and a fingerprint sample. Unverified identity claims often take the form of personal access numbers or magnetic cards encoded with the owner's identity. The authentication system uses the unverified identity to obtain a fingerprint for the comparison process. Before the comparison can begin, however, the new fingerprint sample must be processed.

The second step of the authentication process involves cleaning the fingerprint so that the features of the print may be located. The cleaning process begins with the conversion of the print to a representation that the system can manipulate. The fingerprint is converted to a large matrix of 0's and 1's [5.18]. The 0's represent the valleys, or low points, of the print and the 1's represent the ridges, or high points, of the print. This results in a rough fingerprint pattern with ridge gaps and smudges; a result of dirty or damaged fingers. These irregularities are mathematically removed and the complete print is smoothed and thinned. For additional information on this process, see Rao [5.17].

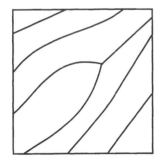 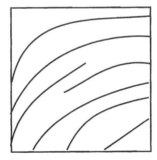

Figures 5.4a & b. Illustrations of a fingerprint fork and ridge ends, respectively.

The third step, feature extraction, involves the location and demarcation of specific pattern features such as forks and ridge ends. Forks are the points of a fingerprint where two ridges join together and continue as one. Ridge ends are the points of a fingerprint where a ridge stops. Figures 5.4a and b illustrate examples of forks and ridges.

Once every fork and ridge end is located, their relative positions must be recorded. Recording the points in terms of their positions to each other allows the authentication process to account for inconsistent alignments and orientations of finger placement on the pad. An alternate method of fingerprint representation employs B-spline functions [5.6]. Each line of a fingerprint is represented by a B-spline function. The end result is a series of B-spline functions as opposed to single points. Research by Chong et al. [5.6] indicates that these representations will not only require less storage space than relative position values, but will improve the processing time required to analyze fingerprints as well. Since both fingerprint representation methods perform the desired task of mathematically describing a fingerprint, either may be implemented.

The fourth step, fingerprint comparison, uses the unverified identity and the fingerprint sample to determine whether the user is authorized to use the computer system. The authentication system uses the unverified identity information to select the fingerprint that will be the basis for identification of the user. Characteristics of the fingerprints are compared and the results used to determine whether the user should be granted or denied access. Depending on the fingerprint representation used, the comparison characteristics will either be the relative placement of the forks and ridge ends or the B-spline functions.

The final stage of the process, system response, occurs when the authentication system either grants or denies a user access to the system. In either case, the authentication system, like the voice print system, should log the time and date that access was attempted. This log will assist in determining which users are regularly denied access and having difficulty with the system. Unlike voice print authentication logs, these logs are unnecessary for locating compromised accounts. This is not because unauthorized users will not attempt to access the system, rather it is a direct result of the difficulty in forging fingerprints. With rapid advancements in technology, however, fingerprint authentication may need to take additional biometric measurements, such as finger size or temperature, to decrease the possibility of unauthorized access.

While forgery is currently not a concern with fingerprint authentication, remote access to a system is a concern. Like magnetic cards, the only way a user will be able to authenticate themselves is with the use of additional hardware. While providing authorized users portable fingerprint readers is possible, it is impractical and costly. Additional concerns involve the trustworthiness of any portable hardware. The fingerprint pattern produced by the hardware cannot be trusted as any knowledgeable user can alter the device to produce the desired results regardless of the fingerprint used. For these reasons, remote access should always be denied and users requiring remote access required to make other computing arrangements.

5.2.3.3 Retinal Prints

Retinal authentication is the process of granting or denying a user system access based on the blood vessel pattern on the back of their eyes [5.19]. Like fingerprint authentication, retinal scanning is hyper-accurate and currently impossible to forge or duplicate. This makes retinal scanning an attractive authentication method.

Retinal authentication requires placement of retinal scanners at selected security points such as at each terminal or at the entrances to restricted labs. To be guaranteed future access to the computing facilities, each user must enroll in the authentication system and have their retinal pattern scanned. As the process is hyper-accurate and a user's retinal scan will not change or age, only one scan is required to enroll. Rescanning may be necessary, however, in the event that a user's eye suffers damage.

Once the authentication system is in place, a user will be required to claim an unverified identity and look into a retinal scanner to gain access to the computer system. Like other biometric authentication methods, the unverified identification can take the form of either a personal access number or magnetic card. The authentication system uses this unverified identity to recall a claimed user's authenticated retinal pattern. The authenticated retinal pattern becomes the yardstick by which a user's pattern will be measured. This retinal pattern is obtained by scanning a user's eye with a low level infrared beam [5.5, 5.19]. The beam makes the blood vessels on the back of the eye appear in varying degrees of gray on a light background [5.5]. The light intensity at hundreds of predetermined points on the retina is recorded for comparison.

The authentication system compares the recorded intensities of the two retinal patterns to determine whether they agree with each other. When the patterns agree, the user is the person he claims to be and may be granted access. In the event that the two patterns do not agree, however, the user should not be given access. In either case, the authentication system should log all attempted accesses. This log will have limited usefulness as the retina cannot be forged and the authentication system is hyper-accurate. It will be useful, however, in identifying hardware problems that arise.

The greatest problems with retinal scanning are not forgery or accuracy, rather providing remote access. These problems are identical to those of the fingerprint authentication system. Not surprisingly, the solution is also the same — remote access should always be denied. In the event this is not practical, less secure means of authentication must be used.

5.2.3.4 Facial Profiles

Facial profile authentication grants or denies system access by examining a user's facial profile, or silhouette [5.11, 5.19]. This is accomplished by comparing two profiles: the profile of the user requesting access and the authenticated profile of the user. If the two profiles match, the user is authenticated. This process requires installation of imaging hardware and analysis software.

Installation of the facial profiling system includes the placement of imaging cameras and plain backgrounds. With the increasing availability of inexpensive terminal-based cameras for teleconferencing and multimedia systems, this is no longer impractical.

In addition to the imaging hardware, each user must prime the system with multiple profile images. Over an extended period of time, each user must record weekly facial profiles to be used in the analysis of future authentication. These profiles are recorded in this manner to account for normal facial changes and aging [5.10]. Users will also be required to update their profile images periodically to account for any drastic changes. When authorized users find the authentication system incorrectly denying them access, they should re-authenticate their profiles.

Once the hardware is installed and the users have primed the system, they will be required to use the profile authentication system. The authentication process occurs in four steps: (1) obtain information, (2) imaging and calculations, (3) profile comparison, and (4) system response [5.11, 5.20].

The first step of profile authentication, as with other biometric methods, is to obtain an unverified user identity and image sample. The unverified identity claim would be in the form of either a personal access number or magnetic card encoded with the owner's identity. The authentication system uses the unverified identity to obtain an authenticated profile for the comparison process.

The second step of the profile authentication process is the imaging and calculating step. Imaging begins with locating several key points on each of the two profile images. Harmon et al. [5.10] and Campos et al. [5.4] each suggests a specific set of points, and corresponding calculations, that produce results relatively unique to each user. Figure 5.4 shows points commonly used by various profiling techniques. Once the relative location of each of the selected points is found, calculations of various angles, distances, triangular areas, and curve fittings are computed [5.4, 5.10, 5.20]. The results of these calculations are used in the comparisons made in Step three.

The third step of the authentication process is the comparison of the calculation results. The values of the calculations made on the two profiles are compared to determine whether the profiles are from the same person.

The final step of profile authentication is system response. When the calculations are within a tolerance level, the user is granted access to the system. In the event that the calculations do not fall within the specified tolerances, the user should be denied access to the system. In either situation, the access attempt should be logged.

As with other authentication methods, the log files produced by facial profiling authentication will assist in locating profiles that may need updating, profiles that have been compromised, and faulty hardware. These problems are easily noticed upon examination of the log files. For example, repeated, intermittent denial of access for one particular profile would indicate that the profile most likely needs updating. Consistent denial of access for one particular user, however, would possibly indicate that an unauthorized user was attempting to subvert the system. In a similar manner, continuous denial of access to all users by one camera location may indicate the presence of faulty hardware. These conclusions, however, could not be made without further investigation.

5.2.3.5   Hand Geometry

Hand geometry authentication relies upon hyper-accurate measurements of a person's fingers and finger webbing to determine whether a user should be granted access to a computer system [5.8, 5.19]. For this method to function properly, measurement devices must be installed and the system primed with authenticated prints.

The installation process for the hand geometry authentication system includes placing hand measurement devices at each terminal or restricted lab entrance. Unlike the previous biometric authentication devices, the physical size of many hand geometry measurement devices may be too large to conveniently place at each terminal. Most hand measurement devices measure approximately eight inches in each dimension. While the installation process is proceeding, each authorized user must create an authenticated hand measurement for comparison once the system is functional. Unless a user finds his newly authenticated measurement inaccurate, measurement updates will only need to be made when a user damages his hand.

Once a user has primed the authentication system and the hardware is installed, he must use the hand geometry measurement device to gain access to the system. This process is similar to those used by other biometric devices such as fingerprint authentication and follows a like process of obtaining the necessary input and measurements, comparing the values, and responding to the authentication request. Each of these steps is discussed below.

The authentication process begins when a user presents an unverified identity in the form of either a personal access number or magnetic card. The system uses this identity to locate the expected hand measurements for the user.   Along with the unverified identification, a user must place his hand upon the measurement device. For the system to correctly measure a user's hand, it must be properly placed upon the device. Proper hand placement is achieved when the user comfortably places the pegs protruding from the device between his fingers, as low as possible [5.24]. The user's fingers must also lay across the guides on the pad [5.19, 5.24]. Proper hand placement is shown in Figure 5.5. Once the hand is properly situated, a light from above the hand will shine down and sensors below the uncovered portion of the finger guides will record hyper-accurate measurements of the length of the user's fingers [5.13, 5.19].

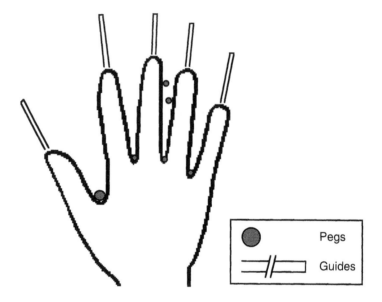

Figure 5.5. Proper hand placement on a hand geometry measurement device.

Once the hand measurements have been recorded by the system, they are compared to the expected values of the unverified identity entered by the user. For the user to gain access to the computer system, the measurements must fall within acceptable tolerances. In the event that the difference between the measured length and the expected length does not closely match, the user is denied access to the computer system. As with other biometric authentication methods, keeping a log of the attempted accesses, whether successful or failed, will assist in locating problems and subversive behavior.

Log files will provide assistance in locating and resolving problems that may occur with the hand geometry authentication system. Since hand geometry authentication is not as secure as fingerprint or retinal scan authentication, the logs will be useful in locating possible attacks. Multiple, concurrent accesses will be one such indication of possible attack. Additional concern should be raised by log files that indicate multiple, unsuccessful authentication attempts by either a single user or multiple users within a short period of time. While either case may indicate that an unauthorized user is attempting to access the system, further investigation would be required.

While log files will be useful in resolving problems within the system, solutions must be found to resolve the concerns resulting from use of the system. One such concern is remote access authentication. For users to remotely access a system employing hand geometry authentication, portable hand measurement devices would be needed. This is both impractical and inadvisable as the device may be neither reliable nor trustworthy. Thus, users wishing to access the system remotely must make other arrangements.

5.2.3.6 Signature Analysis

As signature analysis relies more on habitual actions rather than uncontrollable characteristics, some researchers do not consider it a biometric measurement [5.7, 5.15]. A person's signature, however, relies on biometric characteristics as well as habitual actions [5.7, 5.12]. The manner in which a person writes his signature depends upon the size and development of his arm and muscles [5.12]. The pressure placed upon the writing instrument also depends on the development of a person's muscles [5.12]. Regardless of whether signature analysis is a biometric of many personal traits or a habitual action, it is widely used for user authentication and therefore discussed here.

Signature analysis authentication examines the characteristics of how a user writes his signature to determine whether the user should be granted access to the computer system. For the authentication system to grant access to a user, the signature sample provided by the user must reasonably match in content as well as technique. These features are measured by a specially designed stylus, or pen, which must be installed at each terminal.

In addition to the installation of modified pens, signature analysis authentication requires the user to provide numerous signature samples for comparison. These signature samples should be written in a normal fashion such that they can be easily duplicated by the original writer. When normally written, these signatures rarely need updating.

Once the system has been installed and the users have recorded samples of their signatures, they will begin using signature authentication to gain access to the computer system. Like other authentication methods, the signature authentication process may be separated into multiple steps: (1) obtain information, (2) measure characteristics, (3) signature comparison, and (4) system response [5.12].

The first step of the signature authentication process is obtaining the necessary information. To gain access to the system, the user must provide an unverified identity and sample signature. Like the previous authentication system, the unverified identity will most likely take the form of a personal access number or magnetic card.

The second step in the authentication process, measuring the signature characteristics, occurs both during and after the signature is written. During the writing of the signature the time duration, pen pressure, pen acceleration, pen up-and-down pattern, and the order in which lines are written are measured and recorded [5.12, 5.16]. After the signature is complete, line slopes, signature length, and signature content are recorded [5.12, 5.16].

The third step in the authorization process occurs when the sample signature is compared to the authenticated signatures belonging to the unverified user identity obtained in Step 1.

The final step in the process determines how the system responds to the user's request for access. For the user to be granted access to the system, these signatures must be sufficiently similar by comparison. In the event the signatures do not closely match, the user will be denied access. As with the other authentication methods, an access attempt log should be kept by the authentication system. Access logs are especially important in a signature authentication system as it is prone to attack.

Extensive use of these logs and concern for forgeries can be avoided, however, if the signature measurement process is complete. The characteristics that will improve the authentication's ability to identify and reject forgeries are timing measurements and pressure measurements [5.16]. Most forgeries are written slowly as the forger is attempting to create a visibly similar signature [5.16]. Sensitive timing constraints will reject this type of signature as being too slow. In the event that an unauthorized user is capable of producing a reasonable forgery within the necessary time constraint, the pressure placed upon the pen should identify the signature as a forgery [5.16]. Pressure measurements have proven to be a reliable means of identifying users as pen pressure is a difficult writing characteristic to reproduce accurately [5.16].

5.3 Summary

Most computer systems have a first line of defense: the authentication system. The purpose of the authentication system is to prevent unauthorized users from using the system and accessing the information within the system. This is accomplished by forcing all users to provide either secret or unique information. Common examples of secret information are passwords and questionnaires. Examples of unique information include smartcards and fingerprints. As the degree of security provided by the different authentication systems vary, system administrators will have to determine the most appropriate means of authentication for their computer system. This will require a careful evaluation of both the needs of the computing environment and the features, both positive and negative, of each system.

5.4   Exercises

5.1   There are three advantages of biometric keys over physical or informational keys. What are they and why are they advantages? Do biometric keys have any disadvantages? If so, what?

5.2   Besides entering a user name, what are other ways a user can present their claimed identity when doing voice authentication? What are the advantages and disadvantages of each of these methods?

5.3   What other reasons may explain why questionnaire profiling is not often used?

5.4   Could facial profiling be forged? If so, how?

5.5   Limited research has been done into the possibility of using ear measurements for authentication purposes. Which authentication method is this most similar to? How would the similar authentication system need to be modified to accommodate ears?

5.6   All biometric authentication systems discussed in this chapter require the user to identify who they claim to be by providing either a personal access number or magnetic card. Is this necessary? How can this be avoided? What are the advantages and disadvantages of not requiring an identity claim?

5.5   References

5.1   American National Standards Institute, *American National Standard ANSI/ISO 7810-1985: Identification cards – physical characteristics*, New York, New York, May 20, 1988.

5.2   American National Standards Institute, *American National Standard ANSI/ISO 78106/21988: Integrated circuit(s) cards with contacts – part 2: dimensions and location of contacts*, New York, New York, December 12, 1990.

5.3   Brown, M. K., McGee, M. A., and Rabiner, L. R., "Training Set Design for
           Connected Speech Recognition", *IEEE Transactions on Signal Processing*,
           Vol. 39, No. 6, June 1991, pp. 1268-1281.

5.4   Campos, J. C., Linney, A. D., and Moss, J. P., "The Analysis of Facial
           Profiles Using Scale Space Techniques", *Pattern Recognition*, Vol. 26, No.
           6, June 1993, pp. 819-824.

5.5   Chinnock, C., "Eye-Based Systems Show Promise for Security Use",
           Military and Aerospace Electronics, November 1994, pp. 6-11.

5.6   Chong, M. M. S., Gay, R. K. L., Tan, N. H., and Liu, J., "Automatic
           Representation of Fingerprints for Data Compression by B-Spline
           Functions", *Pattern Recognition*, Vol. 25, No. 10, October 1992, pp. 1199-
           1210.

5.7   Davies, D. W. and Price, W. L., *Security for Computer Networks, 2ed.*,
           John Wiley & Sons Publishing Co., New York, New York, 1984.

5.8   Fites, P. and Kratz, M. P. J., *Information Systems Security: A Practitioner's
           Reference*, Van Nostrand Reinhold, New York, New York, 1993.

5.9   Garfinkel, S. and Spafford, G., *Practical UNIX Security*, O'Reilly &
           Associates, June 1991.

5.10   Harmon, L. D., Khan, M. K., Lasch, R., and Ramig, P. F., "Machine
           Identification of Human Faces", *Pattern Recognition*, Vol. 13, No. 2,
           February 1981, pp. 97-110.

5.11   Harmon, L. D., Kuo, S. C., Ramig, P. F., and Raudkivi, U., "Identification
           of Human Face Profiles by Computer", *Pattern Recognition*, Vol. 10, No. 3,
           March 1978, pp. 301-312.

5.12   Herbst, N. M. and Liu, C. N., "Automatic Signature Verification Based on
           Accelerometry", *IBM Journal of Research and Development*, Vol. 21, No.
           3, May 1977, pp. 245-253.

5.13   Holmes, J. P., Wright, L. J., and Maxwell, R. L., "A Performance
           Evaluation of Biometric Identification Devices", *Sandia Nation Laboratories
           Technical Report SAND91-0276•UC-906*, June 1991.

5.14   Kashyap, R. L., "Speaker Recognition from an Unknown Utterance and
        Speaker-Speech Interaction", *IEEE Transactions on Acoustics, Speech, and
        Signal Processing*, Vol. ASSP-24, No. 6, December 1976, pp. 481-488.

5.15   Morris, R. and Thompson, K., "Password Security: A Case History",
        Communications of the ACM, Vol. 22, No. 11, November 1979, pp. 594-
        597.

5.16   Nagel, R. N. and Rosenfeld, A., "Computer Detection of Freehand
        Forgeries", *IEEE Transactions on Computers*, Vol. C-26, No. 9, September
        1977, pp. 895-905.

5.17   Rao, C. V. K., "On Fingerprint Pattern Recognitions", *Pattern Recognition*,
        Vol. 10, No. 1, January 1978, pp. 15-18.

5.18   Rao, T. Ch. M., "Feature Extraction for Fingerprint Classification", *Pattern
        Recognition*, Vol. 8, No. 2, February 1976, pp. 181-192.

5.19   Russell, D. and Gangemi Sr., G. T., *Computer Security Basics*, O'Reilly &
        Associates, July 1991.

5.20   Samal, A. and Iyengar, P. A., "Automatic Recognition and Analysis of
        Human Faces and Facial Expressions: A Survey", *Pattern Recognition*, Vol.
        25, No. 1, January 1992, pp. 65-77.

5.21   Svigals, J., "Smartcards — A Security Assessment, Computers & Security",
        Elsevier Advanced Technology, Vol. 13, No. 2, April 1994, pp. 107-114.

5.22   White, G. M. and Neel, R. B., "Speech Recognition Experiments with Linear
        Prediction, Bandpass Filtering and Dynamic Programming", *IEEE
        Transactions on Acoustics, Speech, and Signal Processing*, Vol. ASSP-24,
        No. 2, April 1976, pp. 183-189.

5.23   Wilpon, J. G., Rabiner, L. R., Lee, C.-L., and Goldman, E. R., "Automatic
        Recognition of Keywords in Unconstrained Speech Using Hidden Markov
        Models", *IEEE Transactions on Acoustics, Speech, and Signal Processing*,
        Vol. 38, No. 11, November 1990, pp. 1870-1990.

5.24   Wilson, B., "Hand Geometry Boasts Simplicity, Convenience", *Access Control*, March 1992.

5.6   Extended Bibliography

5.25   Boccignone, G., Chianese, A., Cordella, L. P., and Marcelli, A., "Recovering Dynamic Information from Static Handwriting", *Pattern Recognition*, Vol. 26, No. 3, March 1993, pp. 409-418.

5.26   Brault, J.-J. and Plamondon, R., "A Complex Measure of Handwritten Curves: Modeling of Dynamic Signature Forgery", *IEEE Transactions on System, Man, and Cybernetics*, Vol. 23, No. 2, March/April 1993, pp. 400-413.

5.27   Guerfali, W. and Plamondon, R., "Normalizing and Restoring On-Line Handwriting", *Pattern Recognition*, Vol. 26, No. 3, March 1993, pp. 419-431.

5.28   Huang, C. L. and Chen, C. W., "Human Facial Feature Extraction for Face Interpretation and Recognition", *Pattern Recognition*, Vol. 25, No. 12, December 1992, pp. 1435-1444.

5.29   Ikeda, K., Yamamura, T., Mitamura, Y., Fujiwara, S., Tominaga, Y., and Kiyono, T., "On-Line Recognition of Hand-Written Characters Utilizing Positional and Stroke Vector Sequences", *Pattern Recognition*, Vol. 13, No. 3, March 1981, pp. 191-206.

5.30   Liu, C. N. Herbst, N. M., and Anthony, N. J., "Automatic Signature Verification System Description and Field Test Results", *IEEE Transactions on Systems, Man, and Cybernetics*, Vol. SMC-9, No. 1, January 1979, pp. 35-38.

5.31   Moayer, B. and Fu, K. S., "An Application of Stochastic Languages to Fingerprint Pattern Recognition", *Pattern Recognition*, Vol. 8, No. 2, February 1976, pp. 173-179.

5.32   Paquet, T. and Lecourtier, Y., "Recognition of Handwritten Sentences Using a Restricted Lexicon", *Pattern Recognition*, Vol. 26, No. 3, March 1993, pp. 391-407.

6

ACCESS AND INFORMATION FLOW CONTROLS

In Chapter 5 we discussed identification and authentication methods used to limit access to a computer system. Early computers had no internal controls to limit access and any user could thus interact with any portion of the system desired. In today's larger and much more complex environments, however, just because individuals have been confirmed as authorized users does not mean that they should have access to all information contained on the system. It is the job of the *Access Control* security services to determine which information an individual can access.

Conceptually, what access controls are designed to do can be depicted as a protection table such as the one illustrated in Figure 6.1. The table contains every user who may have access to the system on one axis and every file stored on the system on the other axis. The entries located at the intersection of any user/file pair shows what type of access this user has for that specific file. Typical access modes that might be found in the table include:

- *Read* — allow the user to read the file or view the file attributes.
- *Write* — allow the user to write to the file; this may include creating, modifying, or appending onto the file.
- *Execute* — the user may load the file and execute it.
- *Delete* — the user may remove this file from the system.
- *List* — allows the user to view the file's attributes.

Often some of these may be implied in another. A user given *Read* access to a file will generally also be able to view that file's attributes. In Figure 6.1, User 2 has *Read* and *Write* access for File 1 but only *Read* access for File 2. We may also be able to assume that User 2 can view both file's attributes even though *List* is not specifically stated. The table lists User 2's access to File 3 as *List*, however, which means User 2 can view the attributes of the file but not the file itself. A location in the table where there is no entry means that the user has not been granted any type of access for this file. If desired, the table can be expanded to also include a list of specific hardware devices in order to limit access to them as well. This is illustrated in the last two columns of Figure 6.1, which includes Printer 1 and Disk 1. While access control seems like a simple problem with a simple solution, in reality it is seldom implemented in this fashion. The reason for this is the table created is extremely large and sparsely populated. Most users will have access only to their own files and not to files created by another user. This results in a table in which most entries will be blank. Storing a large, mostly empty table is a tremendous waste of space. Consequently, other methods have been created to address the problem.

Object

User	File 1	File 2	File 3	File 4	File 5	Printer 1	Disk 1
1			Read Write		Read Write	Write	
2	Read Write	Read	List			Write	
3		Read Write		Execute		Write	Read Write

Figure 6.1. A protection table [6.5, 6.6].

Working in conjunction with Access Controls are *Information Flow Controls*. These controls incorporate methods to regulate the dissemination of information among the subjects and objects on the system. The policies that dictate the permissible flow of information center around the security model chosen for the system (see Chapter 4 for a discussion of security models). While Access Controls play a major role in controlling which subjects are permitted to view and use information, they are not sufficient to control all aspects concerning the flow of information. Discretionary Access Controls, as defined in the DOD *Trusted Computer Systems Evaluation Criteria*, for example, will clearly delineate who may access a file but do not cover what the person does with the information once it is viewed. The user may make a copy of the accessed information and then pass it along to others not originally intended to receive it. The flow of this information, then, has exceeded its intended scope. Mandatory Access Controls, on the other hand, also govern how the accessed files may be manipulated in certain ways, such as copying, and thus restrict the flow of information. We will begin our discussion of

Access and Information Flow Controls with a discussion of various techniques to govern initial access to the objects protected by the computer system.

6.1   File Passwords

The usage of passwords as an access control technique is similar to their usage for controlling access to the computer system itself. In order to gain access to a file, the user must present the system with the file's password. This password is separate from, and should be different than, the one used by the user to gain access to the system. In this technique, each file is assigned a password and each user who is to be given access to the file must be told the password. The original assigning of the password can be done by the system manager or the owner of the file itself. In order to control the type of access granted to the file, multiple passwords for each file may be necessary. For example, the system might use one password to control reading and a separate one to control writing.

While this technique is easy to understand and fairly easy to implement, it is cumbersome and suffers from several problems that renders it unsuitable for most of today's computing environments. The first problem is with the passwords themselves. Since users have to remember a separate password for each file they have access to, this will result in a large number of passwords that would have to be memorized. Most people will not, however, attempt to memorize the large number of passwords but will instead write them down and keep them on a paper which they tape to their terminal, keep in the top drawer of their desk, or store in their wallet. Obviously this defeats the whole purpose of having the passwords in the first place. In addition, this technique places a great amount of responsibility on the users to not tell anybody the password to a file. Users are notorious for disregarding security policies when they are pressed for time and any technique that relies so heavily on the users themselves will usually result in numerous violations.

The second problem with password file protection is that there is no easy way to keep track of who has access to a file. The passwords are distributed manually, often by word of mouth, which leaves no automated trail to keep track of them. This lack of any kind of list describing who has access to a specific file leads to another problem, revoking a user's access to a file. Actually it is easy to revoke a user's access to a file: simply change the password. The problem is doing so without affecting all of the other users who need the file. Since there is no list of authorized users, when the file's password is changed, each of the other users will have to come forward to identify themselves to obtain the new password. This problem can be partially solved through the use of multiple passwords for each file. Now a user may be considered part of a group. Each file may have a number of groups that have been given access to it. If a user's access is to be revoked, only the group that the user is part of will be affected. All other groups may still access the file using their own password. This technique is especially useful when a user is to be granted access for only a limited time. A group consisting of only the single user can be created and the password eliminated when that user's need for the file is over. There is an obvious amount of extra overhead associated with this multiple password technique, which makes it cumbersome to use.

The final problem with a password-based file protection scheme is encountered when we have a file (e.g., program) that needs to access other files. One way to handle this is to embed the passwords for the other files inside the program itself but this means that a user granted access to the program is immediately granted access to the other files too. Another way to handle this would be to require the user to specify all file passwords up front but this assumes that the user knows which files will need to be accessed before the program is executed. A third method is to have the user supply the password for each additional file as it is accessed but this method is cumbersome and slows processing. There really is no suitable way to handle the problems associated with file passwords.

6.2   Capabilities Based

A capabilities-based access control scheme can be thought of as dividing our protection table from Figure 6.1 by rows. Associated with each user is a list of the objects that the user may access along with the specific access permissions. This list is called a Capability List with each entry being a capability. An example of the capability list for User 2 in our previous example is shown in Figure 6.2.

Object   Permissions

File 1	R,W,-,-,L
File 2	R,-,-,-,L
File 3	-,-,-,-,L
Printer 1	-,W,-,-,-

Figure 6.2. Capability list for User 2 [6.6].

Instead of the actual name of the object, a capability list may instead store a pointer to the object. An additional field may then be added which would describe the type of object that is pointed to. The permissions field in Figure 6.2 can be implemented using a bit map with each bit representing one of the possible access modes or permissions. In our example, the possible access modes are R (read), W (write), E (execute), D (delete), and L (list). Notice that the L bit is set whenever the R bit is set; however, the inverse is not necessarily true. This illustrates the point that a user will have List access whenever Read access is granted.

Capabilities can also be implemented as a *ticket* possessed by the user which will grant a specified mode of access to a specific object. The system maintains a list of these tickets for each user. This approach also allows a user to give access to an object to another user by passing copies of the ticket. Some systems may allow a user to revoke access to files they own by recalling the tickets given to other users.

Just like password file access techniques, both capability lists and capability tickets suffer from some cumbersome operational problems. The system is forced to maintain a list for each user. A single file may be accessible to all or a large number of users and will thus have its access information or ticket repeated many times for each of these users. This leads to tremendous overhead as the system must maintain capability lists with large amounts of repeated information. In addition, systems employing capability techniques have no efficient way of knowing exactly which users have access to a specific object. Revoking access to a file is also a cumbersome proposition since the ticket to grant access may have been passed to a number of different individuals. The system will need to check everyone's capability list to revoke access. A method that makes it easier to revoke access is to have the pointer in the capability list point to an indirect object which then points to the object itself. For an immediate revocation of access, the indirect object pointer can be deleted, thus breaking the chain. Of course this revokes everyone's access including those who may still legitimately require access.

To understand both the capabilities list and ticket techniques it may be useful to use an analogy. We can compare these techniques for granting file access to an attempt to secure a file cabinet by employing a guard to monitor it. Individuals who are to be granted access to a file within the cabinet will be given a special pass (the tickets) to show the guard. The ticket only grants access to a specific file and many users may have a copy of the ticket. The capability list, which contains a list of all files in the cabinet the user is authorized access to, is similar in that it will be shown to the guard who checks and upon verifying that the list includes the file cabinet, allows the user access. Obviously capability techniques need to include measures to keep users from forging tickets and lists so they can't obtain access to objects they are not entitled to. A simple method to do this is to make capabilities accessible only to the operating system and provide limited user commands to manipulate them.

6.3 Access Control Lists

While capability techniques can be thought of as dividing our protection table example by rows, Access Control Lists (ACLs) divide it up by columns. Instead of maintaining a separate list for each user which details the objects that a user has access to, ACLs are created for each object and list the subjects that have permission to access the object. There are several different ways that ACLs can be implemented. One example using our protection table from Figure 6.1 is depicted in Figure 6.3.

There are several obvious advantages in using Access Control Lists over the other techniques previously described. The first is the ease in which a list of all subjects granted access to an object can be determined. In a password scheme there was no way to accomplish this at all since passwords could be passed by word of mouth. In a

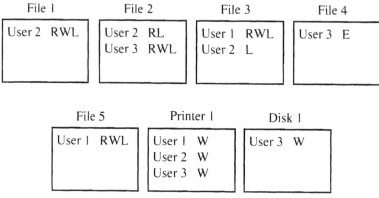

Figure 6.3. Access Control Lists.

capabilities-based scheme all of the subjects capability lists would have to be scanned to determine which had access to a specific object. Now the ACL is simply consulted. A second advantage is the ease in which access can be revoked. The owner of the object can simply remove (or change) any entry in the ACL to revoke or change the type of access granted to any subject. A third advantage is the storage space that is saved using this method (although an even more storage conscious scheme will be discussed later). The tables do not have to list each subject for every object, just those that have access permission and the specific mode of access granted. One drawback to this method, which is traditionally not thought of as such because it is seldom requested, is how difficult it is to list all objects a specific subject has access to. In this case, all of the ACLs would need to be scanned to determine which contained a reference to the subject in question. A capabilities-based scheme, on the other hand, could accomplish this very quickly by simply providing the capability list for the subject in question.

An approach often used on systems to aid in access control is to divide the users into groups which would coincide with real-world divisions such as all individuals working on a specific project. This additional feature can easily be accommodated with ACLs. Figure 6.4 depicts an ACL with groups added in a fashion similar to one used by the Multics and VMS operating systems [6.2]. In this example each entry consists of a user name and a group separated by a period. The user SMITH in group SALES has been granted *Read, Write,* and *List* access to File 1. The '*' is used as a wildcard which matches any user or group; so, the second entry states that any user in group SALES has *Read* and *List* access to File 1. Specific users can be denied access as depicted in the third line which states that user JONES in group PERSONNEL may not access this file at all. The last entry states that all other users are granted *List* access only.

File 1

SMITH.SALES	RWL
*.SALES	RL
JONES.PERSONNEL	N
.	L

Figure 6.4. An ACL employing Groups [6.2, 6.6].

One further feature that can be easily added to Access Control Lists is to provide the ability to restrict access based on such factors as the time of day or location the user is accessing the system from. This can be done by either specifying when and where access is to be granted or by providing times and locations when they are to be denied. The only real difference between the two is the default settings that result. Figure 6.5 shows how these can be added to specify any restrictions on time and location for the ACL of File 1. In this example, User SMITH in group SALES has been given access to the file at any time from any location since no restriction is listed. User JOHNSON in group PERSONNEL can only access the file from 8:00 AM to 6:00 PM and can only do so from a local terminal. Should user JOHNSON attempt to access the file in the middle of the night, or from a dial-in line, access would be denied.

File 1

SMITH.SALES	RWL		
JOHNSON.PERSONNEL	R	8:00-18:00	local

Figure 6.5. ACL with time and location restrictions [6.1].

Due to the fine granularity implemented in ACLs, the example in Figure 6.5 could easily be modified to allow groups or users different modes of access based on the location and time of access. Figure 6.6 shows a modification where user SMITH in group SALES is allowed *Read, Write,* and *List* access to File 1 during normal business hours (8:00 AM to 6:00 PM) and can access it from any location. After hours, however, SMITH only has been granted *Read* and *List* access and must do so from a local terminal.

File 1

SMITH.SALES	RWL	8:00-18:00	
SMITH.SALES	RL		local
JOHNSON.PERSONNEL	R	8:00-18:00	local

Figure 6.6. ACL with multiple individual user access restrictions [6.1].

6.4 Protection Bits

A modification to the Access Control List Approach uses only a few bits to describe the access permissions for each object. Similar to ACLs, Protection Bits are attached to each file but instead of providing a complete list of all users and their allowed access modes, they specify permissions for specific classes of users. Figure 6.7 shows how Protection Bits can be used on a system to implement an **Owner/Group/World** scheme for our *Read/Write/Execute/Delete/List* access modes. Instead of a large list being attached to each object, the Protection Bits use only fifteen bits of memory. The fifteen bits are broken into three sets of five. The first set of five bits represent the permissions for this object given to the owner of this file. The second set are used to delineate the access permissions given to users in the same group as the owner of the file. The final set of bits describes the permissions for all other users on the system. The first bit in each set of five is used to grant *Read* access mode permission. If the bit is set to one, *Read* access is granted. If the bit is set to zero, *Read* access is denied. The second bit of each group is used for *Write* access, the third for *Execute*, and so forth.

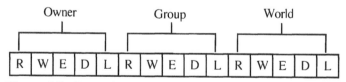

Figure 6.7. Protection Bits for Owner/Group/World scheme.

The most common example of the use of Protection Bits is the UNIX environment. UNIX systems employ an Owner/Group/World strategy for their file access with three access modes specified: *Read, Write,* and *Execute*. (Directories have a separate interpretation of what each of these access modes mean. See Question 6.3 at the end of this chapter.) Associated with each file on a UNIX system is the set of nine required access bits to implement this scheme. Each file also has an owner specified and a group which the user was part of when the file was created. A user is able to be part of many different groups and can freely change between these groups during a session by executing a command to change the current group. This enables the user to limit the access granted to any specific file to a designated number of individuals in a particular group. The result of this is to allow the user to actually limit access to a particular file to only a very few people by defining a special group for these select few to be part of. While extremely flexible, this method is somewhat cumbersome as users have to be aware of which group they are currently executing within. Often, because of the cumbersome nature of groups, the user simply gives everybody (the UNIX World category, sometimes on different systems referred to as Other or All-Other permissions) access to the file. This cumbersome nature of the group structure is the only real drawback to this technique, which is far outweighed by the greatly reduced storage requirements for the access control information. The only other drawback is the lack of an easy way to list all objects for which a specific subject has access to.

6.5 Controls for Mandatory Access

So far in this chapter we have addressed a variety of techniques that can be used to provide Discretionary Access Control. As was discussed in Chapter 4, Mandatory Access Controls place additional restrictions on access by way of an attached label to all subjects and objects which indicates each clearance or security level classification. While the purpose of Discretionary controls was to allow the users to limit access to the files they owned (i.e., access was granted at the "discretion" of the user), the purpose of Mandatory controls is to limit access to files based on the security classifications of the files. Even if a user wants to grant file access to another user, the system would not permit it unless the new user's clearance was sufficient to allow it.

Besides placing restrictions on users as subjects, Mandatory Access Controls also limit what processes or programs can do as subjects. A program will not be able to change the security restrictions imposed by the rules governing clearances and classifications for itself or other objects even if the same user owns them. A program will also be restricted from creating and using a shared file to pass information to another subject which would violate the security restrictions. It should be remembered that Mandatory controls do not replace Discretionary controls; they enhance them and serve as an additional restriction on the access of objects and flow of information. Only if both the Discretionary and Mandatory restrictions are followed will a subject be allowed access to an object.

An interesting problem that Mandatory Access Controls partially solve is the issue of Originator Controlled (ORCON) data [6.3]. ORCON data is information that may only be passed to another with the permission of the owner (originator) of the information. Normal Discretionary controls would allow the originator to specify another individual but would not prevent the second individual from copying the file and passing it along. Mandatory controls, on the other hand, would allow the owner to grant access to another user by creating a new category of information. Mandatory controls operate at two levels, the security level (which can be thought of as a vertical structure separating levels such as Secret and Top Secret) and categories (which are a horizontal separation within a level containing such identifiers as NATO or Nuclear). Since only the originator and those other users the originator grants access to are authorized the special category, the Mandatory controls would prevent anybody from making copies of the data and passing it along. The only problem with this scheme is for organizations that handle a large volume of ORCON data. In such an organization the number of additional categories created to handle every instance of ORCON data could quickly exceed the capacity of the system. There are organizations in the Federal Government that handle thousands of different ORCON documents [6.3]. Mandatory controls were not designed to handle such a large volume of categories.

As a final comment, we should remember that while Mandatory Access Controls inevitably apply more severe restrictions on object access, this is not done to limit the user but rather to protect the objects. A possible threat to the system (addressed in Chapter 3) is covert channels. They may be used to transfer information to subjects not authorized to have it. The techniques discussed to address this threat (required in the Orange Book Mandatory Access Division) should be implemented to lessen this threat to Information Flow Controls. It is because the restrictions are so strong that Mandatory Access Controls actually go a long way towards eliminating another problem that Discretionary Access Controls don't effectively address: Trojan Horses.

6.6   Trojan Horses

The four Access Control techniques previously described all have a major drawback when used to perform as Discretionary Access Controls or their equivalent. Programs that are executed by a user are free to access and modify all objects accessible by that user. This generally includes the ability to modify the access modes of the files. The operating system can't tell the difference between a legitimate request to change the permissions for an object owned by the user, and a request made by some malicious software to do the same. In this case, the specific malicious software we are concerned with is a Trojan Horse.

The simple definition of a Trojan Horse is software that appears to the user to be performing one function while it hides some other, often malicious, function. A more extensive definition would include five requirements:

  • An individual, hereafter referred to as the creator of the Trojan Horse, must have some purpose in mind which the Trojan Horse will fulfill. For example, the creator of the Trojan Horse may want to have access to all files on the system; so, the Trojan Horse will simply change the permission on all files in the current directory to Read accessible for the world.

• The creator of the Trojan Horse must write or modify a program to perform the hidden function while appearing to perform some other function.

• The Access and Information Flow Controls implemented on the system must be non-restrictive enough to allow the hidden function to be performed. This does not necessarily mean that the controls in place are lax, but rather that other methods have been introduced to handle the threat of Trojan Horses.

• The program that has been created or modified must have some way of being made accessible to the targeted victims. The program containing the Trojan Horse may be placed in a system library or a public directory of useful programs (a common one might be the "games" directory), or simply transmitted to the victim.

• The intended victim must run the program. Even the best Trojan Horse in the world won't work unless somebody executes the program to activate the hidden function.

Limiting the possibility of a Trojan Horse being able to perform its function requires several defensive measures. As was already mentioned, if the Access Control scheme employed by the computer system allows programs to modify the permissions of files the user owns, then the Trojan Horse will be able to easily function on the system. Simply changing to more restrictive Access Controls, which would cancel the ability of programs to modify permissions, would not by itself be sufficient to eliminate the threat from Trojan Horses. Instead of modifying the access permissions, the Trojan Horse would now make copies of files in the Trojan Horse creator's own directory. If the ability to do this was also eliminated, the Trojan Horse might then send files via electronic mail to its creator; so, this ability needs to be curtailed as well. Of course by limiting the ability of the Trojan Horse to be able to function by restricting the possible ways that information may flow within the system, we are also severely restricting what legitimate users can be doing.

Another approach to addressing the Trojan Horse threat is to eliminate one of the other requirements for a Trojan Horse. Eliminating the ability of users to develop programs would, for example, make it hard for them to create the Trojan Horse in the first place. This, however, severely limits the usefulness of the system and delegates it to operating only a select group of application programs. Placing voluntary procedural controls on the users to keep them from executing untried software is highly unreliable and doesn't address the possibility of Trojan Horses in system software. A particularly insidious Trojan Horse, described by McDermott |6.4|, could be installed in the system's compiler itself. A Trojan Horse installed here would infect all other programs that are compiled and result in numerous other Trojan Horses. In this case, the compiler Trojan Horse does not perform the ultimate function but instead plants this function in the other programs that it compiled. The best way to eliminate this threat is to severely restrict access to the source code for the compiler and also restrict the ability of individuals to compile and replace existing system software. This particular Trojan Horse serves to illustrate the tremendous dependency we must place on the system software. Some organizations requiring extreme security measures go so far as to not accept any compiled vendor software. Instead they will only accept the source code and will compile the executable modules themselves. This, of course, means that they either have to trust the source code to not contain a Trojan Horse, or they must inspect the source code itself to insure that it does not contain one. Inspection of source code is a tedious process and it is extremely difficult to spot malicious code.

Perhaps the best way to limit the possibility of Trojan Horses is to implement the type of Access and Information Flow Controls used for Mandatory Access. While this will limit the ability of a Trojan Horse to send files or grant permissions to subjects at other security levels, it does not eliminate the problems associated with same-level copying of files. Assigning numerous categories to subjects and objects will further restrict the ability of the Trojan Horse to function but it also creates an environment that is more restrictive for the users. In the end, the best way to handle the possibility of Trojan Horses is to select the security model, enforce the resulting Access and Information Flow Controls, and continually monitor the system to check for possible Trojan Horses. An additional discussion on Trojan Horses is covered in Chapter 13.

6.7 Summary

Once authentication techniques have been used to validate a user's right to gain access to a computer system, it is up to the Access and Information Flow Controls to insure that the proper handling of information takes place. Access Controls determine what permissions a subject has for a particular object. Information Flow Controls handle what may happen to information once it has been accessed.

Several techniques were discussed to implement Access Controls. Perhaps the easiest is a File Password scheme in which access to any object is governed by a password for that object. The drawbacks to this method are that it is cumbersome (a user will have to remember many different passwords), there is no way to determine who has access to any given object since passwords can be transmitted by word-of-mouth, and there is no easy way to revoke a single user's permission to access an object without affecting other users as well.

The second technique described was a capability-based scheme. In this technique, a list of capabilities is kept for each user, which shows which objects the user has permission to access. The problems associated with this technique include the drawback that there is no easy way to determine who has access to a particular object without reviewing all of the user's capability lists. Depending on how the system is implemented, revoking a user's access permissions may also be a difficult matter. There is also the issue of wasted storage space associated with the use of capability lists since access information is duplicated numerous times among the various user's lists.

A third technique described was the Access Control List method which associated a list with each file instead of with each user. This makes it much easier to determine who has access to a specific object and also makes it extremely easy to revoke or change a single user's (or group's) access permissions. This method also uses much less storage space than the capability-based technique. A drawback, not viewed as severe since it is not often called for, is the lack of an easy way to determine which objects a particular user has access to.

Perhaps the most common method, since it is employed in operating systems such as UNIX, is the Protection Bits method. In this technique, a series of bits grouped in sets are associated with each object which describe the type of access the owner, individuals in the same group, and all other users have. Since only a few bits are associated with each file this technique requires very little overhead. It also is easy to revoke or modify access permissions and it is easy to determine what users have access to any particular object.

All of these techniques can be used to implement Access Controls and rudimentary Information Flow controls needed to implement protections at a level akin to Discretionary Access. In order to further prevent the unauthorized flow of information, further controls such as those seen in Mandatory Access Controls are required. Controls at this level will keep programs from transferring information between security levels. These additional controls also help to address the threat of Trojan Horses since such malicious code will not be able to easily transmit information or change access permissions.

6.8   Exercises

6.1   How groups could be used to partition users in order to match real-world
           organizational structures was shown for both Access Control Lists and
           Protection Bit schemes of access control. How can groups be implemented in
           File Password and Capability-based schemes? How could time-of-day and
           location restrictions be added?

6.2   In an Owner/Group/Other protection bit scheme, the first set of bits
           represents the permissions that owners may grant to themselves. Why might
           owners want to limit the permissions they give themselves?

6.3   How might the *Read*, *Write*, and *Execute* modes of access be interpreted for directory structures? If you have access to a UNIX-based system, determine whether your interpretations were correct.

6.9   References

6.1   Ford, W., *Computer Communications Security: Principles, Standard Protocols and Techniques*, Prentice Hall, Englewood Cliffs, NJ, 1994.

6.2   Gasser, M., *Building A Secure Computer System*, Van Nostrand Reinhold, New York, New York, 1988.

6.3   Graubart, R., "On the Need for a Third Form of Access Control", *Proceedings of the 12th National Computer Security Conference*, Baltimore, Maryland, October 1989, pp. 296-304.

6.4   McDermott, J., "A Technique for Removing an Important Class of Trojan Horses from High Order Languages", *Proceedings of the 11th National Computer Security Conference*, Baltimore, Maryland, October 1988, pp. 114-117.

6.5   Silberschatz, A. and Galvin, P., *Operating System Concepts, 4ed.* Addison-Wesley Publishing Company, Reading, Massachusetts, 1994.

6.6   Tanenbaum, A. S., *Modern Operating Systems*, Prentice Hall, Englewood Cliffs, New Jersey, 1992.

6.10   Extended Bibliography

6.7   Abrams, M., Heaney, J., King, O., LaPadula, L., Lazear, M., and Olson, I., "Generalized Framework for Access Control: Towards Prototyping the ORGCON Policy", *Proceedings of the 14th National Computer Security Conference*, Washington D.C., October 1991, pp. 246-256.

6.8   Boebert, W. and Ferguson, C., "A Partial Solution to the Discretionary
          Trojan Horse Problem", *Proceedings of the 8th National Computer Security
          Conference*, Gaithersburg, Maryland, October 1985, pp. 141-144.

6.9   Bonyun, D., "Rules as the Basis of Access Control in Database Management
          Systems", *Proceedings of the 7th National Security Conference*,
          Gaithersburg, Maryland, September 1984, pp. 38-47.

6.10   Denning, D.E. and Denning, P.J., "Certification of Programs for Secure
          Information Flow", *Communications of the ACM*, Vol. 19, No. 8, August
          1976, pp. 461-471.

6.11   Foley, S. N., "A Universal Theory of Information Flow", *Proceedings of the
          1987 IEEE Symposium on Security and Privacy*, Oakland, California, April
          1987, pp. 116-122.

6.12   Guttman, J., "Information Flow and Invariance", *Proceedings of the 1987
          IEEE Symposium on Security and Privacy*, Oakland, California, April 1987,
          pp. 67-73.

6.13   Karger, P., "Limiting the Damage Potential of Discretionary Trojan Horses",
          Proceedings of the 1987 IEEE Symposium on Security and Privacy, Oakland,
          California, April 1987, pp. 32-37.

7

AUDITING AND
INTRUSION DETECTION

Audit trails were originally designed to be used for accounting purposes, not as an aid to security. Dorothy Denning presented a paper at the IEEE Conference on Security and Privacy in 1986, however, in which she described how audit trail data could be used to enhance the security of a computer system [7.2, 7.3]. Since that time, several research projects have resulted in programs that use a system's audit trail to help detect intrusive activities. These systems, known as Intrusion Detection Systems (IDS), have been extended to work in mostly limited networked environments. This chapter will examine this relatively new field in computer security and will examine several current systems to see how intrusive activity can be detected.

7.1 Audit Trail Features

In terms of system security, there are five goals for audit trails. These goals, as outlined in the Rainbow Series *A Guide To Understanding AUDIT in Trusted Systems* [7.10], are:

- To allow the review of patterns of access to individual objects, access histories of specific processes and individuals, and the use of the various protection mechanisms supported by the system and their effectiveness.
- To allow discovery of both user's and outsider's repeated attempts to bypass the protection mechanisms.
- To allow discovery of any use of privileges that may occur when a user assumes a functionality with privileges greater than his or her own.
- To act as a deterrent against perpetrators' habitual attempts to bypass the system protection mechanisms.

- To supply an additional form of user assurance that attempts to bypass the protection mechanisms are recorded and discovered.

Thus, audit data serves two main purposes: to detect unauthorized and intrusive behavior and to deter the same activities by its mere presence. There are two parts to auditable data at the C2 level of security: *auditable events* and *auditable information*. Auditable events are those actions that may be of concern from a security standpoint. Auditable information is the actual data relating to an occurrence of one of the specified auditable events. Examples of auditable events include:

- Use of identification and authentication mechanisms.
- Introduction of objects into a user's address space.
- Deletion of objects from a user's address space.
- Actions taken by computer operators, system administrators or system security administrators.
- All security-relevant events as outlined by the goals stated above.
- Production of printed output [7.10].

The type of information that should be collected on the occurrence of each of these auditable events includes:

- Date and time of the event.
- The unique identifier for the subject generating the event.
- Type of event.
- Success or failure of the event.
- Origin of the request for identification/authentication events.
- Name of the object introduced, accessed, or deleted from a user's address space.
- Description of modifications made by administrators to a security database [7.10].

Thus, for example, all failed login attempts would be recorded with the date and time the attempt occurred. If an unauthorized individual does somehow gain access to the system, the audit trail would provide a record of the activities taken by the intruder, including the date and time of each action. While this would not restore files that are destroyed, it does help to determine the extent of the damage caused by the intruder. In addition, authorized users may be deterred from attempting to perform certain unauthorized activities because they know that a record of their actions is being created. In this sense the audit trail feature serves to deter unauthorized activities.

A number of computer vendors have attempted to comply with the DoD C2 audit requirements. Sun Microsystems, for example, has released a version of their SunOS which includes optional facilities providing equivalent data to that specified in the AUDIT guide [7.4]. Sun uses a number of categories to specify the events the system administrator might want to audit. These categories are listed in Table 7.1.

Table 7.1 Sun Microsystems categories of auditable events [7.4]

```
• dr - Reading of data, open for reading, etc.
• dw - Write or modification of data.
• de - Creation or deletion of an object.
• da - Changes in object access.
• lo - Login, logout.
• ad - Normal administrative operation.
• p0 - Privileged operation.
• p1 - Unusual privileged operation.
```

For each of the categories in Table 7.1, the administrator can choose to log either a successful or unsuccessful attempt, or both. In addition, the security features allow selected users to be monitored without wasting disk space with data from other individuals who are not believed to be a threat. Thus, administrators can closely monitor the actions of individuals whose current or past actions are suspicious.

The type of information that may be recorded by audit trails listed in Table 7.1 is indicative of what is available from modern operating systems. The question remains, however, as to how this information is used. One can imagine the voluminous amount of information recorded for even a moderate sized system if all user accounts and activities are monitored. How does one go about searching through this data to find the few items that may indicate unauthorized activity? It is this problem that Dr. Denning addressed and which is the purpose of current IDS.

7.2 Intrusion Detection Systems

IDS can be designed to detect both attempted break-ins by outsiders as well as unauthorized activity performed by insiders. The types of activities these systems check include:

- Attempted/successful break-ins
- Masquerading
- Penetration by legitimate users
- Leakage by legitimate users

- Inference by legitimate users
- Trojan Horses
- Viruses
- Denial-of-Service [7.2, 7.3]

Break-ins are one of the most widely known threats to computer systems. It is common to hear reports in the news regarding a computer system or network that has been penetrated by an individual or group of "hackers". A break-in is nothing more than an individual who is not authorized to use the system or network gaining access to it. Simply looking through an audit file for unsuccessful attempts to log on to a computer system is not enough since normal users will periodically make a mistake when they enter their password or userid, or they may occasionally forget them. Providing a list of unsuccessful login attempts is only the first step. IDS are designed to do more.

Masquerading often goes hand-in-hand with break-ins. It involves an individual, who has gained access to another's account, trying to appear as that individual. It may also involve such things as the modification of messages or files so that they appear to have been sent or modified by somebody else.

Also similar to break-ins are penetrations by legitimate users. This involves an authorized user of the computer system or network attempting to gain privileges or to perform actions which the user is not authorized to have or perform. A common example is a user attempting to gain system administrator privileges (such as logging in as *superuser* on a UNIX system).

Leakage of information by legitimate users is of special concern in systems that operate in a multi-level security mode. A user authorized access to Top Secret information who attempts to send a file to a user authorized access to only Secret information should be detected by an IDS. This may also involve other actions such as an individual attempting to print a file on a printer located in an area with individuals not authorized access to the file or a user attempting to store a file on a storage device not authorized to handle it.

Inference by legitimate users is an interesting issue. It involves the attempt by a user to obtain information the user is not authorized through the aggregation of several pieces of data. This is a common problem in multi-level databases where an individual may not be authorized access to all information stored in the database but can infer certain information from other entries in the database.

A Trojan Horse is a program that appears to be designed for one purpose but actually performs another (often malicious) action. It in fact may also perform the actions it appeared to be designed for in the first place. An IDS often attempts to discover the hidden activity. One way this can be done is by noticing the amount and type of resources the program used and comparing them with the amount and type that should have been used for the advertised purpose of the program. Also, ordinary sounding processes attempting actions in violation of established security policies might indicate something hidden inside the code.

Somewhat in a manner similar to Trojan Horses, viruses are a threat IDS search for. A virus is a program that attaches itself to other programs in order to replicate. It also may hide some malicious intent beyond its own propagation. Unusual file accesses by programs could be an indicator that a virus may have infected the system.

A final activity an IDS looks for is a denial-of-service attack. In this threat, the attacker attempts to monopolize specific resources in order to deny the use of them, and the system in general, to legitimate users. Unusual patterns of resource activities and requests may indicate such an attack is occurring. This is especially true if these requests have been generated from a user who is not normally associated with these specific requests. Denial-of-service attacks may, in some circumstances, originate from outside of the system or network. In these cases, the attack would still be indicated by an unusually high pattern of requests for specific actions (e.g., multiple logins) or network traffic (e.g., flooding a system with electronic mail messages).

IDS can use one of several methods to perform their assigned detection activities. In the past, they have been based on user or group profiles designed to look for specific user actions or attempts to exploit known security holes. Another method uses an intruder's profile as its basis of comparison.

7.2.1　User Profiling

The basic premise behind user profiling is that the identity of any specific user can be described by a profile of commonly performed actions. The user's pattern of behavior is observed and established over a period of time. Each user tends to use certain commands more than others, access the same files, login at certain established times and at a specific frequency, execute the same programs and so forth. A characteristic profile can be established for each user based on these activities and is maintained through frequent updating. An intruder masquerading as an authorized user will generally not perform the same operations or be logged on at the same time as the authorized user. The intruder can thus be detected by comparing current activity against the previously established pattern of behavior exhibited by the user. Since the intruder's activity will fall outside of the established profile, the intrusion can be detected. Authorized users performing unauthorized activity can similarly be detected since the unauthorized activity would also fall outside of their normal profile. A variation of this method is to establish group profiles that describe the normal activities a member of a group would be expected to perform. Groups might be established, for example, along functional lines in an organization such as programmers, administrators, and various types of application program users.

Generic profiles are often assigned when a user is first given access to the system. This profile is then updated as the user interacts with the system for normal activities. One problem with profiling, especially when designed to detect unauthorized activity by authorized users, is the ability of the users to gradually change their profiles over time. Gradually extending the hours when a user normally logs on (over a period of several months) would allow the user to start logging in at midnight when the normal activity should have been during standard daylight hours. If the user had suddenly logged in at midnight, the activity would have been detected. By gradually extending work hours or the login time, the profile would also correspondingly change so the activity would not be recognized as abnormal. Outsiders can also escape detection in user-profile based systems as long as they don't perform too many activities or attempt to access unusual files.

7.2.2   Intruder Profiling

The idea behind intruder profiling is similar to law enforcement descriptions of profiles for certain types of criminals. Outsiders and unauthorized users will perform certain activities or act in a certain way when they gain access to a computer system. These activities, if they can be identified and put in the form of a profile, can be searched for and, if found, may indicate that intrusive activity is occurring. An example of this activity, frequently observed, occurs when an intruder gains access to a computer system for the first time. Intruders will often immediately check to see who else is logged on. They may then examine the file systems and wander through the directory structure, occasionally looking at files. They usually don't stay connected very long; simply logging on, performing a few actions, and then logging off. An authorized user normally doesn't act in such a seemingly paranoid manner.

7.2.3   Signature Analysis

Just as an individual has a unique written signature, which can be verified through handwriting analysis, individuals likewise have a "typing signature" which can also be verified through keystroke analysis [7.5]. The time it takes to type certain pairs or triplets of letters can be measured and the collection of these *digraphs* and *trigraphs* together form a unique collection which can be used to characterize individuals. Certain digraphs and trigraphs, because of their frequency, can be considered more important and a minimal set of these important di- and trigraphs can be used in the identification process. In fact, a set of the five digraphs *in, io, no, on,* and *ul* has been found to be sufficient to distinguish touch typists from each other, with a reasonable level (95% confidence level) of accuracy [7.5].

Of course this type of identification technique requires specialized monitoring equipment that would be difficult to implement across a large network. Instead, however, another type of signature might be used, one in which common mistakes may be identified and used to help identify the authenticity of a user. While this technique is much less reliable than the keystroke analysis, it could be used to afford an additional level of security.

7.2.4   Action Based

Another approach to identify intrusive activity is "action-based intrusion detection". In this approach, specific activities or actions that are known to be common activities performed by intruders are checked. For example, a common occurrence on UNIX systems is for an intruder to attempt to gain access to *root*; therefore an action-based system might look for all occurrences of individuals attempting to become *root*. This does not mean that all individuals who become *root* are immediately tagged as being an intruder but rather limits the number of users whose actions must be fully monitored.

A similar method is to check for attempts to exploit known security holes. There are a number of common holes in systems and application software that can be exploited by knowledgeable individuals. An individual attempting to exploit any of these holes is therefore a suspected intruder. The obvious problem with this approach is that it requires knowledge of the most significant holes, or intruders will simply exploit those not monitored. The way to implement an action-based system is to allow for easy addition of newly discovered holes.

Another type of action that might indicate intrusive activity is the attempted use of commands for a different operating system. New users to a computer system, unfamiliar with the specific operating system in use, may attempt commands they are used to perform on another system. Using VMS commands in a UNIX environment, for example, might indicate an intruder has somehow gained access to the system. New users may make similar mistakes but established users should make fewer.

7.2.5   IDES

Originally developed in 1985 at SRI International [7.8], the Intrusion Detection Expert System (IDES) uses a user profile approach to intrusion detection as well as an expert system to check for activities that match known attack scenarios or attempts to exploit known system vulnerabilities [7.8, 7.9]. The structure of IDES is shown in Figure 7.1.

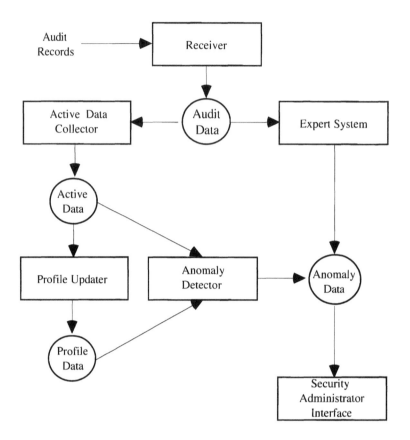

Figure 7.1. IDES structure [7.8].

IDES compares the current behavior of a user to an historical profile to determine whether the current activity is within norms. If the current behavior is abnormal, it may indicate intrusive activity. IDES does not keep a record of all activity for each user but uses a subset of measures to describe normal activities. The measures chosen by the IDES researchers include [7.8]:

- CPU usage
- Input/output usage
- Connect time
- Location of use
- Command usage
- Mailer usage

- Compiler usage
- Editor usage
- Directories accessed and/or modified
- Errors
- Hour and day of use
- Network activity

Some of the measures record a count of a specific activity while others simply record whether the activity occurred at all. An example of this is *command usage*. One measure records the number of times each command was used during a session, while another records (in a binary format) simply whether a command was used. The user profiles are updated once each day using a series of weights to give the most current data more influence over the new profile.

It is the arrival of the audit records that drives IDES. After receiving an audit record, the *Receiver* parses and validates it and places valid records into the *Audit Data*. The *Audit Data* database is used by both the statistical anomaly detector portion of IDES as well as the *Expert System*. In the statistical anomaly detector, the record is first used by the *Active Data Collector* to generate the *Active Data*. *Active Data* consists of information on all user, group, and remote host activities since the last time the profiles were updated. This data is in turn used by the *Anomaly Detector* to see if it indicates activity that could be considered outside of the norm when compared to the established user's individual or group *Profile Data*. If it is abnormal, an anomaly record is created and stored in a database of *Anomaly Data* which can be accessed through the *Security Administrator Interface*. The level of sensitivity for the anomaly detector is set by the security administrator through this interface. Profile updating takes place daily and is performed by the *Profile Updater*.

Operating in parallel with the statistical anomaly detector is the *Expert System*. This system receives the *Audit Data* as did the *Active Data Collector*. An expert system analysis is also included in recognition of the fact that, while some users have a profile based on well-established patterns of behavior, others have patterns that are sporadic and thus much harder to describe. With this sort of "loose" profile, almost any type of behavior would be viewed as normal and an intruder gaining access to such an account would probably go unnoticed. The *Expert System* looks for specific actions that can be viewed as indicators of possible intrusive activity independent of whether the action was considered outside of the user's profile. An example of this type of action would be the execution of a command to query the status of a specific account followed by an attempt to log into that same account (e.g., a *finger* command followed by a *login* command) [7.8]. Another example would be a user attempting to exploit a known hole or vulnerability in the security of the system. The obvious weakness with this expert system approach is that only known attack methods and vulnerabilities are checked. Exploitation of unknown (to IDES) holes would go undetected.

An enhancement to IDES has extended its intrusion detection functions to a networked environment. Several interconnected hosts transfer their audit trail information to a central site, which then uses the same methodology to determine whether intrusive activity is or has been taking place.

7.2.6   MIDAS

The Multics Intrusion Detection and Alerting System (MIDAS) is an intrusion detection system specifically designed to work with the Multics operating system [7.11] as used by Dockmaster. Dockmaster, NSA's unclassified computer system, is used to provide information on security related topics to the computer security community. MIDAS consists of several components as depicted in Figure 7.2. A portion of the processing is performed on the Multics system while the rest is run on a separate Symbolics Lisp machine [7.11].

As an *audit record* is generated on the Multics system, the *Preprocessor* filters out data not used by MIDAS and formats the remaining information into an assertion for the fact base. This assertion is sent to the *Fact Base* via the *Network Interface*, which links the Multics and Symbolics machines. The *Command Monitor* captures command data that is not audited by Multics and sends it to the *preprocessor* where it is handled in the same manner as the audit records. The introduction of an assertion into the *Fact Base* may cause a binding between this new fact and a rule contained in the *Rule Base*. It may, in fact, cause a series of rules to be activated. This assertion may thus change the state of the system and may result in a system response to a suspected intruder. The *Statistical Database* contains both user and system statistics and defines what normal activity is for Dockmaster. Should the current record fall outside of the defined norm, a rule would be instantiated which in turn may change the state of the system and cause a system response.

It is obvious that how well MIDAS performs is a function of the strength of the rules in the rule base. There are three types of rules used by MIDAS: *immediate attack heuristics, user anomaly heuristics,* and *system state heuristics* [7.11]. The *immediate attack heuristics* do not use any of the stored statistical data. They are designed to perform a superficial examination of the records, looking for events that by themselves indicate that a security violation may have occurred. *User Anomaly heuristics* use the statistical profiles to determine if the current activities of the user are outside of the norm defined by previous sessions. The *system state heuristics* are similar to the user anomaly heuristics except these are applied to the system itself and not a specific user. An example of this is an inordinate number of unsuccessful logins system-wide, which might indicate an attempt by an individual to break into the system but which might not be noticed at the individual user level.

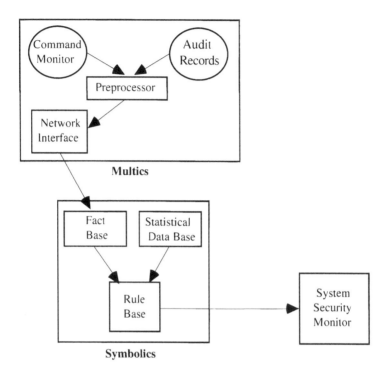

Figure 7.2. MIDAS architecture [7.11].

7.2.7   Haystack

Haystack was developed for the Air Force as an audit trail reduction and intrusion detection tool [7.12]. Unlike the two previous systems, Haystack was not designed to work in a real-time environment but is run in an off-line batch mode. Haystack initially existed as two components, one on the Unisys 1100/60 mainframe and the other on a Zenith Z-248 IBM PC compatible machine (shown in Figure 7.3).

The audit trail on the Unisys 1100 first passes through a *Preprocessor*, which extracts the necessary information required by the analysis program. This information is placed into a Canonical Audit Trail (CAT) file and is written to a 9-track tape. The tape is later read by a PC and the records are processed.

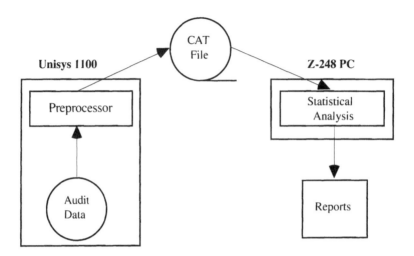

Figure 7.3. Haystack organization [7.12].

The processing of the data is performed in two parts. Each record is checked to see if it indicates a security-relevant event and is logged if it does. The records are also used to update a database that contains information on the user's past behavior. There are two types of statistical analysis that Haystack performs. The first is a trend analysis, which uses the information in the database to determine if the current user's actions are significantly different from that of the past sessions. The other analysis compares the actions of a user's current session with a "target intrusion", which is a description of the activities for one of the types of intrusions, Haystack is trying to detect. This analysis will yield a "suspicion quotient" which indicates how closely this session resembles a target intrusion.

Calculation of the suspicion quotient is a four step process.   The first step entails the generation of a session vector X from the audit records, which represents important details about the current user's session [7.9].   These details consist of current session counts for specific attributes. Each element of this session vector is then compared with its corresponding threshold value found in a threshold vector.   The threshold vector describes what the system considers normal activity. The result of this comparison is a binary vector indicating the session attributes that fall outside a 90% threshold range based on historical data. The binary vector B is thus calculated as follows [7.9]:

$$b_i = \begin{cases} 0 & t_{i.\min} \leq x_i \leq t_{i.\max} \\ 1 & otherwise \end{cases}$$

The third step of the process consists of calculating a weighted intrusion score by summing the result of multiplying all elements in the binary vector with a corresponding value found in a weighted intrusion vector. Each element w_i of the weighted intrusion vector represents the relative importance of that attribute to detecting the specific target intrusion. The weighted intrusion score is then used to obtain the suspicion quotient by determining what percentage of all sessions have a weighted intrusion score less than or equal to the one just obtained for the current session.

An obvious drawback to the way Haystack performs intrusion detection is that it is not designed to be used in a real-time environment. This results in a considerable amount of time passing before an intrusion is noticed. A tremendous amount of damage could have occurred between the time an intruder gained access and the time the intrusion is detected. Another problem experienced by the developers of Haystack, a problem common to all profile-based systems, was the determination of what attributes were significant indicators of intrusive activity. Despite these drawbacks, the Haystack algorithms used to determine whether an intrusion occurred have been used in other intrusion detection systems.

7.3   Network Intrusion Detection

The intrusion detection systems described up to this point were designed to detect intrusions on a single host. With the increasing number of systems that are part of a networked environment, it has become necessary to consider intrusions not only of single hosts but of networks as well. Some early attempts at solving this problem consisted of nothing more than taking existing individual host intrusion detection systems and expanding their scope to a network. This was the case with both IDES and another system called the Information Security Officer's Assistant (ISOA). Other efforts have built upon the lessons learned in the single host intrusion detection systems while taking into account the additional characteristics found in a networked environment.

7.3.1   Network Attack Characteristics

Connecting a computer to a network increases the possibility that a system will be attacked since a larger number of users have access to it. At the same time, if the systems can work together, certain attacks will be easier to spot from a network perspective. For example, consider what is known as a "doorknob rattling attack. Similar to an individual who walks around a building checking each door in an attempt to find a door that was left unlocked, this attack consists of an intruder attempting to gain access to a computer system by repeatedly trying single logons. If unsuccessful, the intruder doesn't attempt to access this same system but moves on to another. In terms of the individual hosts, a single unsuccessful attack is not enough to raise suspicions. Observed from a network perspective, however, multiple hosts — each experiencing a single unsuccessful logon — would indicate a systematic network attack. Another aspect of the network environment that makes it significantly different than single host systems is that not only are there multiple hosts to worry about, but the hosts may not be of the same type nor will they all be individually monitored. By taking advantage of the broadcast nature of a network, unmonitored individual hosts can still be considered monitored (to a certain degree) if all traffic to and from them is monitored. In addition, all traffic on a network can be monitored without making significant changes to the operating system. Often this will provide more information than what is available on individual host audit trails.

7.3.2   NSM

The Network Security Monitor (NSM), developed at the University of California, Davis, does not use audit trails to perform its intrusion detection functions. Instead, it monitors the broadcast channel to observe all network traffic. As a result of this, it can monitor a variety of hosts and operating system platforms. A significant advantage to this method is that an intruder will not be able to tell that the network is monitored. This is an important point, since intruders have been known to turn off the audit trail features on systems that were known to be monitored [7.9]. The logical architecture of NSM is shown in Figure 7.4.

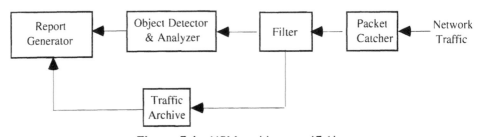

Figure 7.4.   NSM architecture [7.6].

The challenge for NSM is in constructing a picture of what individual users are doing from the numerous individual captured packets. NSM takes a layered approach to this problem, the bottom most layer being the individual packets in the form of a bit stream. The second layer is the thread layer, which forms the packets into unidirectional data streams associated with specific hosts and organized into thread vectors [7.9]. The next layer takes the thread vectors and attempts to pair them with another thread vector, representing the bi-directional (i.e., host-to-host connections) nature of network communication. This pairing forms what is referred to as a connection vector. The fourth layer entails the development of host vectors, which use the connection vectors to draw conclusions about what each host is doing.

The host and connection vectors are used as inputs to an expert system to analyze the network traffic. The expert system also uses several other types of information to determine if intrusive activity has occurred. The first is a profile of expected traffic behavior. This information consists of, for example, which data paths are expected to occur (i.e., which hosts normally connect to which other hosts) using what type of service (e.g., *telnet, ftp, mail,* etc.). This expected behavior is based on the past performance of the network. The expert system also knows what level of authentication is required for each service and the level of information that can be obtained using that service. For example, *ftp* does not provide as much capability as does *telnet* but also requires less authentication. All of this information is then compared with signatures of past attacks to ascertain whether particular connections appear to be abnormal and indicate intrusive activity.

NSM was extensively tested with some very interesting results. During a period of two months at UC-Davis, NSM analyzed in excess of 110,000 connections, correctly identifying over 300 intrusions. More significantly, only about 1% of these intrusions had previously been noticed by the system administrators [7.9]. This would seem to validate the need for intrusion detection schemes.

7.3.3   DIDS

The Distributed Intrusion Detection System (DIDS) is a project sponsored jointly by UC-Davis, the Lawrence Livermore National Labs (LLNL), Haystack Laboratory, and the U.S. Air Force [7.9]. It is an extension of NSM and is designed to take care of several deficiencies with NSM. The first deficiency is that NSM does not have the ability to monitor the actions of a user directly connected to a system on the net either through the console or via dial-up lines. Second, DIDS is designed to allow intrusion detection activities to take place even in the face of encrypted data traffic (a problem that handicaps NSM). DIDS consists of three components as depicted in Figure 7.5.

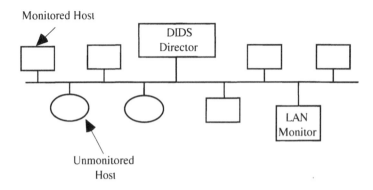

Figure 7.5. DIDS components [7.13].

The individual *Host Monitors* scan their own system's audit trails looking for events that may indicate intrusions as well as other events that are important to the network. These other events include such activities as network access attempts using *rlogin* or *rsh*. The individual monitors also employ the same algorithms used by Haystack to form their core intrusion detection scheme [7.9]. All important events occurring on the individual hosts are reported to the *DIDS Director* by the *Host Monitors*. The function of the Director is to coordinate the network's intrusion detection activities. The Director communicates with both the individual host and the *LAN Monitor* to request more information on particular subjects as well as to report the current security state of the network. The purpose of the *LAN Monitor* is to observe all traffic on the network and report on network activity such as *rlogin*, *telnet*, and *ftp* connections. Currently, the *LAN Monitor* is a subset of NSM [7.9, 7.13].

Another interesting aspect of DIDS is its ability to track users as they travel across the network. DIDS assigns a unique Network-user IDentification (NID) to all users as soon as they enter the monitored environment. All subsequent actions by an individual user are then associated with the NID and not a userid or name. In this way, DIDS knows that actions performed by *tom@host1* are to be credited to the same individual as *mary@host2*, even though the user has changed names on the individual hosts [7.9, 7.13]. An even more interesting problem is to track users as they travel through unmonitored hosts. It is a difficult matter to know when user *tom@monitoredhost1* accesses *unmonitoredhost2* and then uses it to log into another system as *mary@monitoredhost3*. A possible solution is to compare packets traveling between hosts. The data portion of packets should be the same for the same individual no matter how many different hosts exist in the individual's trail. To do this, however, involves careful timing and comparison functions and is currently not performed by DIDS.

7.3.4   NADIR

Designed for the Los Alamos National Laboratory's Integrated Computing Network (ICN), the Network Anomaly Detection and Intrusion Reporter (NADIR) is an expert system-based anomaly and misuse detection system [7.7]. NADIR takes audit records from the network and generates weekly summaries of network and individual user activity. The associated network, ICN, is not a general purpose network but is tailored to the organization. As such, NADIR is not immediately transferable to other networked environments.

The ICN is divided into four partitions, each processing at a different security level [7.7]. Any workstation connected to a partition can access other systems in its own partition or in a partition at a lower security level. The partitions are linked by a system of dedicated service nodes which perform such functions as access control, file access and storage, job scheduling, and file movement between partitions [7.7]. The audit records used by NADIR come from these service nodes. NADIR compares the summary of the weekly audit data with a series of expert rules that describe security policy violations and suspicious activity. Each user has a "level-of-interest" value (initially set to zero), which indicates the level of suspicion that an intrusion or some other anomalous activity has occurred with that account. Each time a rule in the expert system matches the profile generated from the week's audit data, the level-of-interest is increased. The amount this value is increased depends on the importance of the matched rule. At the conclusion of the analysis process, a report is generated which lists all users whose level-of-interest value has exceeded a predefined threshold. The rules used in NADIR were developed by interviewing security auditors and administrators tasked with enforcing the laboratory's security policies.

7.3.5   CSM

The Cooperating Security Manager (CSM) is an intrusion detection system designed to be used in a distributed network environment. Developed at Texas A&M University, this system runs on UNIX-based systems connected over any size network. The goal of the CSMs is to provide a system that can detect intrusive activity in a distributed environment without the use of a centralized director. A system with a central director coordinating all activity severely limits the size of the network. Instead of reporting significant network activity to a central director, the CSMs communicate among themselves to cooperatively detect anomalous activity. The way this works is by having the CSMs take a proactive, instead of a reactive, approach to intrusion detection.

In a reactive approach with a centralized director, the individual hosts would report occurrences of failed login attempts, for example, to the central director. In a proactive approach, the host from which the intruder was attempting to make the connections would contact the systems being attacked. The key to having a proactive approach work is to have all hosts (or at least the vast majority of hosts) on a network run a CSM. While this may at first appear to be somewhat idealistic, with the current interest among some vendors to develop "security on a chip", the concept of an intrusion detection system provided in hardware may not be that far off.

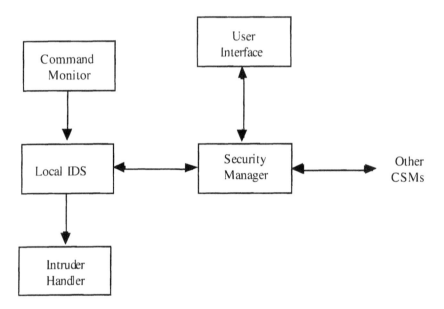

Figure 7.6.   CSM components.

The CSMs consist of five components as illustrated in Figure 7.6.   The *Command Monitor* is responsible for capturing the commands issued by the users and sending them to the *Local IDS*. The *Local IDS* is in charge of intrusion detection for the local CSM host. Messages relating to important network activity (commands such as *login. ftp,* and *telnet*) are sent to the *Security Manager,* whose job it is to coordinate between the other CSMs on the network. Whenever a connection to another host is made, both CSMs keep track of the connection and any action on the one host is also considered paralleled on the other. This keeps an intruder from attempting a few attacks from one host, and then moving to another host before suspicion has been raised. If a host determines that intrusive activity is occurring, the CSM sends a message to the other hosts in the user's chain of connected systems to notify them of the incident. Each of these CSMs can continue this notification if the individual originated from still other hosts. The ultimate result is that all involved hosts are notified of the intrusive activity.

The *User Interface* is used by system or security administrators to query the CSM on the current security status of the host. The administrator can query the CSM on individual user's origin and trails, and can request the current level of suspicion for any user. The *Intruder Handler* is designed to take appropriate action when an intrusion is detected. The first course of action is to simply notify the administrator that an intrusion is occurring. Since modern computer systems no longer require constant operator care, there is a good chance that the administrator will not be available when an attack occurs. In that case, the CSM will take further action if the activities of the intruder are viewed as destructive. These actions include terminating the current session and locking the account.

7.4 Monitoring and the Law

An issue that remains is the legality of monitoring actions of users on computer systems. At first it may appear that an organization has the right to monitor its own computer systems in order to protect itself from damage that could be caused by outsiders or disgruntled employees. The issue, however, is not as clear to the courts and there have been few cases related to monitoring to help set any consensus in terms of legal precedents. Consider, for example, a 1992 related case ruled on by the Pennsylvania Supreme Court dealing with a new telephone service, then being introduced, called *Caller*ID*. This service identified the caller to the receiver of a telephone call. The court ruled that, since *both* parties had not consented to the disclosure of the caller's identity, the service violated the federal law and 1988 amendments to the Wiretap Act [7.1]. Basically, current law prohibits surveillance without obtaining a court order with only a few exceptions. One of these exceptions is for individuals to record communication they are part of, with a few states requiring both parties to consent to the recording. In an earlier case in 1978, directly related to computer monitoring, a Court of Appeals ruled that keystroke monitoring did not constitute an illegal wiretap, since it was performed by private individuals and not by a law enforcement agency [7.1].

So what does all of this mean for intrusion detection systems? With so few rulings, it becomes essential for those wishing to monitor their systems to take precautions against possible future suits. In December of 1992, the Computer Emergency Response Team (CERT) issued advisory CA-92:19 which addressed the Department of Justice advice on Keystroke Logging. The advisory basically stated that organizations that intend on monitoring their systems should include in the system banner, at login, a message that states that monitoring will occur, and that anyone using the system, by the mere act of using the system, consents to this monitoring and its use. It is not enough to notify all authorized users when their initial account is set up; it must be displayed at each login, so those not authorized access to the system can also view it.

This may actually result in the side effect of scaring off potential intruders, since they know their actions will be monitored.

7.5 Summary

Audit trails that record various actions performed by computer users have been part of modern operating systems for a number of years. The audit trails, which were first used for accounting purposes, were discovered to also have the potential to be used to detect intrusive activity on the computers they monitored. The problem with using the audit trails, however, is that they produce too much information for security managers to effectively handle. The development of a variety of IDS, however, has made the use of audit trail information possible.

There are several approaches the IDSs use to detect intrusive activity. The most common is a profile-based approach in which current user activity is compared with a stored profile of typical activities for that user. If the current actions are not reflective of normal activity for the user, it may indicate somebody else is using the account. Another approach is action-based in which a user's actions are examined for specific actions known to be indicative of intrusive activity. A third approach, which currently is not used due to a lack of available data, is intruder profiling. In this approach, instead of defining typical user behavior, typical intruder behavior is identified. If the current user's activities match the pattern of a typical intruder's, then intrusive activity is indicated. A fourth technique is signature analysis. This method uses physical characteristics, such as typing speed and/or common errors made, to authenticate user identity.

A number of IDSs have been developed using a variety of these techniques. Several are designed to operate in a networked environment. Most, however, are still under development, with only a couple being commercially available.

7.6 Exercises

7.1   For a non-PC-based system of your choice, describe specific actions that you would look for to detect attempted/successful break-ins of your system and masquerading. How are these two different? How are they the same?

7.2   List several similarities and differences in using audit trail data to detect unauthorized activities performed by insiders and intrusive activities performed by intruders. Which do you think is harder to detect? Defend your answer.

7.3   Each of the four discussed methods to detect intrusive activity have their strong and weak points. Which of the four do you feel has the most merit? Why? If a combination of methods would work best, what combination would you choose? Defend your choice(s).

7.4   One of the most difficult problems in implementing a profile-based system is identifying the attributes or measures that enable the system to positively identify a user. What attributes or measures do you feel provide the best indicators of individual activity? Defend your choice(s).

7.5   The problem of tracking users on a network, as they travel between a combination of monitored and unmonitored hosts, is a tricky one. A method proposed by the developers of DIDS is to compare packets. List some of the problems associated with implementing this solution and how you would go about resolving them. (Hint: Consider problems associated with a lack of a global clock as well as problems associated with the splitting up of packets.)

7.6   Three responses mentioned to handle intrusive activities were to notify the system/security administrator, terminate the session, and lock the account so the individual cannot log back in. What are the advantages and disadvantages of each of these responses? Describe other responses that could be used to limit the damage an intruder can cause while not interfering with authorized users.

7.7   References

7.1   Cheswick, W. R. and Bellovin, S. M., *Firewalls and Internet Security*, Addison-Wesley, Reading, Massachusetts, 1994.

7.2   Denning, D., "An Intrusion-Detection Model", *Proceedings of the 1986 IEEE Symposium on Security and Privacy*, Oakland, California, April 1986, pp.118-131.

7.3   Denning, D., "An Intrusion-Detection Model", *IEEE Transactions on Software Engineering*, Vol. SE-13, No. 2, February 1987, pp. 222-232.

7.4   Ferbrache, D. and Shearer, G., *UNIX Installation Security & Integrity*, Prentice Hall, Englewood Cliffs, New Jersey, 1993.

7.5   Gaines, R. S., Lisowski, W., Press, J. S., and Shapiro, N., "Authentication
        by Keystroke Timing: Some Preliminary Results", RAND Technical
        Report, R-2526-NSF, May 1980.

7.6   Heberlein, L.T., Levitt, K.N., and Mukherjee, B., "A Method to Detect
        Intrusive Activity in a Networked Environment", *Proceedings of the 14th
        National Computer Security Conference*, Washington, DC, October 1991,
        pp. 362-371.

7.7   Hochberg, J., Jackson, K., Stallings, C., McClary, J.F., DuBois, D., and
        Ford, J., "NADIR: An Automated System for Detecting Network Intrusion
        and Misuse", *Computers & Security*, Vol. 12, No. 3, May/June 1993, pp.
        235-248.

7.8   Lunt, T., Jagannathan, R., Lee, R., Listgarten, S., Edwards, D. L.,
        Neumann, P. G.; Javit, H. S., and Valdes, A., "IDES: The Enhanced
        Prototype, A Real-Time Intrusion-Detection Expert System", SRI
        International Report, SRI-CSL-88-12, October 1988.

7.9   Mukherjee, B., Heberlein, L. T., and Levitt, K., "Network Intrusion
        Detection", *IEEE Network*, Vol. 8, No. 3, May/June 1994,
        pp. 26-41.

7.10   National Computer Security Center, *A Guide To Understanding Audit in
        Trusted Systems*, NCSC-TG-001, Version 2, June 1988.

7.11   Sebring, M., Shellhouse, E., Hanna; M. E., and Whitehurst, R. A., "Expert
        Systems in Intrusion Detection: A Case Study", *Proceedings of the 11th
        National Computer Security Conference*, Gaithersburg, Maryland, October
        1988, pp. 74-81.

7.12   Smaha, S., "Haystack: An Intrusion Detection System", *Proceedings of the
        IEEE Fourth Aerospace Computer Security Applications Conference*,
        Orlando, Florida, December 1988.

7.13   Snapp, S. R., Brentano, J., Dias, G. V., Goan, T. L., Heberlein, L. T., Ho,
        C.-L., Levitt, K. N., Mukherjee, B., Smaha, S. E., Grance, T., Teal, D. M.,
        and Mansur, D., "DIDS (Distributed Intrusion Detection System) —
        Motivation, Architecture, and an Early Prototype", *Proceedings of the 14th*

National Computer Security Conference, Washington, DC, October 1991, pp. 167-176.

7.8   Extended Bibliography

7.14   Banning, D., Ellingwood, G., Franklin, C., Muckenhirn, C., and Price, D., "Auditing of Distributed Systems", *Proceedings of the 14th National Computer Security Conference*, Washington, DC, October 1991, pp. 59-68.

7.15   Clyde, A. R., "Insider Threat Identification System", *Proceedings of the 10th National Computer Security Conference*, NIST, September 1987, pp. 343-356.

7.16   Dowell, C., "The COMPUTERWATCH Data Reduction Tool", *Proceedings of the 13th National Computer Security Conference*, Washington, DC, October 1990, pp. 99-108.

7.17   Frank, J., "Artificial Intelligence and Intrusion Detection: Current and Future Directions", *Proceedings of the 17th National Computer Security Conference*, Baltimore, Maryland, October 1994, pp. 22-33.

7.18   Halme, L. R. and Van Horne, J., "Automated Analysis of Computer System Audit Trails for Security Purposes", *Proceedings of the 9th National Computer Security Conference*, Gaithersburg, Maryland, September 1986, pp. 71-74.

7.19   Hansen, S. E. and Atkins, E. T., "Centralized System Monitoring with Swatch", Technical Report, Electrical Engineering Computer Facility, Stanford University, available via *anonymous ftp* from *mojo.ots.utexas.edu* /pub/src/swatch-1.8.6.tar.Z, March 1995.

7.20   Heberlein, L. T., "Towards Detecting Intrusion in a Networked Environment", Technical Report CSE-91-23, University of California, Davis, June 1991.

7.21   Heberlein, L.T., Mukherjee, B., and Levitt, K.N., "Internetwork Security Monitor: An Intrusion-Detection System for Large-Scale Networks", *Proceedings of the 15th National Computer Security Conference*, Baltimore, Maryland, October 1992, pp. 262-271.

7.22   Heberlein, L. T., "Thumbprinting: A Technical Report", Draft Proposal, Department of Computer Science, University of California, Davis, 1994.

7.23   Hochberg, J. G., Jackson, K. A., McClary, J.F., and Simmonds, D. D., "Addressing the Insider Threat", *Proceedings of the DoE Computer Security Group Conference*, Albuquerque, New Mexico, May 1993.

7.24   Jackson, K. A., DuBois, D., and Stallings, C., "An Expert System Application for Network Intrusion Detection", *Proceedings of the 14th National Computer Security Conference*, Washington, DC, October 1991, pp. 214-225.

7.25   Jackson, K., "Management Issues in Automated Audit Analysis: A Case Study", *Proceedings of the 8th European Conference on Information Systems Security, Control, and Audit*, Stockholm, Sweden, September 1993.

7.26   Kuhn, J. D., "Research Toward Intrusion Detection Through Automated Abstraction of Audit Data", *Proceedings of the 9th National Computer Security Conference*, Gaithersburg, Maryland, September 1986, pp. 204-208.

7.27   Kumar, S. and Spafford, E., "A Pattern Matching Model for Misuse Intrusion Detection", *Proceedings of the 17th National Computer Security Conference*, Baltimore, Maryland, October 1994, pp. 11-21.

7.28   Lunt, T. F., "Automated Audit Trail Analysis and Intrusion Detection: A Survey", *Proceedings of the 11th National Computer Security Conference*, Gaithersburg, Maryland, October 1988, pp. 65-73.

7.29   Marshall, V. H., "Intrusion Detection in Computers", *Summary of the Trusted Information Systems (TIS) Report on Intrusion Detection Systems*, Unpublished report, January 1991, available via *anonymous ftp* at *csrc.nist.gov* /pub/secpubs/auditool.txt.

7.30   Puketza, N., Mukherjee, B., Olsson, R. A. and Zhang, K., "Testing Intrusion Detection Systems: Design Methodologies and Results from an Early Prototype", *Proceedings of the 17th National Computer Security Conference*, Baltimore, Maryland, October 1994, pp. 1-10.

7.31   Schaefer, L. J., "Employee Privacy and Intrusion Detection Systems: Monitoring on the Job", *Proceedings of the 14th National Computer Security Conference*, Washington DC, October 1991, pp. 188-194.

7.32   Sisbert, W. O., "Auditing in a Distributed System: SunOS MLS Audit Trails", *Proceedings of the 11th National Computer Security Conference*, Gaithersburg, Maryland, October 1988, pp. 82-90.

7.33   Snapp, S. R., Brentano, J., Dias, G. V., Goan, T. L., Grance, T., Heberlein, L. T., Ho, C.-L., Levitt, K. N., Mukherjee, B., Mansur, D. L., Pon, K. L. and Smaha, S. E., "Intrusion Detection Systems (IDS): A Survey of Existing Systems and a Proposed Distributed IDS Architecture", Technical Report CSE-91-7, University of California, Davis, February 1991.

7.34   Spirakis, P., Katsikas, S., Gritzalis, D., Allegre, F., Androutsopoulos, D., Darzentas, J., Gigante, C., Karagiannis, D., Putkonen, H., and Spyrou, T., "SECURENET: A network-oriented intelligent intrusion prevention and detection system", *Proceedings of the IFIP SEC'94*, Curacao, June 1994.

7.35   Winkler, J.R., "A UNIX Prototype for Intrusion and Anomaly Detection in Secure Networks", *Proceedings of the 13th National Computer Security Conference*, Washington, DC, October 1990, pp. 115-124.

7.36   Winkler, J.R. and Landry, J.C., "Intrusion and Anomaly Detection: ISOA Update", *Proceedings of the 15th National Computer Security Conference*, Baltimore, Maryland, October 1992, pp. 272-181.

8

DAMAGE CONTROL AND ASSESSMENT

In August 1992, the Texas A&M University Supercomputer Center (TAMUSC) was the victim of a well-organized Internet attack. Over the course of a 2-week period, the intruder's activities were monitored and logs of their activities were made for future analysis [8.8]. The initial impulse of the TAMUSC was to sever the intruder's connections to the system and assess the damage. Circumstances, however, led them to passively monitor the intruder's actions. The intrusive activity monitored by the TAMUSC led to the development of a set of network security tools and improvements to the security of the Texas A&M computing services. Network attacks such as this are not uncommon; in early 1991 an attempt was made to subvert the security of the computing systems at AT&T Bell Laboratories [8.1]. Security administrators at this site decided not only to monitor the intruder, but to goad him into revealing his techniques by providing the necessary bait. For a period of four months Bell Laboratories limited the intruder's activity, thus controlling possible damage, as the intruder became an experiment in network security and hacker techniques. After this time, Bell Laboratories closed the door to their intruder. What makes this attack different from the attack on TAMUSC is the manner in which Bell Laboratories handled the intruder. Instead of just monitoring the intruder's actions, they placed obstacles in his way and observed his reactions. This provided valuable information not normally available with passive monitoring, all the time controlling the possible damage inflicted upon the system. These reactions to network intruders gave the security administrators what they desired — a better understanding of a hacker's techniques.

Intruder manipulation is not the only means by which an administrator can control damage inflicted as a result of a system security breach. Other common damage control techniques include patching exploited system holes, invalidating compromised user accounts, repairing and preventing further file corruption, and increasing the level of user authentication. Each technique has its advantages, and each provides an administrator different solutions to the intruder problem. The selection of the techniques to implement will depend upon the goals of the intended security system, the availability and applicability of each solution, and whether the intruder is logged in or has left the system.

Damage control is only half of the response equation. System security administrators must also assess the damage caused by an intruder after an attack. This is often difficult as intruders tend to hide their activity and presence by modifying audit logs and appropriately adjusting file modification dates to appear unaltered. System administrators should therefore take the necessary precautions so that an accurate account of an intruder's actions can still be made. With such an account in hand, a more accurate damage assessment can be made. Together, this damage assessment plan and the necessary damage control techniques form a comprehensive intrusion response system.

8.1   Damage Control

As mentioned above, damage control techniques are those actions that are taken while an intruder is logged into a system. Since intruders often limit the amount of time they stay logged into a system, the techniques must be quickly activated and operate in real time. The benefits of affecting any of these techniques are severely hindered, if not useless, once the intruder logs out of the system. Execution speed and response time are therefore of the utmost importance regardless of which damage control techniques are implemented.

Selecting the damage control technique, or set of techniques, to implement will depend largely upon the computing environment under attack and the goals of the administrator. While Texas A&M University and Bell Laboratories were interested in toying with their intruders, most organizations will wish to remove the intruder from their system, as organizations often do not have the time, human resources, and interest required to trifle with an intruder. Furthermore, many organizations do not wish to risk additional system damage by allowing an intruder access to their system. For this reason, each organization must plan a standardized course of action when an intruder is detected. Six possible actions are discussed below; no single action is such that it cannot be combined with any number of the others.

8.1.1   Inform the Authorities

Once it has been determined that an intrusion is in progress or has occurred, a system security administrator should be immediately notified. Communications to an administrator should be done either via telephone or in person as opposed to email or any other means of computer communications. Using a computer system to inform the system administrators of an intrusion has two significant problems. First, the intruder may prevent it from reaching the appropriate administrators. Second, the intruder may be able to intercept the communiqué, if not prevent it. In either case, an intruder has the advantage of knowing his presence has been detected. At this point, an intruder may decide to quietly leave the system and avoid being caught or tracked. Most likely, however, the intruder will either ignore the threat or begin to seriously damage the system knowing that access will soon be denied. Clearly, neither action is desired.

Once contact has been made with the security administrator, key information will need to be communicated. The administrator will need to know how the intruder was detected, what the intruder was doing, and what actions the user has performed since detecting the intruder. This information will assist the administrator in tracking the intruder and determining if the intruder has been tipped off, or is otherwise aware that they have been detected. Additional, unsolicited information that may be of value should also be given to the administrator.

Upon gathering all available information and verifying the presence of an intruder, the administrators will begin to protect and fortify the system. The exact actions taken will depend largely upon how the administrators wish to handle the intruder. The administrators may choose to research the intruder's techniques and methods by monitoring the intruder's actions. Many businesses and professional organizations do not wish to burden themselves with an intruder and therefore attempt to remove all intruders. Two administrative actions that are sure to occur with any intrusion are creating, or updating, file backups and notifying the Computer Emergency Response Team (CERT).

8.1.2 Backup System Data

Once an intruder's presence has been positively identified, sensitive files should be backed up to a safe location. This may not be necessary, however, if backups are made on a regular basis. The objective of this process is to prevent damage to any sensitive information within the system. Depending on how long the intruder has been able to access the system, this may be useless as the data may have been altered at an earlier time. Nonetheless, this will be useful in the event that the intruder becomes noticeably more hostile and begins to act maliciously. This may occur if the intruder believes he has been noticed or becomes frustrated by an unsuccessful or unfruitful attack. It is therefore important to covertly perform the backups This can be accomplished by using accounts not normally associated with system administrator privileges to back up files. These backups should be performed in small, inconspicuous parts so as not to attract unwanted attention. Voluminous amounts of file duplication or migration by a superuser may serve to tip-off an intruder that a problem is suspected by the administrators. Furthermore, activation of a superuser account will most likely scare the intruder from the system. If an automated job, such as an *at* job or *cron* job, can be activated, this should be done. These types of activities are common to most systems and may be ignored by an intruder. Depending on the sophistication of the intruder, the utility programs that will be used to perform these actions may have been modified. All actions performed when an intruder has compromised a system should be carefully observed as they may not perform their intended task or may be modified to act as a Trojan Horse. The possibility of this occurring can be better assessed at the time of the attack.

After the process is verified to properly function, but before the backup process begins, an unused backup medium should be prepared for use. The benefit of using a new medium is threefold. First, it prevents corruption or damage to existing backup data. This provides extra protection against corruption to what may be the only available data for restoration. Second, it provides an independent set of data to use for comparison to other, non-modified data. It may be useful to compare possibly corrupted data to that which is believed to be correct and accurate. Third, it begins the logging of the intrusion for future analysis. Many organizations, such as CERT, use all available intrusion information to determine how and why intrusions occur in search of a means to prevent further, similar attacks.

In the event that the backup process does not go unnoticed by the intruder, it may be necessary to forcibly remove the intruder from the system.

8.1.3   Remove the Intruder

Unauthorized user access is never welcome in a computer system. Many organizations whose livelihood relies on the security and integrity of their computer system attempt to work to remove any and all intruders. Other organizations, such as universities and other research institutes and labs, are interested in learning from the intruders actions and allow intruders to remain on their system for some time [8.1]. Eventually these organizations decide to conclude their investigations and remove the intruder from the system [8.1]. While this is a wise decision, it may also be difficult.

Research has shown that one of the first actions an intruder takes upon gaining unauthorized access is to modify the system in an attempt to retain their access for an extended amount of time [8.2, 8.12]. This is often accomplished by adding new users to the authorized access lists, obtaining existing authorized user account names and passwords, planting Trojan Horses to obtain passwords, modifying the trusted access permissions, or installing back door access paths [8.1, 8.2, 8.12]. Many of these access paths can be quickly identified and patched. All it takes, however, is one unnoticed means of entry for an intruder to get back into the system. In addition, if the original security compromise is not located and patched, any preventative measures taken will be useless. Incomplete patching will result in two undesirable effects: (1) warning the intruder that his presence is known and (2) indicating to the intruder how unfamiliar the administration is with their own systems. Furthermore, it may provoke the intruder into causing serious damage to the system. This is not to say that an intruder should not be stopped. Every reasonable means necessary should be employed to keep an intruder from accessing a system.

As expected, all of the security holes mentioned above must be patched. Once the files have been repaired or restored, the passwords and trusted system lists changed, and the original security hole found and removed, the intruder should no longer have access to the system. It can be expected, however, that the intruder will continue to attempt to access the system. If the patchwork was complete, these attempts should fail. Eventually, the intruder will either stop or find another security hole. Hopefully, the intruder will choose to stop before another hole is found.

8.1.4 Contain and Monitor the Intruder

While removing an intruder is the safest action, allowing an intruder to remain can be a valuable research method [8.1, 8.8, 8.12]. Passively monitoring an intruder's actions can yield information about how the intruder compromised the system, what the intruder does to remain undetected, how the intruder further compromises the system, and the intruder's purpose for invading the system. The results of such an undertaking, however, may not bear fruit. One such incident where monitoring an intruder yielded little useful information is detailed later in the book (see Chapter 15). Other similar efforts, however, have shown the value of monitoring an intruder's actions (see Chapter 15). Both of these incidents required care and planning, as will any similar administrative response [8.1, 8.8].

Planning and implementing a monitoring system requires the system administrator to take precautions to prevent damage. For example, an intruder should not be allowed to successfully delete or modify system files. This can be accomplished by either reducing the number of available commands, hiding the correct results of a command's execution and showing the expected results, or by sacrificing one computer to the intruder's actions. Each of these options will require significant manpower to implement and support.

The first monitoring technique, reducing the number of available commands, requires the administrator to (1) provide a reason for the reduction, and (2) select the commands to implement. If a believable reason for a sudden reduction in functionality is not provided, an intruder may become suspicious about being monitored. The administrator must also select the commands that will be made available. The criteria for selecting a command will vary from system to system, but a good beginning is to choose commands that are not destructive to the system.

The second, and more difficult, monitoring technique is to alter the effective results of each command so that they only appear to properly function. This can be quite difficult as the execution of various commands may produce contradictory output. This process requires the administrator to carefully determine, and provide, reasonable output.

The third, and most reasonable, approach is to offer up a sacrificial computer that will be completely restored after the exercise. A sacrificial computer is one whose files and settings can be modified or deleted by an intruder without concern. The benefits of this approach are that the computer will function as expected with little modification other than severing dangerous network connections. Since the full complement of commands and most network services are available, an intruder's actions will not be limited. Thus, the audit logs will yield a more accurate chronicle of how an intruder operates. The difficulty with implementing this method, however, is that it requires an additional computer. While all of the monitoring methods may require additional printers, storage devices, or other peripherals, this method requires a complete computer. For many organizations, this may be difficult to obtain, thus forcing an alternate response.

8.1.5   Lock Stolen User Accounts

Most intrusions begin with the compromise of a single user account. This account may be either a system default account, such as guest, or an authorized user account. In either case, the administrator should consider locking the account from further use. This will not prevent an intruder from exploiting the account at the time of the attack, but it will prevent further access from the account. This may be useless, however, as an intruder may have compromised other accounts or system vulnerabilities. Unfortunately, locking an account may bring the administrator into disfavor with the account's authorized user. Depending on the user's circumstances, this may be a simple nuisance or possibly a significant problem. The administrator should therefore inform the authorized user as soon as possible so that the denial of service is expected and can be worked around.

This process does not require a complete denial of service to the authorized user. The administrator may choose to provide the user with a replacement account or simply change the password of the existing account. This decision will depend upon the severity of the attack, the needs of the administrator, and the needs of the affected user. If the administrator wishes to monitor the account or fears that it may have been further altered or compromised, the authorized user should be given a new account to use. In the event that the administrator plans to simply eradicate the intruder, and the risk of additional account compromise seems minimal, a simple password change may suffice.

8.1.6   Require Additional Authentication

Locking an account can be a very drastic measure. As mentioned above, circumstances may be such that only the authorized user is inconvenienced by this. In an effort to further slow down the activity of an intruder, and possibly halt it altogether, the system may require the current user (an intruder) and every subsequent user to provide additional authentication information to continue to function. For example, a system may require an additional password be provided before file removal or modification is performed. One of the key benefits of requiring the additional authentication is that it may seem natural to the intruder and therefore arouse little suspicion.

The additional authentication used for the protection scheme is based upon information provided by a user at the time an account is established. This information, and the way in which it is used, is similar to that of questionnairebased user authentication (see Chapter 5). That is, the information is of a personal nature and not readily discernible from the information within the computer system. This information will require periodic updates as it becomes outdated. It will also need to be changed after it has been used and the offending intruder has been removed. This will prevent the intruder from taking advantage of any captured authentication information.

While the process of maintaining and using additional authentication may be inconvenient to authorized users, it does not completely prevent them from using the system. The additional authentication further provides an authorized user with the knowledge that their account has been compromised. As the additional authentication is only employed after an account has been compromised, its presence will also signal an authorized user that his account was stolen. This notification will inform a user to take the appropriate actions and protect his data.

8.2 Damage Assessment

While damage control concerns the response to an attack in progress, damage assessment concerns the post-intrusion response. More precisely, damage assessment refers to the two-stage process of first identifying and recovering from an attack, then preventing future attacks. The identification and recovery stage includes such tasks as examining log files, identifying stolen information and user accounts, identifying and locating modifications to both system and user files, and restoring the system to its pre-attack state. Once these actions have been performed, the prevention process may ensue. This process includes searching audit logs for vulnerabilities, patching existing security holes, locking unused and stolen accounts, changing passwords, implementing shadow password files, possibly reducing system services, and creating a clean system backup. As can be seen, many of these actions are performed in both stages of the damage assessment process. As much of the processes in each stage overlap, the stages are often performed simultaneously, as one indistinguishable process.

The complete damage assessment process does not require a system be free from intruders; however, it is best applied when intruders are not logged into a system. An intruder's presence would only be destructive to this process as the intruder may actively work to thwart an administrator's actions. The implementation of any damage assessment technique would therefore be best applied after the affected system were placed into some form of single user mode. In the event the computer cannot be effectively removed from service, or more than one computer has been compromised, an alternate solution would be to restrict off-site access. Even though this will only allow on-site users to continue their work, it may be more acceptable to denying service to every authorized user.

8.2.1   Attack Recovery

The primary goal in the recovery process is to restore the system to its pre-attack state. This requires the system to be carefully scrutinized to locate all changes that have been implemented by the intruder. This process begins with examination of the audit trails, or log files. The audit trails will indicate how the intruder initially gained access and may also indicate what the intruder did once inside the system. The knowledge gained by the examination of the audit trails will assist in identifying stolen or unauthorized accounts. This may not be enough, however, so additional password file comparisons and examination will be required. After the accounts and passwords have been restored to their original state, the system must be examined for unauthorized modification to files, both system and user. This will include searching for such things as Trojan Horse programs. Naturally, once the modifications are located and studied, they must be removed. Upon completion of these steps, the system, theoretically, should be completely restored to its original state. Each of these steps is discussed in detail.

8.2.1.1   Examine Audit Trails

The first step in the recovery and restoration process is the examination of audit trails, or log files. Audit trails are on-line records of every command that has been executed on a system. Audit trails were originally intended for computer usage accounting and billing purposes; however, they have since become a valuable tool in identifying the activities of system users, particularly unauthorized users [8.3, 8.10]. For this reason, they are the first items an administrator should examine after a successful attack has occurred.

Examination of audit trails often yields valuable information concerning the activity of an intruder. This information may indicate the type of information an intruder desires, the steps an intruder took to obtain system administrator, or superuser, privileges, and how the system was modified to provide an intruder with easy access in the future [8.3, 8.10]. Figure 8.1 is a segment of an audit trail where an intruder is attempting to obtain superuser privileges. This file excerpt comes from an audit trail that records all attempts to become the superuser. In this example, the person on user account "smith" was attempting to obtain superuser status and was finally successful on his fourth attempt.

The administrator will have to determine if this was an authorized user having difficulties logging in or if this was truly an intruder. Examination of other audit logs and discussions with the authorized user of the "smith" account will help to answer this question.

```
smith *UN*successfully su'd to *ROOT*    on Thu Feb  2 00:25:03 CST 1995
smith *UN*successfully su'd to *ROOT*    on Thu Feb  2 00:25:43 CST 1995
smith *UN*successfully su'd to *ROOT*    on Thu Feb  2 00:26:17 CST 1995
smith      successfully su'd to *ROOT*   on Thu Feb  2 00:26:25 CST 1995
```

Figure 8.1. Audit trail records of attempted superuser access.

Directly logging on as the superuser is not the only way an intruder may attempt to obtain additional system privileges. Another means of obtaining superuser privileges as exploiting ignored system vulnerabilities such as a *sendmail* or *emacs* hole. Audit trail records of activity such as this may indicate the accounts that have been performing these unwanted and overtly hostile actions. Further examination of these accounts and their activities would be an excellent beginning in the search for other hostile behavior and system modification.

Once an account is suspected of being stolen and exploited by an intruder, the account's activity should be examined. The actions recorded by the system will often indicate how an intruder further compromises the security of the system. For example, an intruder may create additional user accounts for future access. Depending upon the configuration of a system's auditing services, the recorded information may indicate that the user account and password files were modified with the *vi* editor. In some instances, the auditing services may record less. The auditing services may also record modifications made to system files and commands. For example, one common intruder activity is to modify the system login program to record a copy of an authorized user's password for later use. While the recording process may not be apparent, the modification to the login program may still be recorded in the audit trails.

Once an intruder presence in a system has been secured, the next logical step is to either look for data or work to gain access into other systems. This is accomplished by searching files, directories, and personal mail. Like file modifications, these actions can also be recorded in the audit trails if so instructed. Examination of the commands executed by an intruder may reveal the intruder's subject of interest. Knowing what an intruder is looking for will be useful in the event traps are to be placed.

In addition to data searches, attempted accesses to remote systems will also be recorded in the audit trails. In some cases, use of the *telnet, FTP, rlogin, rsh,* or *rexec* commands will result in the recording of the remote site's name or IP address. This may also provide insight into the type of information an intruder desires. For example, continuous attempts to access various military sites would be a good indication that an interest in strategic military information exists. A second reason for having the remote site names is so that their administrators can be warned and a cooperative effort can be made towards capturing or stopping the intruder.

Clearly, the benefits of audit logs are numerous. This fact, however, is also known to many intruders. This is evident by the number of intruders that disable the activity recording and remove any record of their presence or activity from the existing logs. A system administrator will therefore need to take a proactive stance in the prevention of damage to the audit trail files. One method to prevent damage or modification is to use a write-once-read-many (WORM) recording medium. Using specialized equipment, however, is often too cost prohibitive for many organizations. A less effective alternative such as audit trail backups is the next best course of action.

8.2.1.2   Identify Stolen Accounts and Data

One of the benefits of audit trails is the assistance they provide in locating stolen accounts or information. As mentioned above, audit trails may capture an intruder's actions and identify password theft, or the threat thereof. More precisely, this is accomplished by looking for suspicious actions that could be associated with password or information theft. Common actions that indicate accounts are being attacked include the modification, downloading, mailing, or displaying of the password file or other files containing passwords (i.e., a UNIX .netrc file) in part or in whole. Positive identification that a user is stealing information, however, is more difficult to obtain. The only way to identify stolen information is to examine the search patterns of an intruder. For example, if an intruder is able to locate and review information regarding defense contractors, it could be easily misconstrued that the intruder is most likely to download similar information. Unfortunately, assumptions based upon an intruder's activity are not always correct. Said intruder could just as easily be looking for recreational entertainment. Looking further into the actions of an intruder may assist in bringing an intruder's actions into focus. This same intruder would appear different if they were also attempting to access known military installations. This process clearly requires a thorough examination of the available audit trails.

The benefits of audit files are no doubt great; however, they are not always available. Attempting to locate stolen passwords or information without the aid of audit trails requires an excellent knowledge of user activity and system operation. This knowledge will be required to locate unusual account and system activity. Unusual activity that should be further investigated includes accounts that appear unusually active after long periods of dormancy, passwords that are easily determined with the latest password cracking programs, and abnormal account usage times and patterns. Since an intrusion has already occurred at this stage, this information will help to identify accounts that have possibly been compromised. It should be noted that this type of analysis is not appropriate for identifying the unknown existence of an intrusion; its value is only in locating a starting point for an informal investigation of an existing attack. Conspicuously missing from the list of unusual activity is abnormal behavior from the superuser (root) account. Much of what is abnormal activity by a user's standards is common to a superuser; abnormal superuser activity is difficult to generalize and define and thus difficult to detect. Furthermore, the superuser account should always be assumed to be stolen. The additional privileges that come with the superuser's account makes it a common and valuable target. Additionally, the fact that the audit trails are either erased or no longer being updated should raise concern and suspicion that the administrator's account has been stolen.

Unlike stolen passwords, stolen information is difficult to detect without the assistance of audit trails. When information is stolen, untraceable copies are created or downloaded with little record that any activity took place. Logic and reason will therefore be required to determine what may have been stolen. Administrators will have to determine what files and information the intruder had access to. The accessible information will have to be reviewed to see what would be of value or interest to the intruder. For example, information about last weekend's company softball game will undoubtedly be of little value to an intruder. Scientific research, however, may be of value to an intruder and should therefore be suspected of being stolen. This does not necessarily mean that the information was stolen without audit logs; simply that it was an easy and possibly attractive target to the intruder. Unfortunately, educated guessing is the only way to determine what information could have been stolen.

8.2.1.3   Locate System Modifications

Of equal importance to locating stolen accounts and information is identifying unauthorized system modifications. These modifications are often performed to provide an intruder with either an additional means of accessing the system or a safer means of accessing the system. Common modifications to search for are listed in Table 8.1. This list is not intended to be complete, but rather provides a place to begin the search. Each system will have different traits and vulnerabilities that provide different opportunities for an intruder.

Each of the modifications listed in Table 8.1 provides an intruder the means of returning to the system without detection or with what appears to be a valid user account. Unauthorized and unnoticed access like this will invariably lead to the compromise of the system administrator's superuser account.

Table 8.1 Possible intruder installed system modifications

```
• Modification to the login program
• The introduction of old, presumably patched
  system vulnerabilities
• Addition or modification of network services
• Addition or modification of user accounts
• Modification of system shells
• Addition of trusted users or systems
• Removal or modification of system auditing
  services and files
```

Locating the types of modifications listed in Table 8.1 proves to be a straightforward task when assisted by audit trails. Audit trails are only of limited assistance, however, as at best they can only indicate what files or programs were modified, not how they were modified. A knowledgeable user will therefore be required to scrutinize the files and locate all unauthorized changes. Locating every modification is a difficult and imprecise process even with an expert knowledge of the system. As can be expected, locating newly installed holes becomes even more difficult when audit trails are unavailable.

Without the assistance of audit trails, a system administrator will need to thoroughly search the system for newly placed vulnerabilities that may not even exist. One means of doing this is the examination of file modification dates. Files that have recently been modified without a legitimate reason should be more closely examined. Most intruders, however, are quick to restore any tell-tale file modification dates so as not to attract unwanted attention to their access paths. Laboriously examining every file for modifications could be greatly simplified, however, if some precautions were taken before the attack. One such precaution is the calculation of file checksums. File checksumming is the process of hashing large amounts of data, usually a single file, down to a simple, significantly smaller, and more manageable value [8.6, 8.7]. As long as the original data remains unchanged, the checksum value will remain unchanged [8.6]. In the event that the original data is modified, the related checksum value will change. Thus, if a file's original checksum value does not match a newly calculated checksum value, the file has been changed. Some people may question whether modifications can be made without a change appearing in the associated checksum value. While some early checksum algorithms may have produced the same checksum value for both the original data and the modified data, newer checksum algorithms have made this near impossible [8.10]. The value of the checksum algorithm is meaningless, however, if a trusted set of checksums was not previously created and updated.

8.2.1.4   System Restoration

Once files have been identified as requiring replacement or recovery, unaltered files should be loaded into the system. If at all possible, these replacement files should come from the original operating system distribution disks. The administrator should also verify that any subsequently released patches are also applied. Failure to do this could result in the removal of one set of vulnerabilities at the cost of introducing an older, more widely known set of vulnerabilities. In the event that distribution copies of files do not exist, as is the case with the user account and password files, the most recent, and unaltered, set of files should be reinstalled. This too may result in the reintroduction of vulnerabilities, such as compromised passwords. These holes, however, should have been previously identified and easily patchable. In the event that an unmodified version of a file does not exist, the modified version will have to be repaired. This should be rare, however, as many systems follow a rigid and periodic file backup process.

8.2.2   Damage Prevention

Once a system has been restored to its pre-attack state, or before an attack ever occurs, action should be taken to prevent future damage and system compromise. This can be accomplished with a few simple techniques. These techniques are not intended to completely protect a system from attack and compromise, rather, they serve as a minimalist effort that should prevent a large number of possible system break-ins. The six security techniques discussed below improve the posture of a computer system and should always be enforced. These techniques are: patch security holes, lock stolen user accounts, change account passwords, employ shadow password files, backup information, and reduce network services. They are not intended to compromise a complete and thorough security system — such a system would include many of the other concepts discussed throughout this book.

8.2.2.1   Patch Security Holes

Previous audit trail and system examinations should reveal weaknesses in a system. These weaknesses, whether maliciously applied or previously existing, must be patched. Many will be well-known and therefore well-documented. Other system vulnerabilities will be new and possibly unique to a particular system. In either case, the patches should be applied and documented. This will not only protect the system from future attacks, but will also provide a record of patches and modifications that have been applied or need to be applied.

A list of previously applied patches will be helpful when reinstalling a new copy of the operating system or just verifying the presence of patches. This list will help ensure that all known system holes are again protected and no longer present a threat to the system. It is easy to forget one or two special patches or system modifications when a system is reinstalled. Even though many systems are configured to install many existing patches, the documented list will guarantee that site-specific modifications are reapplied as well. Furthermore, the list will also serve the purpose of providing a list of patches to examine after an attack. It cannot be guaranteed that every previously installed patch will exist, or even function after an attack. Many intruders remove or modify existing patches as this is not as easily noticed by an administrator. Administrators often wrongly assume that existing patches still exist and function properly. Administrators should therefore verify that a patch not only exists but properly functions by means of thorough testing.

8.2.2.2 Lock Stolen User Accounts

Stolen user accounts are a valuable tool to an intruder. They provide an intruder the means of accessing a system under the appearance of an authorized user. For this reason, system administrators must work to keep intruders from stealing user accounts and masquerading as authorized users. One way to reduce the vulnerability of user accounts is to work with users in controlling their accounts. Users and administrators must keep each other abreast of changes in an account's activity and privileges. Users must inform administrators of the times their accounts will be inactive and discuss their needs and usage patterns. Similarly, administrators should safely provide the resources required by a user, but also monitor unusual activity and restrict the privileges allotted to an account. When administrators and users work together, stolen accounts can be quickly detected.

One of the greatest problems in locating stolen accounts and preventing their theft is the inevitable breakdown in communication between the administrators and users. Administrators must be informed of changing account usage patterns as soon as possible. This will allow the administrators to provide a continued level of high performance in a user-transparent fashion. Changes worthy of administrator notification include on-site only use to remote use when traveling, temporary inactivity such as when going on vacation, and permanent inactivity such as when changing employers. This notification will allow administrators to keep unauthorized usage to a minimum while providing authorized users the resources and security they require.

Despite poor communications, administrators should actively search for and lock or remove accounts that have been dormant for some time. These accounts are attractive to intruders as the authorized users are not likely to notice the unauthorized use of their account. Additionally, an intruder can hide in a dormant account without raising additional suspicion. In an effort to reduce this type of abuse, administrators must strictly adhere to an account lock out and removal policy. This policy may simply require users to periodically revalidate their accounts or lose them. Other policies may lock an account after a predetermined amount of inactivity. Regardless of the rules enforced by a lock out plan, the goals remain the same: reduce the means by which unauthorized access is possible.

8.2.2.3   Change Passwords

The concept of changing an account's password is both simple and obvious. Nonetheless, it must be carefully planned so that the changes are thorough. This is accomplished by taking a three-phased approach to change passwords. Briefly, these phases are: (1) protect privileged accounts, (2) protect user accounts, and (3) prevent future password compromises. Together, these phases provide a comprehensive means of protecting a system from intrusion through compromised accounts.

The first phase, protecting privileged accounts, requires an administrator to change the passwords of all superuser, or root, accounts as well as system default accounts. Most people would believe that this would be quite obvious and need not be mentioned. Surprisingly, however, this is a real problem and concern. Experience has shown that many administrators do not change system default passwords, thus giving uncontrolled access to anyone with a passing familiarity of a system [8.12]. To protect a system from this type of usage, the passwords should be changed not only after an attack, but on a regular basis. For many organizations, this is standard operating procedure. Even still, compromising system accounts by trying default passwords is a very common, and successful, attack method.

The second phase of protecting a system from attack via compromised accounts is to change the passwords of the user's accounts. Clearly, the known stolen account passwords should be changed; they are a liability to the security of a system. In addition, all users should be instructed to change their passwords. This will prevent accounts whose passwords are known to an intruder from being attacked. It will also prevent an intruder from accessing accounts that the administration does not realize are stolen. One problem that may result from informing all users to change their passwords is wide spread panic and concern. Care must therefore be taken as not to cause such a problem. One such way would be to introduce a plan similar to that discussed in Phase three.

The third phase in protecting a system is to introduce a means of protecting user accounts from further abuse. One such way is to institute a plan that requires users to change their password on a regular basis. This will force users to change the password they used at the time of the attack, thus invalidating any existing password lists obtained by the intruder. The drawback to this plan will be the backlash from users who do not want to change their password. While serving and assisting the users is one of the tasks of an administrator, the importance of providing a secure computing environment is an administrator's primary concern and should be treated as such.

Once these phases have been completed, stolen user accounts should no longer be an immediate concern. This is not to suggest that this will not be a problem in the future, but rather current vulnerabilities of stolen accounts should no longer pose an immediate threat. The need to prevent any further accounts from being stolen, however, is great. One such method to reduce the possibility of account theft is the use of shadow password files.

8.2.2.4   Employ Shadow Password Files

Many existing operating systems, including various derivations of UNIX, store user account information in the same file as the account passwords. This was initially done in an effort to improve system performance and conserve storage space [8.2]. An unfortunate drawback of this data organization is the requirement that the data be made readable to many utilities, and thus readable to every user. Because this allowed anyone to obtain every authorized user's encrypted password, it presented a significant security breach. In an effort to prevent the encrypted passwords from being made public, shadow password files were introduced [8.2].

Shadow password files are access-restricted files that contain the encrypted passwords of each system account [8.2, 8.5]. This enables the encrypted passwords to be removed from the account information file, thus increasing system security without negatively effecting the daily operation of a system [8.4, 8.5]. An example of a shadowed and non-shadowed user information file from a Sun Microsystems Solaris operating system is shown in Figures 8.2(a) and 8.2(b). The general information in both Figures 8.2(a) and 8.2(b) differs only in that the encrypted password information has been removed from the account information file in the non-shadowed file, Figure 8.2(b). The removal of the encrypted passwords promotes system security as the freely available account information files provide only limited information about the system and its users.

```
fred:Qhih7H25GG:144:144:Fred's account:/home/usr/fred:/bin/tcsh
wilma:i9H45d8Sh:145:145:Wilma's account:/home/usr/wilma:/bin/csh
barney:hgrD4496a:146:146:Barney's account:/home/usr/barney:/bin/csh
betty:Huyt6G4x8:147:147:Betty's account :/home/usr/betty:/bin/bsh
```
(a)

```
fred:x:144:144:Fred's account:/home/usr/fred:/bin/tcsh
wilma:x:145:145:Wilma's account:/home/usr/wilma:/bin/csh
barney:x:146:146:Barney's account:/home/usr/barney:/bin/csh
betty:x:147:147:Betty's account :/home/usr/betty:/bin/bsh
```
(b)

Figures 8.2. (a) Part of a non-shadowed password file. (b) An equivalent shadowed user information file.

Encrypted passwords are key in retaining access to a computer system. As previously mentioned, once an intruder gains access to a system, the intruder will work to retain that access. This is often accomplished by stealing accounts or, more precisely, stealing the encrypted passwords. Once the encrypted passwords are stolen, they may be compared against an encrypted version of a dictionary. The results of this comparison are the known, plain-text passwords that make up many of the encrypted passwords used to access a system. Therefore, preventing an intruder from obtaining a copy of the encrypted passwords will help prevent an intruder from accessing a system. For this reason, shadow password files are now used and supported by most operating systems. Regardless of whether an intrusion has occurred or not, administrators should seriously consider employing shadow passwords on their systems.

8.2.2.5 Backup Information

One of the key goals in recovering from an attack is to restore a system as quickly as possible. This is an issue primarily because the down time after an attack is equivalent to lost computing time and therefore lost money. System administrators must therefore provide a means to expeditiously recover from an attack. One way to do this is to restore a clean operating system and then work to recover any compromised accounts and passwords. This process requires a clean operating system to exist in some fashion. If periodic system backup is performed, then this is not a concern. In the event that system administration has been lax and backup files are either out of date or non-existent, recovery will be a more involved process.

Most system administrators and users understand the importance of backing up data — many administrators have had to load backup files when a user accidentally deletes a file. Besides protecting users from themselves, backup files may provide a copy of a complete and properly configured operating system. Thus, in the event that a disk fails, recovery is as quick and easy as reading from a tape. The same is true for intrusions — if system modification becomes too great, recovery from a backup file may resolve much of the damage. This only solves part of the problem, however, as the recovery system still contains the same vulnerabilities that allowed the intruder to access the system. Thus, for this to be a viable solution, the system must be recovered to a known, pre-intruder state and the exiting vulnerabilities should be patched. The determination of such a backup time and the necessary system patches will be aided by examination of the intruder's activity, some of which may be in any existing system audit trails. Once the system is restored and patched, a fresh backup should be made. This backup should also be somehow identified as "intruder-free" for expeditious recovery in the future.

Not every system has the benefit of backup files. In such a case, a corrupt system can either be completely recovered from distribution files or patched as needed. Because patching is often an incomplete process, it may be in the best interest of all users and administrators involved to reinstall a system from the distribution files.   While this process is neither enjoyable nor quick, it may be more complete than patching an overly stressed system. This process may also be aided by the automatic application of newly available patches that protect a system from similar attacks. This may not result in a complete recovery, however, as site specific modifications may still need to be applied — modifications that would be present if recovering from personal backups as opposed to a system distribution file. On its own, this process may require extensive efforts and long periods of time to complete. Once this laborious process has been completed, the system administrator would be well advised to begin to backup the system in an effort to prevent similar problems from occurring in the future.

8.2.2.6   Reduce Network Services

Many network attacks begin with the compromise or exploitation of existing network services. One such well documented attack exploited the UNIX *finger* command [8.9]. In an effort to reduce intrusion susceptibility from similar attacks, a system administrator may wish to remove any unnecessary or underutilized services. Some such network services that should always be considered for removal are *finger*, *TFTP* (Trivial File Transfer Protocol), *rexec* (remote execution), *rsh* (remote shell), and *rlogin* (remote login).   While other services exist and should also be considered, these are excellent candidates as they provide services that are useful but unnecessary for most authorized users. Furthermore, these protocols make an intruder's work easier unless properly configured.

The Trivial File Transfer Protocol, *TFTP*, is a simple file transfer scheme. This protocol is similar to its more feature-filled counterpart, the File Transfer Protocol (*FTP*). The key differences between the two protocols is that *TFTP* provides no user authentication and is based on a User Datagram Protocol (UDP) as opposed to a Transmission Control Protocol (TCP) [8.11]. These missing features reduce the security provided by the *TFTP* service. One such security shortcoming is *TFTP*'s allowing sensitive system files, such as password files, to be downloaded to a remote system [8.2]. With the ever present possibility that user passwords are easily determined, this should be prevented. This problem can usually be resolved by altering the execution options of the *TFTP* daemon [8.2].   This alteration will often be necessary as many manufacturers distribute their operating system software with the *TFTP* vulnerability present [8.2].

The *finger* service, much like the *TFTP* service, is commonly removed in an effort to reduce the security vulnerabilities of a system. While older holes in the *finger* services allowing commands to be executed by a remote system have been removed, the information produced by most default *finger* services can be dangerous in the wrong hands.   This information often includes an individual's last use of a system, an individual's user account name, the site of a user's last connection, and personal information that may be useful in guessing passwords [8.4]. As this information is frequently enough to begin a successful attack on a computer system, many organizations remove the *finger* service [8.4]. In the event that an organization finds value in the *finger* service, a less revealing version of the *finger* service may be created and easily installed. In either case, the default *finger* service should be evaluated and removed.

Remote access service such as *rsh, rexec,* and *rlogin* are also excellent candidates for removal from a computer system. Unlike the *TFTP* and *finger* services, the various remote access services are only useful when access to a particular system has been granted [8.4]. These services are intended to allow authorized users access to trusted systems without providing any password authentication [8.4]. This unchallenged access, however, is not limited to authorized users. Once an intruder has obtained access to one system, the remote services will allow the intruder to access other trusted systems without being challenged for a password. In an attempt to confine the effects of a system compromise, these services should be denied as well as the *TFTP* and *finger* services.

The *TFTP, finger,* and remote services are worthy of removal when attempting to improve system security. As previously stated, however, they are not the only services whose presence should be reevaluated. Other services that should be considered for removal are: *biff, link, netstat, NFS, NIS, sprayd, systat, tcpmux,* and *uucp.* As is to be expected, the specific services that should be removed from a system will depend upon the needs of the users and the requirements of a system.

8.3 Summary

Damage control and assessment is the activity of restricting the damage that an intruder inflicts upon a system as well as determining what damage an active intruder has already done. The means of damage control range from simply informing the necessary authorities to monitoring and manipulating an intruder's activity. Many of the techniques employed for damage control require careful planning and thought so that they can be rapidly executed in response to an intruder's actions. As damage control techniques are being implemented throughout a system, damage assessment procedures can commence. Damage assessment techniques are intended to restore a system to its pre-attack state. These techniques alone are not enough to protect a system from attack. They are presented as a minimalist set of actions that can be performed to improve the basic security of system. A more complete damage prevention package will address such additional issues as firewalls and encryption.

8.4   Exercises

8.1.   One possible reaction to a system intrusion is direct communication with the intruder. What are the advantages and disadvantages of this communication? Would you recommend it to a system administrator?

8.2.   Not every intruder breaks into a system to steal the data it contains. It is common for intruders to gain a strong foothold in one system and use that as a base for attacking other systems. Is it important to identify what information could have been stolen from those systems whose primary purpose is as a stepping stone to other systems? Why or why not?

8.3.   Table 8.1 lists some possible system modifications that an intruder may attempt. What other system modifications can be made? How will these modifications affect the security and integrity of the system? How can they be detected and prevented?

8.4.   When does the feasibility of performing individual file restorations give way to performing a complete system restoration? What are the side effects of doing a complete system restoration?

8.5   References

8.1   Cheswick, W. R. and Bellovin, S. M., *Firewalls and Internet Security*, Addison-Wesley Publishing Co., Reading, Massachusetts, 1994.

8.2   Curry. D., *UNIX System Security*, Addison-Wesley Publishing Co., Reading, Massachusetts, 1992.

8.3   Denning, D., "An Intrusion Detection Model", *IEEE Transactions on Software Engineering*, IEEE Press, New York, New York, Vol. SE-13, No. 2, February 1987, pp. 222-232.

8.4   Ferbrache, D. and Shearer, G., *UNIX Installation Security and Integrity*, Prentice Hall, Englewood Cliffs, New Jersey, 1993.

8.5   Frisch, Æ., *Essential System Administration*, O'Reilly & Associates Inc.,
         Sebastopol, California, 1991.

8.6   Garfinkel, S. and Spafford, G., *Practical UNIX Security*, O'Reilly &
         Associates Inc., Sebastopol, California, 1992.

8.7   Russell, D. and Gangemi Sr., G. T., *Computer Security Basics*, O'Reilly &
         Associates Inc., Sebastopol, California, July 1991.

8.8   Safford, D., Schales, D., and Hess, D., "The TAMU Security Package: An
         Ongoing Response to Internet Intruders in an Academic Environment",
         Proceedings of the Fourth USENIX Security Symposium, Santa Clara,
         California, October 1993, pp. 91-118.

8.9   Seeley, D., "A Tour of the Worm", Technical Report, The University of
         Utah, available via *anonymous ftp* from *cert.sei.cmu.edu*
         /pub/virus-l/docs/tour.ps, January 1990.

8.10   Stalling, W., *Network and Internetwork Security: Principles and Practice*,
         Prentice Hall, Englewood Cliffs, New Jersey, 1995.

8.11   Stevens, W. R., *TCP/IP Illustrated, Volume I*, Addison-Wesley, Reading,
         Massachusetts, 1994.

8.12   Stoll, C., *The Cuckoo's Egg*, Doubleday Books, New York, New York,
         1989.

8.6   Extended Bibliography

8.13   Chantico Publishing Co., *Disaster Recovery Handbook*, TAB Professional
         and Reference Books, Blue Ridge Summit, Pennsylvania, 1991.

8.14   Hansen, S. E. and Atkins, E. T., "Centralized System Monitoring with
         Swatch", Technical Report, Electrical Engineering Computer Facility,
         Stanford University, available via *anonymous ftp* from *mojo.ots.utexas.edu*
         /pub/src/swatch-1.8.6.tar.Z, March 1995.

8.15   Baker, M. and Sullivan, M., "The Recovery Box: Using Fast Recovery to
        Provide High Availability in the UNIX Environment", *1992 Summer
        USENIX Conference in San Antonio, Texas*, June 1992, pp. 31-43.

8.16   Blaze, M., "NFS Tracing by Passive Network Monitoring", Technical Report
        TR-355-91, Department of Computer Science, Princeton University,
        available via *anonymous ftp* from *ftp.dsi.unimi.it*
        /pub/security/docs/papers/nfsspy.ps.gz, January 1994.

8.17   Brand, R. L., "Coping with the threat of Computer Security Incidents: A
        Primer from Prevention through Recovery", Technical Report, available via
        anonymous ftp from *csrc.nist.gov* /pub/secpubs/primer.ps, December 1992.

8.18   Farmer, D. and Venema, W., "Improving the Security of Your Site by
        Breaking Into It.", Technical Report, available via *anonymous ftp* from
        ftp.dsi.unimi.it /pub/security/docs/papers/sag_to_crack, January 1994.

8.19   Pethia, R. D. and Van Wyk, K. R., "Computer Emergency Response – An
        International Problem", Computer Emergency Response Team, Software
        Engineering Institute, Carnegie Mellon University, Pittsburgh, Pennsylvania.

8.20   Spafford, E. H. and Weeber, S. A., "Software Forensics: Can We Track Code
        to its Authors?", *Purdue Technical Report CSD-TR-92-010*, Department of
        Computer Sciences, Purdue University, February 1992.

9

NETWORK SECURITY

Before the invention of computers, information security was for the most part a physical security problem. Information was protected behind locked doors and kept secure in safes and locked file cabinets. The situation didn't change much with the introduction of early computing systems which were also kept secure behind locked doors. With the advent of remote access card readers and terminals, however, security became harder to maintain since every room with one of these devices had to be kept secure. Additional security was added so that only authorized individuals could use the computer. Authentication techniques, such as accounts with userid/password combinations, were used to verify the authenticity of users. Even with authentication techniques, physical security still played a large part in maintaining control of these early computer systems. With the introduction of networks, however, physical security began to play a less important role. Today, with the global nature of the Internet, physical security can only be counted on to protect the computer system from theft. It can't be relied on to protect the information contained on the computer systems connected to a network. Individuals can now "travel the digital highways", journeying from the United States to the Far East, Europe, and back to the United States in a matter of a few seconds. None of the machines except the actual terminal (workstation or PC) the individual is sitting in front of can rely on physical security measures to protect it. Authentication and access control techniques are part of the solution but networks must also rely on other techniques to maintain the integrity of the data they contain. It is these other techniques, used to secure computer systems attached to networks, that are the subject of this chapter.

9.1   Network Fundamentals

Before examining how security is applied to networks, a basic understanding of network organization is required. There are a number of reasons computer systems are connected together in a network including resource sharing, communication, reliability, and increased processing power. Communication between computers in a network can be accomplished in a *point-to-point* fashion where each system transmits to another specific system, or in a *broadcast* manner where systems transmit in general to the media accessible to all other systems. There are several ways that the computer systems can be connected in a network. Figure 9.1 depicts two topologies found in broadcast networks. Figure 9.2 depicts two other topologies found in point-to-point networks.

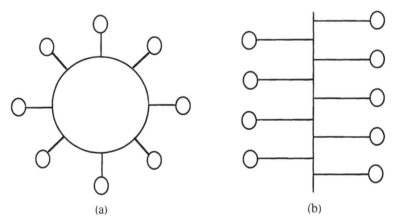

(a)   (b)

Figure 9.1. Broadcast network topologies. (a) Ring. (b) Bus [9.5].

In order to reduce the complexity of networks, most are organized in a series of layers. Each layer is built upon the layer below it to standardize and simplify communication between them. The purpose of each layer can be thought of as to provide

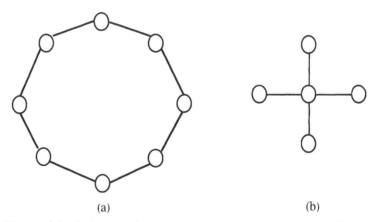

(a)   (b)

Figure 9.2. Point-to-point topologies. (a) Ring. (b) Star [9.5].

specific services to the layer above it. This effectively hides the details of communication between lower level layers and the upper levels and serves to modularize the protocols for each layer. The purpose is to also create an environment where each layer on a system communicates with the same layer on another system using the protocol developed for that layer. Each subsequent lower level takes the information passed to it from the level above and formats it to meet its protocol needs before sending it along. Figure 9.3 illustrates this process.

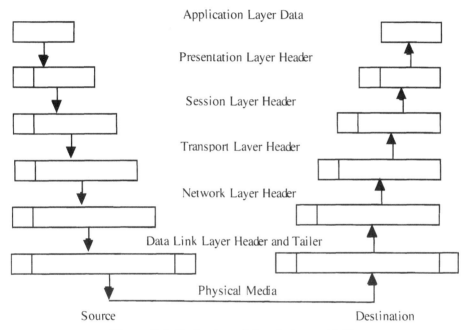

Figure 9.3. Packaging of data in layers |9.3|.

In this example, a 7-layer model is assumed. Data to be sent is created at Layer 7 of the source host destined for Layer 7 on the destination host. As far as the application at Layer 7 on the source host is concerned, the message only needs to be formatted in the Layer 7 protocol, and is then passed to the next level below, Layer 6. At this next layer, the message is sent along formatted so that it conforms to the Layer 6 protocol and is passed to Layer 5 where the process continues. It is possible at any of these layers that the message may have to be split into different parts. At any of the layers a header or tailer may also be attached to the message. If the message is split, each portion is treated as its own entity by all layers below the split. Each portion may then receive its own header and/or tailer. The packaged data is eventually passed to the physical media where it is transmitted to the destination source. As the message is received at the destination host, it is passed back up through the layers. Each layer strips off its header and if the message had been split into separate parts, reassembles it. The advantage of this layered approach can be seen at Layer 3 and below where splitting of packages normally occurs. The application program at Layer 7 does not have to worry about splitting a large message into parts; this will be handled at the lower layers where constraints are imposed by network protocols. The lower layers in turn don't worry about the contents of the message; this is the responsibility of the application layer.

The most commonly encountered layered model is the 7-layer International Standards Organization (ISO) Open Systems Interconnection (OSI) Reference Model. This model, including what is known as the communication subnet, is depicted in Figure 9.4.

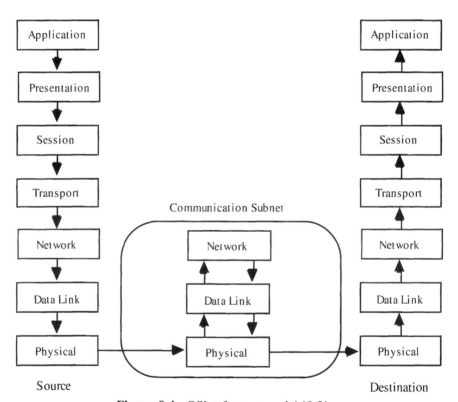

Figure 9.4. OSI reference model [9.5].

The lowest layer of this model is called the **Physical Layer**. This layer is concerned with the actual transmission of raw binary bits across a transmission medium. Error detection and correction is not a concern at this layer. Layer 2, **Data Link**, is designed to take the raw bits that have been transmitted and to turn them into what appears to be an error-free line. The next layer up from Data Link Layer is the **Network Layer.** This layer is concerned with the controlling of the subnet. A key issue at this layer is routing. The **Transport Layer** is the fourth layer whose purpose is to provide transmission services to the higher levels without being concerned about cost-effective data transfer. It also insures that all pieces are received correctly. Layer 5 is the **Session Layer,** which provides a way for higher level entities to establish synchronized dialogue (sessions). The **Presentation Layer,** Layer 6, provides certain services that are frequently used by Layer 7. An example of this is data compression. The highest level, Layer 7, is the **Application Layer** which is concerned with a number of different protocols. An example of this is the communication necessary to invoke a full screen editor across a network.

The communication subnet depicted in Figure 9.4 is designed to transmit data between different hosts without the user having to be concerned with routing issues. Often the machine the user is connected to is not the machine the user ultimately wants to communicate with. Any data transmitted between the two will need to be passed to several intermediary machines to relay the information. Several different networks may in fact be involved with the transmission. The entire seven layers worth of protocol packaging does not need to be unpackaged in order to transfer the data, only the subnet portion needs to be addressed.

Another issue related to the services provided by the various layers is whether the service provided is *connection-oriented* or *connectionless*. A connection-oriented service is one in which the connection between the same layer on two different hosts consists of several phases: the establishment, transfer, and termination phases. The transfer phase is where the actual stream of data units is conveyed between the two. The data is generally guaranteed to be received in the proper order and without transmission errors. Connectionless service, on the other hand, involves the transmission of single data units without any guarantee that the units will be received correctly or in the proper order. In addition, it is also possible to receive multiple copies of the data units at the destination host.

9.2 Network Security Issues

Network security isn't any different than single host security in terms of its goal. Network security is still aimed at meeting the objectives of providing confidentiality, integrity, availability, and access for legitimate users of the network resources. The real difference in providing basic security services occurs because of the increased complexity of the networked environment. Providing confidentiality of information, for example, is difficult enough when the entire system resides in a single room. Consider the implications of allowing access to information from multiple locations located in areas separated by tremendous distances. Security for a single host is generally the responsibility of a single individual. In a networked environment, the security of individual systems is the responsibility of numerous individuals. Intruders to networks continually count on finding a single weak link in the network chain which will then allow them access to the rest of the network. Network security measures must account for this, as well as other complexities, in an attempt to maintain the security of the network data and resources.

9.2.1   Basic Network Security Objectives and Threats

The security services of a network have four fundamental objectives designed to protect the data and the network's resources. These objectives are:

- *Confidentiality*: Ensures that an unauthorized individual does not gain access to data contained on a resource of the network.
- *Availability*: Ensures that authorized users are not unduly denied access or use of any network access for which they are normally allowed.
- *Integrity*: Ensures that data is not altered by unauthorized individuals. Related to this is *authenticity*, which is concerned with unauthorized creation of data.
- *Usage*: Ensures that the resources of the network are reserved for use only by authorized users in an appropriate manner.

Opposing these objectives and the network security services are a number of threats. These threats can be described in terms of how they affect the normal flow of information in the network. There are four basic patterns of attack for these threats as depicted in Figure 9.5. The first of these is *denial of service* in which the flow of information is blocked entirely. This can be accomplished in a number of ways including affecting the medium through which that data must travel or the source host itself where the data (or requested network service) resides. The second pattern of attack is *modification* where the contents of messages or the data itself is modified before it is received at the destination host. The third pattern of attack is *interception*. In this attack the normal flow of information is not affected, instead an additional flow, generally to an unauthorized source, is created. Two examples of this form of attack are *eavesdropping*, where another (unauthorized) user gains access to the information as it is transmitted, and *traffic analysis* where information about the network, its services, and its users is obtained by observing the type, destination, and volume of traffic without knowing the contents of the messages or data sent. The last attack pattern is *creation* in which new data traffic is created and inserted onto the network, generally masquerading as data from another, authorized source.

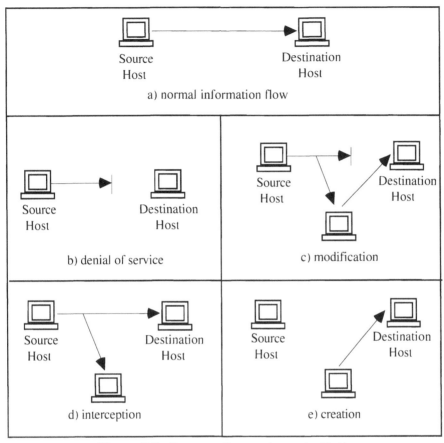

Figure 9.5. Patterns of network attacks [9.4].

9.2.2 Security Services

Defending the network from these patterns of attack is a series of six *security services*. These services are:

- *Access Control*: Protects against unauthorized use of the network or its resources.
- *Authentication*: Establishes the identity of an entity (either a user or another system). Also prevents repudiation of an exchange of previous traffic by either the sender or receiver.
- *Confidentiality*: Protects information from being disclosed to unauthorized entities.
- *Data Integrity*: Prevents the unauthorized modification or deletion of data.

- *Traffic Flow Integrity*: Prevents the collection of information about the network through observation of network traffic characteristics.
- *Assured Usage*: Prevents the denial of service through degradation of network services.

It is important to be able to visualize the environment for these services if we are to understand the difficulty of implementing them. In Figure 9.6 a connection between two hosts has been requested. This connection can be for any of a variety of reasons such as sending or receiving files, electronic mail, or for requesting a specific service. The local networks each host is part of are not directly connected to each other so the transmission between the two must travel through several other intermediate subnets. The path the transmissions take may include different configurations of topology and may include networks supporting different services. In theory the subnets should simply determine that the transmission is not intended for them and forward it onward. In practice, however, the two end systems cannot be assured that the subnets simply forward the data and thus must rely on the network security services to provide the necessary assurances.

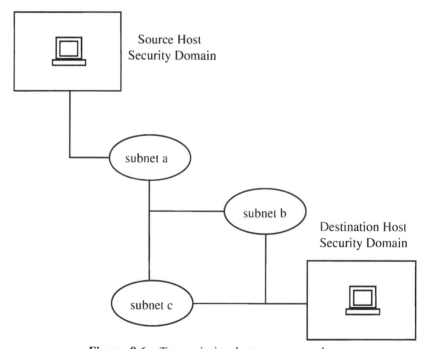

Figure 9.6. Transmission between networks.

The authentication service insures that the source for the received data is correctly identified. Related to authentication is *nonrepudiation*. Often it is important to be able to prevent a sender of a message from denying that it was sent. This is especially true in financial transactions. Similarly, it is also often important to be able to determine that the destination host did indeed receive the message. Another problem that must be addressed by both the authentication and access control servers is the replaying of previously captured transmissions. This technique has been used by unauthorized individuals to trick hosts into believing that the transmission came from an authorized individual. In Figure 9.6, for example, a user on one of the subnets not normally authorized access to the destination host could capture login information that had been transmitted at an earlier time from an authorized user on the source host to the destination host. This information could later be replayed to the destination host in order to obtain access to it. Finally, the authentication service is often used in conjunction with other mechanisms to provide the access control service.

Access control is concerned with protecting against the unauthorized use of the network or its resources. This service directly contributes to the objectives of confidentiality, availability, and integrity by enforcing authorization. Authorization generally assumes a pair of active entities: the *target* and the *initiator*. Authorization, and thus access controls, governs which initiators may access and use which target systems or network services. Access control is also responsible for a process called *selective routing*. The purpose of selective routing is to prevent sensitive information from being transmitted through networks or subnets that are not trusted. In Figure 9.6, for example, if subnet b was not trusted by the source host but subnet c was, selective routing would be responsible for insuring that important transmissions from the source to the destination hosts would avoid subnet b.

Confidentiality services protect transmissions from being revealed to unauthorized users. There are two basic techniques used to provide this service. The first is to trust only entities in a well-defined *security domain*. A security domain consists of all hosts and resources, as well as the transmission medium used to connect them, which abide by a formal security policy and for which we can be assured a certain level of security. Hosts in this domain place a certain level of trust in the other hosts and may thus provide certain services for these trusted hosts which are not available to hosts residing outside of the security domain. An example is the UNIX *rlogin* command, which allows a user on one host access to another host without having to provide a password for this new host. The security domain may also consist of additional networks or subnets for which the same level of trust has been placed. The second technique is to hide important information through the use of *encryption*. Encryption transforms the information to be hidden from an understandable format to one that is unintelligible to any but the intended recipient (who knows how to transform the information back to its original format). This technique is used whenever a transmission has to leave the current security domain in order to travel to its ultimate destination. Since we can't trust systems that are outside of our security domain, we must hide the important information from those who might try to intercept it.

Encryption is also useful in another security service, traffic flow integrity. In this service the goal is to prevent unauthorized individuals from obtaining information through observing characteristics of the transmission itself. Characteristics of importance include the source and destination, frequency, and size of the transmission. The difference between encryption for traffic flow purposes and encryption for confidentiality is the level of the OSI model the encryption is performed at. If, for example, an application running at the seventh layer of the model is communicating with another application on a different host, the data can be passed to the sixth layer and encrypted at that point before passing it along. The information is then sent through the network and isn't decrypted until it arrives at the destination host whose sixth layer knows how to decrypt this specific data. If the data is captured in any subnet between the source and destination hosts, then the information will be useless since it cannot be understood. Encryption at this level is known as *end-to-end* encryption since the encryption process takes place only at the source and destination hosts (the two ends).

Encryption of only the data does not help with traffic flow integrity since the other characteristics of the transmission can still be observed. An alternative approach is to encrypt as the transmission leaves the host. This will encrypt the entire transmission which will also serve to hide the transmission characteristics. Of course the transmission will need to be decrypted at each node in the network or subnets so that it may be properly routed, but it does protect the transmission from analysis through wiretapping or electronic emissions from the physical medium. This form of encryption is called *link* encryption since it is performed at each link of the transmission chain between two communicating hosts. If one can trust all intermediate systems and subnets, this effectively provides the traffic flow integrity desired. A final point on traffic flow analysis; it should be obvious that more than just encryption is needed if one wants to hide the volume of traffic sent from or to a specific host or network. For this reason some organizations (the military in particular) have systems generate false messages during periods of low network usage. These messages are simply ignored by the receiving host but will appear to be just as real to anybody who has tapped into a transmission line as other, official traffic.

The data integrity security service ensures that data is not modified or deleted by an authorized individual. In terms of a network, the concern about modification is not only at the site where the data is stored but also as it is transmitted. It also includes the unauthorized creation of new data items supposedly from an authorized source. While both data integrity and confidentiality services share similar methods to provide their respective service, it is important to understand the difference between them. Suppose, for example, the source and destination hosts in Figure 9.6 represented a bank and one of its remote automated teller machines (ATM). An individual wishing to exploit the system might attempt to tap into the line between the two systems so that a customer's account and personal identification number (PIN) could be obtained. This would be a confidentiality issue. If, on the other hand, a customer wishing to exploit the system attempted to modify the transmission between the two systems (so that the ATM dispensed $100.00 but the bank only received a request for and authorized a $10.00 transaction) it would be a data integrity issue.

Encryption will help with the modification portion of data integrity since the customer would not know what to change in the encrypted message. It will not by itself, however, solve the associated problem of replay. Suppose, for example, that a customer were able to capture all of the transmissions from one transaction between the bank and ATM. Later the customer accesses the transmission line and attempts another transaction. This time, however, the customer blocks all messages to the bank from the ATM and simply resends the authorization recorded earlier thus convincing the ATM to dispense the money without the bank receiving notification of the transaction. One way around this problem is to provide a time-stamp inside of the encrypted message. Thus when the recorded transmission is replayed the time-stamp will reveal the fraudulent nature of this transaction. A field or value included for integrity purposes is often referred to as an integrity check value.

Finally, the assured usage service is concerned with the availability of network resources to authorized users based on some defined level of performance. This defined level of performance is often referred to as the Quality of Service (QoS) and should be stated in the security policy. This service is often more difficult to ensure than the others. It may also actually result in competition between authorized users since the security policy may define different levels of users and may sacrifice service to one level in order to provide service to another level.

9.3   The Trusted Network Interpretation

The Department of Defense has provided guidance as to what is required to secure a network. This guidance is outlined in the *Trusted Network Interpretation of the Trusted Computer System Evaluation Criteria* |9.2|. Commonly referred to as the *Red Book* or the TNI, this guidance provides an interpretation of how the *Orange Book* can be applied to a network environment. The first part of the *Red Book* is the actual interpretation of the various classes found in the *Orange Book* and how they apply to networks. A second part of the *Red Book*, however, is a list of other security services that either do not exist on a stand-alone system or that have increased significance in a network.

There are two viewpoints from which to evaluate secure networks. The first is the Interconnected Accredited Automated Information System View. This viewpoint looks at a network as a series of multiple interconnected Automated Information Systems (AIS) that have been individually accredited to handle certain levels of information. Each AIS will agree with another AIS as to what range of sensitive information can be exchanged between them. A network designed this way really consists of a series of systems, each of which is responsible for enforcing its own security.

The second viewpoint is the Single Trusted System View in which a common level of trust is supported throughout the entire network. A single trusted system is viewed as a single entity rather than a series of individual components. The network formed adheres to a single security policy and is considered a single trusted computing base, referred to as the Network Trusted Computing Base (NTCB). The functions of the NTCB may be partitioned among the various systems connected to the network but all work together to ensure that the overall security policy is enforced.

In terms of the network interpretation of the *Orange Book*, it is generally not practical to apply the various requirements to a network consisting of interconnected AIS. Instead, Part I of the TNI is aimed at networks with a single NTCB viewpoint. Part II, however, is applicable to all networks, no matter what structure they take. We will not discuss the individual network interpretation of any of the various *Orange Book* requirements but will instead concentrate on the security services outlined in Part II of the TNI.

9.3.1 TNI Security Service

The TNI addresses nine security services split evenly among three categories. The categories are Communications Integrity, Denial of Service, and Compromise Protection. For each service, the TNI lists both a brief functional description of the service as well as possible techniques to provide the service. It also lists three criterion (Functionality, Strength, and Assurance) for each and the range of possible evaluations. While the criterion for rating the services is not important in a general discussion of network security, the description of the services themselves, as well as examples of possible mechanisms for implementation, are and provide a glimpse of other factors that need to be considered in securing a network.

The first category, **Communications Integrity**, is concerned with the accuracy, non-corruptibility, and level of confidence in the transmission between two systems in the network. This first category consists of the three services, *Authentication*, *Communications Field Integrity*, and *Nonrepudiation*.

Authentication is concerned with ensuring that an established transmission takes place between the desired entities and not an entity attempting to masquerade as another or to replay a previously captured transmission. If this service is provided for a connection-oriented transmission, the TNI refers to it as Peer Entity Authentication. If it is in support of a connectionless transmission it is called Data Origin Authentication. The methods listed to implement this service include encryption, something known by the entity (e.g., a password), and use of some characteristic of the entity (e.g., biometrics) or a possession owned by the entity (e.g., smartcards).

Communications Field Integrity refers to the protection from unauthorized alteration of the fields in the data transmitted between two entities. This includes any of the header, trailer, and data fields. The TNI does allow the network architect, administrator, and even the user to selectively apply data integrity to certain fields depending on the ultimate security goal of the designer. Countermeasures for this service include policy, procedures, and automated or physical controls. Encryption, however, is generally the primary technique used.

The nonrepudiation service ensures that there is an unforgeable proof of both shipment and receipt of data. This means that neither the sender nor receiver can deny that a legitimate message was sent and received. One technique to implement this service is called Digital Signatures (discussed in the Cryptography chapter), which employ two parts: the signing of a data unit and the verification of a signed data unit. The signing process is accomplished by either enciphering the data unit itself or producing a special cryptographic checksum of the data unit. The verification process employs the appropriate decryption process to determine whether the signature was produced by the stated signer.

The second category of service described by the TNI is **Denial of Service**. This entails maintaining the network at some predefined level of throughput and also maintaining the availability of any remote entity to authorized users. The TNI also states that a denial of service (DOS) condition exists whenever network resources are not available to users on an equitable basis although priorities can be used in the determination of equity. During active times on the network, a DOS condition can be detected by not receiving a response for a specified maximum waiting time. During periods of inactivity, however, DOS conditions are harder to detect unless periodic messages are sent to test connections. It is important to note that DOS conditions may occur either as a result of an attack by an outsider designed to deny the use of the network to authorized users, or simply through failure of the network to handle an extreme or unanticipated load. The three specific services contained in the DOS category are *Continuity of Operation, Protocol-Based DOS Protection Mechanisms*, and *Network Management*.

Continuity of Operations, as its name implies, refers to the assurance that the network is available for use by authorized individuals. This assurance is based on a pre-specified minimum level of service. Approaches to handle DOS conditions include the use of redundant components, reconfiguration of existing network assets, fault tolerance mechanisms, and the distribution of network control functions among the various network systems. An important aspect of this service takes place when the network is implemented and tested. This testing should include service response level measurement under expected extreme conditions to determine the network's ability to handle extreme traffic loads.

Protocol-Based DOS Protection Mechanisms include those measures that use existing or additional protocol mechanisms to detect DOS conditions. Where possible, existing protocols should be used in order to limit network traffic overhead which may by itself lead to a DOS condition. A common protocol defined to detect DOS conditions is the request-response mechanism, which uses periodic "are-you-there" messages to determine the existence of an open path between entities. Another method to detect DOS conditions might involve the measurement of throughput between two entities which use input queuing. Should the measured throughput fall below a predefined minimum, a DOS condition exists.

The TNI Network Management service describes those measures taken to configure the network or monitor its performance which aren't described by current protocol models. Using throughput as a measure of performance may not be sufficient, for example, since service could drop below defined performance standards due to an extremely noisy channel condition. As a result, the TNI takes a two tier approach to DOS resistance. The first tier is the protocol-based mechanisms. The Network Management service provides the second tier. This second tier deals with the health of the network, detection of failures, and identifying overt acts that degrade the service of the network. The second tier is not concerned with lower tier measurements such as throughput.

The last category of service defined by the TNI is **Compromise Detection**. This category is concerned with the non-disclosure of information that is transmitted between two entities of the network. The three specific services covered by this category are *Data Confidentiality*, *Traffic Flow Confidentiality*, and *Selective Routing*.

The data confidentiality service protects data from unauthorized access. The main method used to obtain unauthorized access to data is passive wiretapping, which is aimed at the data itself and not at the other fields used in transmission. Consequently, this service is mainly aimed at protecting against this form of attack. The two principle methods used to implement this service are physical security (keep potential wiretappers physically away from the systems and transmission medium) and cryptography.

Traffic flow confidentiality services are concerned with the fields other than the data field used in a transmission between two entities, as well as other characteristics of the transmitted data itself. This includes the size of the message, the frequency of message traffic, and the source and destination of each transmission. While encryption above the transport layer will effectively hide the data, it does not protect against information obtained from these other sources. The three methods used by the traffic flow confidentiality services to perform their function are physical security (if an individual can't get close enough to the systems or medium to perform a passive wiretap, they can't obtain any information), encryption (below the transport layer), and traffic padding. The problem with encryption applied below the transport layer is that, while it protects against an analysis of fields relating to such things as the source and destination, it also requires all intermediate systems in the transmission path be secure. This is necessary since, at each intermediate system, the transmission data must be decrypted in order to send it to its ultimate destination. The purpose of traffic padding is to maintain a certain transmission level so that, whether during periods of little network activity or heavy usage, the flow of data appears to be constant. For this technique to be effective, the spurious transmissions need to be encrypted so they are not detected as spurious but appear to be valid data.

The final security service, selective routing, is designed to control the path transmitted data takes from source to destination. This control allows the data to either choose or avoid specific networks or links. This means that, if required or desired, only physically secure subnets could be used to transmit the data concerned, thus lessening the risk during transmission. This service can be implemented to allow any combination of either the initiator of a transmission selecting the route (or specific subnets or systems to avoid), or the end-systems dynamically changing routes based on persistent evidence of attacks.

9.3.2   AIS Interconnection Issues

There are two views that can be taken when discussing interconnection of Automated Information Systems. The first is the **Component Connection View**. In this approach, any AIS that is connected to another AIS must enforce an *interconnection rule* which specifies what level of information may be transmitted or received. Each system is then responsible for maintaining separation of multiple security levels of information and determining what information can be sent or received. This means that each system does not need to know the range of possible security levels for all other systems, just the range of levels for its immediate neighbors. The **Global Connection View**, on the other hand, requires that each AIS know the range of security levels processed for all components in the network. While the component connection view is somewhat simpler to implement, it is easier to spot problems, such as the *Cascading Problem*, when the network is addressed from a global connection standpoint.

The cascading problem is a description of a condition that can exist when various systems with different security levels are interconnected. Figure 9.7 illustrates the problem associated with this type of connection. In this figure there are two systems, each designed to maintain separation between two security levels. The first maintains separation between Top Secret (TS) information and Secret (S) information. The second maintains separation between Secret and Unclassified (U) information. Neither system

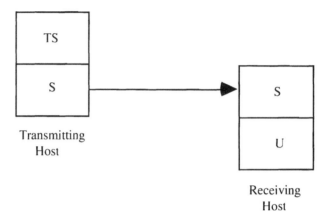

Figure 9.7. Cascading problem [9.2].

has the safeguards in place to guarantee separation between three security levels. If the Transmitting Host fails to maintain its separation of data and Top Secret information is allowed to be accessed by a user cleared for only Secret, this data could be sent to the Receiving Host. If the Receiving Host in turn fails to maintain its separation of information, this Top Secret information may be allowed to be accessed (maybe through the same technique as in the Transmitting Host) by a user only cleared for Unclassified information. In essence, the network is processing information requiring three security levels but its individual systems are only trusted to maintain separation between two levels. The level of trust required to maintain separation between three levels is much greater and would require enhanced security mechanisms. The problem, as illustrated in Figure 9.7, can be detected from both the Global and Component Connection viewpoints. But consider the extension to the network as illustrated in Figure 9.8.

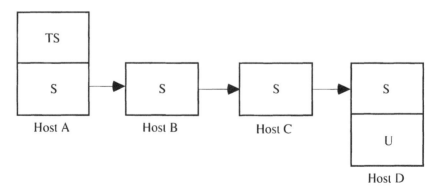

Figure 9.8. Extended cascading problem.

In this second example of the cascading problem, the transmitting host, Host A, is connected to an AIS, Host B, which only processes information at one level. Should Host A's safeguards to separate the Top Secret information it processes from users with a Secret clearance, the level of compromise is no greater should the data subsequently find its way to Host B. The same is true if this information is further sent on to Host C, which is also cleared for Secret only users. Host C, however, is connected to another AIS which is processing information at two security levels and if the Top Secret data, now labeled as Secret, finds its way to Host D, whose separation safeguards also fail, the Top Secret information could be obtained by users only cleared for Unclassified. Looking at the network from a Component Connection viewpoint, where only the immediate neighbors are of concern, the potential for this problem would not be spotted. It is only from the global viewpoint that this possibility would be spotted. This illustrates the need to take a global point of view when making a decision on whether to grant access to additional hosts in a network.

Another AIS interconnection concern is what is referred to as the *Propagation of Local Risk*. This occurs when the administrators for a host have decided to accept certain safeguards that might normally be considered inadequate for the information or levels of information being processed. Often such a decision is based on operational needs for the organization involved. If this AIS is connected to a network, however, other systems connected to the network need to know the acceptance of risk by the administrators of this AIS so that appropriate decisions concerning data transmissions and receivals can be made. Otherwise, the same risk accepted by the one AIS will be passed along to the other systems connected to the network.

9.4   Distributed Systems Security

A recent trend in computing has been towards what is referred to as distributed systems. A distributed system is a combination of hardware and software components connected via a network. The difference between a distributed system environment and a traditional network, however, is that in a distributed environment the software components may execute on two or more of the hardware processors that communicate via the network. The reasons for implementing a distributed system are similar to those for a network, namely resource sharing, reliability, and communication. Added to this list is speed, since in the distributed system a problem may be divided among several processors which together may be able to solve the problem faster than if a single processor had been assigned the task. A common technique seen in distributed computing is to assign certain services to specific processors. A user needing to access this service will need to communicate with the processor assigned this task. The process of accessing this remote service is done transparently to the user. From the user's perspective, all services appear to reside on the systems they are directly connected to.

With the increase in capability provided by distributed systems comes additional security concerns. This is especially true when certain services, such as the security services themselves, are distributed among various processors. Consider, for example, the problems associated with remote access of security services. In order for a user to demonstrate appropriate credentials to all other servers when desiring to obtain access to their services, the user's authority to use the service must be validated. Since the authentication server resides on a separate processor, a method is required to demonstrate to the requested server that the user is authorized access. This is often done through the use of a *ticket* that has been granted by the security server. This ticket serves as a pass that the user gives to the processor running the desired service to validate the user's authority. The ticket is generally encrypted using data known to the desired server and the security server but not to the user. In order to avoid later replay problems, the ticket may also contain a time-stamp or similar technique. This process is illustrated in Figure 9.9. In this example, the user first requests the ticket for the desired service from the security server. The server verifies the user's authority for the desired service and then responds with the encrypted ticket. This ticket is then sent to the desired server, which decrypts it and verifies the user's authority. The user is then allowed access to the service.

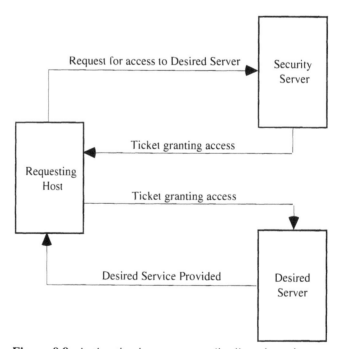

Figure 9.9 Authenticating access to distributed services.

Another problem associated with distributed systems is *delegation of authority*. This occurs when the user requests service from a server which, in order to fulfill the request, must access another server. This problem is illustrated in Figure 9.10. In this illustration, the user has requested a service from Server A. This server in turn requests Server B perform some operation in order to satisfy the user's request. The problem is how to prove to Server B that the user is authorized access to its services. One possible way to solve this problem is to have the user provide tickets for all possible target servers but this would require that users know in advance all the servers they might need. Another solution is to expand the ticket granting function in the Security Server to include tickets for all other servers that the requesting service may need to access. Which solution is best, or if neither is acceptable and a hybrid approach utilizing elements of both approaches may be better, depends on the specific distributed environment and the services offered.

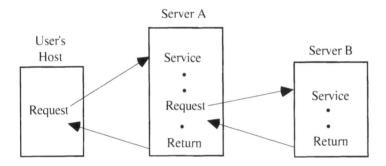

Figure 9.10. Delegation of authority in distributed servers [9.1].

9.5 Summary

The increase in the number of systems connected to networks and distributed systems connected via networks seen in recent years will continue. With networks, an additional level of complexity for security services is introduced. Many of the issues relating to network security are similar to single host environments. Network security is still concerned with the basic security goals of Confidentiality, Availability, Integrity, and Usage. One technique often proposed to solve network security problems is encryption. While encryption does indeed help with certain aspects of the network security problem, it does not solve all problems. Additional measures such as traffic padding and selective routing may need to be implemented to provide the level of security required for the information being transmitted. Even if all of these measures are implemented, the very nature of a network that connects dissimilar systems, often processing information from varying security levels, introduces problems. Often the level of trust one system places in its safeguards may not be shared by other systems on the network. Unless care is used connecting such systems, a propagation of this local risk may ensue. In addition, the network must be viewed from a global viewpoint to avoid the cascading problem where the network as a whole may be processing information at more security levels than any one system can appropriately safeguard.

9.6   Exercises

9.1   A Token Ring network is a point-to-point network in which the systems are
            configured in a ring. Use of the medium is governed through the use of a
            token passed from system to system. A system cannot transmit data unless it
            has the token. If, upon receiving the token, a system has data to transmit, it
            does so and then sends the token along upon completion. If it has no data to
            transmit it simply sends the token along. What are two easy methods to
            affect the performance of this type of network and thus potentially deny its
            use to authorized users?

9.2   Propose a solution to the extended cascading problem described in the text.
            Will detection or prevention be easier for this type of problem?

9.3   Two possible methods to handle the delegation of authority problem in
            distributed systems were discussed. Both methods have associated problems.
            Describe the problems associated with each and propose solutions for them.

9.4   Covert channels have been described in a previous chapter. Describe possible
            network covert channels and provide methods to detect and/or prevent them.

9.5   A current trend in networking is towards the use of wireless transmissions.
            How will this affect network security? Be sure to address each of the network
            patterns of attack and the security services that address them.

9.6   What, if any, would the differences be in the security services provided for
            connection-oriented versus connectionless networks?

9.7   References

9.1   Lockhart, H. W., Jr., *OSF DCE: Guide to Developing Distributed Applications*, McGraw-Hill, Inc., New York, New York, 1994.

9.2   National Computer Security Center, *Trusted Network Interpretation of the Trusted Computer System Evaluation Criteria*, NCSC-TG-005, Version 1, 31 July 1987.

9.3   Pooch, U. W., Machuel, D., and McCahn, J., *Telecommunications and Networking*, CRC Press, Inc., Boca Raton, Florida, 1991.

9.4   Stallings, W., *Network and Internetwork Security: Principles and Practice*, Prentice Hall, Englewood Cliffs, New Jersey, 1995.

9.5   Tanenbaum, A., *Computer Networks, 2ed*, Prentice Hall, Englewood Cliffs, New Jersey, 1989.

9.8   Extended Bibliography

9.6   Arsenault, A., "Developments in Guidance for Trusted Computer Networks", *Proceedings of the 10th National Computer Security Conference*, September 1987, Gaithersburg, Maryland, pp. 1-8.

9.7   Branstad, D., "Considerations for Security in the OSI Architecture", *Proceedings of the 10th National Security Conference*, September 1987, Gaithersburg, Maryland, pp. 9-14.

9.8   DeMillo, R. and Merritt, M., "Protocols for Data Security", *Computer*, Vol. 16, No. 2, February 1983, pp. 39-50.

9.9   Donaldson, A., McHugh, J., and Nyberg, K., "Covert Channels in Trusted LANS", *Proceedings of the 11th National Computer Security Conference*, October 1988, Baltimore, Maryland, pp. 226-232.

9.10   Fellows, J., Hemenway, J., Kelem, N., and Romero, Sa., "The Architecture
        of a Distributed Trusted Computing Base", *Proceedings of the 10th National
        Computer Security Conference*, Gaithersburg, Maryland, September 1987,
        pp. 68-77.

9.11   Ford, W., *Computer Communications Security: Principles, Standard
        Protocols and Techniques*, Prentice Hall, Englewood Cliffs, New Jersey,
        1994.

9.12   Freeman, J. W., Neely, R. B., and Dinolt, G. W., "An Internet System
        Security Policy and Formal Model", *Proceedings of the 11th National
        Computer Security Conference*, Baltimore, Maryland, October 1988, pp. 10-
        19.

9.13   Gasser, M., *Building a Secure Computer System*, Van Nostrand Reinhold,
        New York, 1988.

9.14   Herbison, B.J., "Security on an Ethernet", *Proceedings of the 11th National
        Security Conference*, Baltimore, Maryland, October 1988, pp. 219-225.

9.15   Johnson, H. and Layne, J. D., "A Mission-Critical Approach to Network
        Security", *Proceedings of the 10th National Computer Security Conference*,
        Gaithersburg, Maryland, September 1987, pp. 15-24.

9.16   Kent, S.T., "Network Security: A Top-Down View Shows Problem", *Data
        Communications*, June 1978, pp. 57.

9.17   Kirkpatrick, K., "Standards for Network Security", *Proceedings of the 11th
        National Computer Security Conference*, October 1988, pp. 201-211.

9.18   Losocco, P., "A Security Model and Policy for a MLS LAN", *Proceedings
        of the 10th National Security Conference*, Gaithersburg, Maryland,
        September 1987, pp. 25-37.

9.19   Millen, J., "A Network Security Perspective", *Proceedings of the 9th
        National Computer Security Conference*, Gaithersburg, Maryland,
        September 1986, pp. 7-15.

9.20   Nelson, R., "SDNS Services and Architecture", *Proceedings of the 10th
        National Computer Security Conference*, September 1987, pp. 153-157.

9.21   Shaffer, S. L. and Simon, A. R., *Network Security*, AP Professional,
         Boston, Massachusetts, 1994.

9.22   Sidhu, D. and Gasser, M., "A Multilevel Secure Local Area Network",
         Proceedings of the 1982 Symposium on Security and Privacy, pp. 137-143.

9.23   Tater, G. and Kerut, E., "The Secure Data Network System: An Overview",
         Proceedings of the 10th National Computer Security Conference,
         Gaithersburg, Maryland, September 1987, pp. 150-152.

10

FIREWALLS

"Firewall: a fireproof wall to prevent the spread of fire from one room or compartment to the next." — Webster's New World Dictionary

System administrators have found it increasingly hard to protect their computer systems as the number of computers connected to networks has grown. The idea of disconnecting a machine from a network, or a network from other networks, is in opposition to the very reason networks were created; yet many a frustrated administrator has at times wished they could do just that. An alternative, a method to protect the network from outside intruders without limiting the access to the outside world, would greatly ease their concerns. This is the purpose of firewalls. They are intended to limit the damage that can be caused to a network by limiting the access rights of outsiders to the network. This chapter discusses the purpose and design of security gateways and firewalls, which have seen a recent rise in popularity.

10.1 Simple Damage Limiting Approaches

A firewall in a building is designed to keep a fire from spreading to other parts of the structure or to at least slow its progress until help can arrive. The fire may burn out of control in one portion of the structure; the firewall simply insures that other portions aren't affected at the same rate. This same idea can be applied to networks and computer systems. If an organization places all of its computing assets on a single network, when a security problem arises the entire network can be affected. This is especially true where access methods such as the UNIX *.rhosts* file (which allows users access to other systems listed in the file without having to provide a password) are available. Often, local machines are configured to implicitly trust each other. Instead, if the network was broken into a series of smaller networks connected through secure gateways or routers, a security problem in one of these smaller networks could be better contained without having it affect the other networks. A crucial element of such an arrangement is that no workstation on one network should trust a workstation on another network. As a further precaution, users who have accounts on more than one network should use different passwords for each.

Continuing with our previous analogy to the physical world, another way to limit the possibility of a fire would be to limit access to the building and to control the type of activities each individual granted access could perform. The ability to smoke in the building, for example, could be denied to all thus lessening the chance that a fire might start. The computer version of such policies is to limit individuals who can obtain entrance to a network, and to further restrict what type of activities these individuals can perform. One simple approach to perform this filtering is to force each host to individually determine who and what it will allow to access its services. An example of such an approach is *TCP WRAPPER* [10.6], a tool designed at the Eindhoven University of Technology in The Netherlands and used throughout the UNIX community.

TCP WRAPPER works by specifically identifying which network traffic to allow and which to deny. It uses two files to describe the allowable accesses: */etc/hosts.allow* and */etc/hosts.deny*. Access can be controlled on a host or services basis, or a combination of both. For example, services such as *telnet, ftp*, and *rlogin* could be allowed while others such as *finger* could be blocked. In addition, specific hosts could either be blocked from certain types of access or granted certain access privileges. A drawback to this approach is that it requires that the system administrator configures each system. A mistake in one of the files could allow an intruder access to one of the machines in the network which might then lead to further penetration of the network. A different approach is to place the filtering responsibilities for the network in a limited number of machines. This is the approach taken by most computer network firewalls.

10.2   Network Firewalls

The purpose of a network firewall is to provide a shell around the network which will protect the machines on the network from various threats. The types of threats a firewall can protect against include:

- Unauthorized access to network resources — an intruder may break into a host on the network and gain unauthorized access to files.
- Denial of service — an individual from outside of the network could, for example, send thousands of mail messages to a host on the network in an attempt to fill available disk space or load the network links.

- Masquerading — electronic mail that appears to have originated from one individual could have been forged by another with the intent to embarrass or cause harm.

One way to avoid these problems would be to completely disconnect the network from any other network. This, of course, is not the preferred method. Instead what is needed is a way to filter access to the network while still allowing users access to the "outside world". A typical network firewall can be depicted as shown in Figure 10.1.

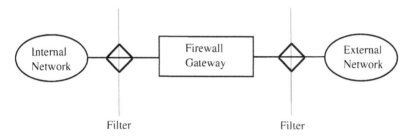

Figure 10.1. Typical network firewall configuration [10.1].

In this configuration, the internal network is separated from external networks by a firewall gateway. A gateway is normally used to perform relay services between two networks. In the case of a firewall gateway, it also provides a filtering service which limits the types of information that can be passed to or from hosts located on the internal network. There are three basic techniques used for firewalls: *packet filtering, circuit gateways*, and *application gateways* [10.1]. Often, more than one of these is used to provide the complete firewall service.

10.2.1 Packet Filtering Gateways

Packet filtering can provide an easy and cheap way to implement a basic level of filtering for a network. Most implementations involve a router used to connect two networks together. The router often is delivered with software that can enable it to discard packets based on the source or destination ports or addresses. The configuration of a typical router used as a firewall matches Figure 10.1. In this example, the router replaces the gateway. The actual filtering can be applied to either incoming packets, outgoing packets, or both. In order to perform the filtering, the router needs to know that packets to accept and which to reject. This information is contained in a file which defines a set of filtering rules. This rule set should include information about which sources and destinations to allow packets to arrive from or be sent to. An example of a set of rules is depicted in Figure 10.2.

operation	source	port	destination	port	description
discard	bad.host	*	*	*	don't trust bad.host
allow	our.host	25	*	*	our outgoing mail

Figure 10.2. Sample packet filtering rules [10.1].

In this example, the rules instruct the router to discard all packets that originated from *bad.host*. It also instructs the router to allow all mail messages originating from *our.host* to any destination. An interesting question at this point is what happens to all of the other traffic that has not been described by the current set of rules? Should the router allow anything that it has not been specifically instructed to discard or should it discard everything that it has not specifically been told to allow? Obviously the safer of the two from a security standpoint is to discard all packets not identified as allowable but this may be too restrictive for some sites. The rules also have to be designed so that a mixture of *accepts*, *discards*, and *allows* can exist for a particular site and so that whole classes of network traffic (or services) can be denied. Consider the example depicted in Figure 10.3.

operation	source	port	destination	port	description
discard	bad.host	*	*	*	don't trust bad.host
allow	our.host	25	*	*	our outgoing mail
accept	bad.host	25	our.host	25	accept bad.host mail
discard	*	*	our.host	21	deny FTP use

Figure 10.3. Additional packet filtering rules [10.1].

In this case, all traffic from *bad.host* except electronic mail (packets with a source and destination of port 25) is discarded. In addition, all FTP traffic (packets with a destination port of 21) is discarded without regard to its originating source. Administrators often deny whole classes of traffic because the class has proven to be too dangerous from a security standpoint. Examples of particularly dangerous classes of traffic include *tftp*, *sunrpc*, *rlogin* , and *rexec* [10.2].

A couple of slightly more complex, yet very common, configurations are depicted in Figures 10.4 and 10.5. In Figure 10.4, which is referred to as a Screened Host Gateway, the router is configured such that the Bastion Host is the only computer system on the internal network that can be accessed from an external network. An exposed host that is designed to be a critical strong point in the security of a network or group of networks is often referred to as a bastion host [10.1, 10.3] (a bastion, historically, is a particularly strong part of a fortification or castle). Since the bastion host is the only system accessible to outsiders, it is imperative that it is protected against intrusions. Should the bastion host become compromised, the rest of the internal network is in danger.

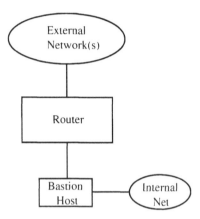

Figure 10.4. A Screened Host Gateway [10.3].

Often, the router is called upon to perform several functions. In Figure 10.5 a single router is used to not only serve as the network firewall but to also route traffic between several internal networks. The first internal net, Net 1, consists of only a gateway which is used for communication with the external world. All traffic destined for an external host must be sent through the gateway. Likewise, traffic from an external host destined for a host on one of the internal nets must pass through the gateway. This arrangement allows for an additional level of security since the gateway (or bastion host) is not part of the secure internal networks. The network inhabited by a gateway acting as a bastion host is often referred to as the demilitarized zone (DMZ) because of the security danger that exists for this system to be exposed to external threats from other networks.

The router will allow any traffic to pass between the non-DMZ internal networks (Net 2 and Net 3). External communication between any host on either Net 2 or Net 3 and any host on an external network, however, must pass through Net 1 and the Gateway. Communication between the Gateway on Net 1 and machines on Nets 2 and 3 can also be restricted, thus adding an additional level of security.

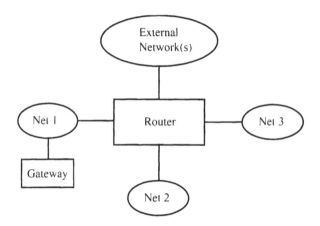

Figure 10.5. Firewall router with two internal subnets.

Sometimes, in order to speed processing, filtering is only accomplished on either input or output packets but not both. In fact, some routers are designed to only filter based on the destination port |10.1|. If only output filtering were to be performed on the network configuration of Figure 10.5, a problem could arise if an individual from an external host attempted to forge a packet address. This individual on an external net, for example, could send a packet to the router that claimed it was from one of the other internal networks. If only output filtering was performed, this sort of attack could not be prevented. If only output filtering is to be performed, the configuration of Figure 10.4 can be slightly modified to handle address forgery. This new configuration uses one router to handle routing functions for the internal networks and another router as the interface to the external world. Thus, an individual who sent a packet from an external address with an address forged to appear as if it came from one of the internal networks would be caught by the second router and not allowed to pass to the internal router and networks. This special configuration is shown in Figure 10.6 and is referred to as a Screened Subnet |10.3|.

One final comment needs to be made about the need to filter routing information as well as other traffic. In the configuration depicted in Figure 10.5, Nets 2 and 3 were not allowed to send traffic directly to any external networks. Another advantage of this is that the paths to hosts on Nets 2 and 3 can be hidden from external networks since the Gateway can be used to correctly direct traffic in the internal nets. This effectively hides the actual paths for machines on Nets 2 and 3. The router, however, needs to keep track of paths to hosts on these networks but it should not send routing information about any hosts on Nets 2 or 3 to external networks. This information needs to be filtered.

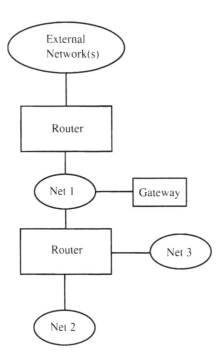

Figure 10.6. Firewall for routers with output filtering [10.1].

10.2.2   Circuit-Level Gateways

Circuit-level gateways simply relay network traffic between two hosts connected via a network's virtual circuit [10.1]. An internal user, for example, might connect to a port on the gateway which would in turn connect to another port on a host residing in an external network. The gateway simply copies the bytes from one port to the other. Normally the gateway will relay the data without examining it but often may keep a log of the amount of data relayed and its intended destination. In some instances the relay connection (forming a "circuit") will take place automatically for specific network functions. At other times, however, the gateway will need to be told the desired destination port. When the connection request is made of the gateway, the decision as to whether this is an allowable transaction is made. If it is allowed, the circuit connection is created and the data relaying begins. If, on the other hand, the requested connection is deemed inappropriate, then the connection is not made and an error message can be returned (or the request simply discarded). Although normally thought of as a relay for TCP traffic, circuit-level gateways can also be used for some UDP applications where a virtual circuit is assumed.

10.2.3   Application-Level Gateways

Application-level gateways (also referred to as *proxy gateways*) usually operate at a user level rather than the lower protocol level common to the other firewall techniques. Instead of routing general purpose traffic, application-level gateways are used to forward service-specific traffic. A common example of this is a mail gateway. Indeed, the use of gateways to direct electronic mail traffic is so common that the Domain Name Service (DNS) has a special feature called MX records (mail exchanger) for their support [10.1]. The use of such gateways not only is valuable from a security standpoint by isolating internal networks, but also aids in the everyday use of this service. Users, for example, can access email from different machines while still keeping the same email address. In addition, just like in circuit-level gateways, application-level gateways provide a centralized point for the logging of activities. The obvious disadvantage to application-level gateways is the need for a special program to handle each desired application. Since this requires quite a bit of work, typically only those services deemed to be extremely important will be supported.

The basic configurations are similar to those found in firewalls utilizing packet filtering routers and bastion hosts. The most basic design for an application-level gateway firewall is similar to Figure 10.4. This configuration is more secure than a filtering router alone, however, since it will only allow certain, very specific, traffic to get through. This is probably the most common configuration for application-level firewalls.

The other common configuration is shown in Figure 10.7. Note that this design is similar to Figure 10.6 with the addition of a second gateway attached to the internal net. In this firewall design the inside router (the one that connects all internal networks as well as the DMZ) serves as a *choke*. The purpose of the choke is twofold: first to block all internal traffic destined for external networks unless addressed to the internal gateway, and second to block all external traffic destined for the internal net unless it is also addressed to the internal gateway. This design (when all routers and gateways are properly configured) results in a very secure firewall.

10.3   Firewall Costs and Effectiveness

It should be obvious that with the additional software and hardware that is required to implement a firewall comes an associated cost both in terms of performance and dollars. There is also the additional cost associated with the not so insignificant amount of time required for the administration of the firewall. System performance may be

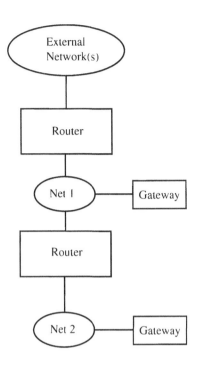

Figure 10.7. A common application-level gateway firewall design [10.1].

affected since certain services may not be available and others are forced to be channeled through a single machine. What happens, for example, when the machine acting as an organization's internal gateway (shown in Figure 10.7) malfunctions? The internal net and its hosts are functioning but they can't communicate with external nets because all traffic is relayed through the gateway. Of course, all of these costs must be weighed against the possible costs associated with a breach in security. How much will it cost in terms of lost business or the time required to "clean up" a system should an intruder gain access to the organization's computing assets?

An additional cost associated with firewalls is the loss of a certain amount of freedom. Anytime restrictions are placed on the provided services a certain segment of users will feel that their ability to perform assigned tasks has been impeded, since access through the firewall is more difficult. For the most part, however, the obvious need for a level of security to protect an organization's (and the individuals in the organization) computing assets results in an acceptance of these limitations.

While firewalls are an important tool to be used in defending a network, they are by no means perfect. One of the largest limitations of firewalls is that they are only as secure as the service whose traffic they allow through. In other words, if the application program/protocol that an organization is running has errors in it that might result in a security hole, the firewall will not be able to catch it. The firewall's job was to simply restrict the traffic that got through. It is not the responsibility of the firewall to monitor the operation and semantics of the applications and services themselves.

Another way to circumvent the protections provided by a firewall is to *tunnel* through them. Tunneling involves the encapsulation of a message of one protocol inside another [10.1]. This encapsulated message then traverses the target networks, traveling through any firewalls that are in place, until it reaches the destination host. At the destination host, the encapsulation is stripped off and the message in its original protocol is inserted into the network. It is obviously important that the outer protocol be one which the firewalls are designed to let through.

10.4   Sample Security Packages

In August of 1992, the Texas A&M University Supercomputer Center was notified that a computer owned by Texas A&M was being used as a platform to launch attacks against other computer systems. After an initial investigation, the machine being used was determined to reside in the office of a faculty member who was at that time out of town. Instead of physically accessing the machine, the decision was made to monitor network connections to the machine and disconnect it electronically from the net should it become necessary. The decision to monitor instead of simply accessing the machine and cutting the intruders off turned out to be a fortunate one as it resulted in gaining much knowledge about the intruders and their techniques. It also led to the development of three security packages: *drawbridge*, a filtering tool; *tiger*, a set of programs that can be used to check machines for security problems; and *netlog*, a series of network intrusion detection programs [10.5].

The first line of defense in the Texas A&M University (TAMU) security packages is *drawbridge*. This package is designed to filter all internet packets transmitted to or from TAMU. It allows access to be controlled on a machine by machine, as well as port by port, basis. *Drawbridge* is a simple tool, more akin to the use of routers for filtering rather than the more complicated firewalls discussed in this chapter. Recognizing that it was only the first line of defense, *netlog* was developed to monitor the incoming network traffic in order to determine if an attempt was being made to circumvent the filter (*drawbridge*). *Netlog*, which actually consists of a set of monitoring tools, checks the incoming traffic for unusual connections (attempts to connect to *tftp*, for example), unusual patterns of connections (based on historical data gathered on "normal" network usage at TAMU), and a wide range of detailed intrusion signatures (including such things as attempts to login using system accounts or to gain *root* access). The third element of the TAMU security package is *tiger*, a series of scripts (and thus generally referred to as the *tiger scripts*) used to check a computer system for signs that an intrusion has occurred, as well as to determine if certain security related configuration items are set correctly. The scripts check target machines for such things as

- Accounts without passwords
- Directories often used by intruders for signs of unexpected files
- World readable home directories
- Digital signatures of system binary files
- .rhost files with '+' entries

The various components of the TAMU security package are shown in Figure 10.8. Additional information on the security package, including details on how to obtain copies, can be found in [10.5].

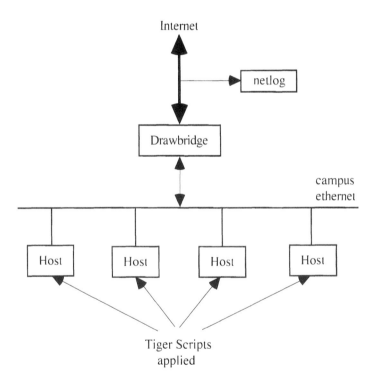

Figure 10.8. Texas A&M University security package [10.5].

Another security package available to help secure a computer network is the Trusted Information Systems (TIS) Firewall Toolkit [10.4]. This toolkit is available at no charge from TIS over the Internet. The TIS Firewall Toolkit is designed for use on UNIX systems using TCP/IP. It can be used to build screened host-based firewalls utilizing a bastion host to enforce security, as was depicted in Figure 10.4.   The security applications provided by the toolkit include:

- An electronic mail gateway
- An FTP application gateway
- An audit log of significant security events
- A TELNET application gateway
- A "plugboard" gateway for other TCP connections (such as network news)

The toolkit requires installation by a systems manager experienced in UNIX systems. Additional information on the toolkit including details on how to obtain copies can be found in |10.4|.

10.5 Summary

The complexity involved in securing computer systems connected to a network increases with the addition of every new machine. Since systems often are designed to implicitly trust other systems they are "close" to, a single insecure system in a network can place the entire network in jeopardy. A stop-gap measure, used to help protect the machines connected to a network from individuals outside of the networked environment, is the introduction of firewalls to the environment.

Firewalls can be implemented at different levels of a network. Packet filtering gateways can be configured in a variety of ways. Most utilize a router to perform some initial filtering for the networks it protects. In addition, many utilize a special *bastion host* which is often the only host on a network that is accessible to the outside environment. This simplifies the security problem since now only a single machine must be trusted to protect against external intruders. Other firewalls have been designed for application at the circuit and application levels.

Many routers are shipped with simple filtering routines, which can be used to build a first line of defense against intruders. Several more extensive packages are available free of charge to organizations in need of firewall protections |10.4, 10.5|. In addition, several vendors have developed their own firewall packages for either internal use or commercial sales.

10.6 Exercises

10.1 What are the problems and tradeoffs associated with having a packet filtering router allow all traffic not specifically identified to be discarded versus having the router discard all traffic not specifically identified as being allowed?

10.2 Special precautions need to be taken for firewalls that consist of routers which only perform output filtering. Are there any special problems associated with firewalls that only filter incoming traffic? Why?

10.3 Explain why the term "proxy gateway" is descriptive of the nature of application-level gateways.

10.4 How can the following two items be used together to detect intrusive activity on networks?

      • Monitoring is an important part of many firewalls.
      • Some sites include dummy users on their system.

10.5 What challenges and problems does the growth of information protocols such as *gopher* and the *World Wide Web* present to firewalls?

10.6 What problems does the Mbone (the Internet's multicast backbone) present to firewalls?

10.7 References

10.1 Cheswick, W. R. and Bellovin, S. M., *Firewalls and Internet Security*, Addison-Wesley Publishing Co., Reading, Massachusetts, 1994.

10.2 Garfinkel, S. and Spafford, G., *Practical UNIX Security*, O'Reilly & Associates, Inc., Sebastopol, California, 1992.

10.3 Ranum, M., "Thinking About Firewalls", Trusted Information Systems, Inc., available for *anonymous ftp* from *ftp.dsi.unimi.it*, pub/security/docs/firewall/fwalls.ps.gz, January 1995.

10.4   Ranum, M. and Avolio, F., "A Toolkit and Methods for Internet Firewalls",
          Trusted Information Systems, Inc., available for *anonymous ftp* from
          ftp.dsi.unimi.it, pub/security/docs/firewall/usenix-paper.ps.gz, January 1995.

10.5   Safford, D., Schales, D., and Hess, D., "The TAMU Security Package: An
          Ongoing Response to Internet Intruders in an Academic Environment",
          Proceedings of the Fourth USENIX Security Symposium, Santa Clara,
          California, October 1993, pp. 91-118, also available via *anonymous ftp* from
          net.tamu.edu, pub/security/TAMU.

10.6   Venema, W., "TCP WRAPPER: Network monitoring, access control, and
          booby traps", *Proceedings of the Third Usenix UNIX Security Symposium*,
          Baltimore, Maryland, September 1992, pp. 85-92.

10.8   Extended Bibliography

10.7   Avolio, F. M. and Ranum, M. J., "A Network Perimeter with Secure
          External Access", Trusted Information Systems, Inc., Glenwood, MD,
          available for *anonymous ftp* from *ftp.dsi.unimi.it*, pub/security/docs/
          firewall/isoc94.ps, January 1995.

10.8   Cheswick, B., "The Design of a Secure Internet Gateway", AT&T Bell
          Laboratories, Murray Hill, New Jersey, available for *anonymous ftp* from
          ftp.dsi.unimi.it: pub/security/docs/firewall/SIG.ps.gz, January 1995.

10.9   Digital Equipment Corporation, "Screening External Access Link (SEAL)
          Introductory Guide", available for *anonymous ftp* from *ftp.dsi.unimi.it*:
          pub/security/ docs/firewall/SEAL.ps.gz, January 1995.

10.10   Livermore Software Laboratories, Inc., "PORTUS Announcement Letter",
          Houston, Texas, available for *anonymous ftp* from *ftp.dsi.unimi.it*:
          pub/security/docs/firewall/lsli_portus.ps.gz, December 1994.

10.11   Mogul, J., "Simple and Flexible Datagram Access Controls for Unix-based
          Gateways", Technical Report 89/4, Western Research Laboratory, Digital
          Equipment Corporation, Palo Alto, California, March 1989, available for
          anonymous   ftp   from   *ftp.dsi.unimi.it*:   pub/security/docs/firewall/
          screen.ps.gz, January 1995.

10.12   Ranum, M., "A Network Firewall", *Proceedings of the World Conference on System Administration and Security*, Washington, DC, July 1992, available for *anonymous ftp* from *ftp.dsi.unimi.it*: pub/security/docs/firewall/f_dec.ps.gz, January 1995.

10.13   Raptor Systems Inc., "Eagle Network Security Management System: User's Guide Version 2.2", Wilmington, Delaware, available for *anonymous ftp* from *ftp.dsi.unimi.it*: pub/security/docs/firewall/Eagle.ps.gz, January 1995.

10.14   Reid, B. K., "The DECWRL Mail Gateway", Digital Equipment Corporation, available for *anonymous ftp* from *ftp.dsi.unimi.it*: pub/security/docs/ firewall/DecMailGateway.ps.gz, January 1995.

10.15   Siyan, K. and Hare, C., *Internet Firewalls and Network Security*, New Riders Publishing, Indianapolis, Indiana, 1995.

10.16   Treese, G. W. and Wolman, A., "X Through the Firewall, and Other Application Relays", Technical Report CRL 93/10, Cambridge Research Laboratory, Digital Equipment Corporation, Cambridge, MA, May 1993, available for *anonymous ftp* from *ftp.dsi.unimi.it*: pub/security/docs/firewall/CRL_firewall.ps.gz, January 1995.

11

DATABASE SECURITY

Database systems affect every person's daily life. They are used in billing systems, subscription services, reservations systems, and numerous other aspects of daily life. For these systems to properly carry out their respective tasks, the database operations must function properly and the information contained within the database must be correct. While the data cannot be guaranteed from accidental changes, it can be protected from malicious system and data attacks. This protection is the subject of this chapter. This chapter begins with a database primer followed by a discussion of various database security vulnerabilities and countermeasures.

11.1 Database Management System Primer

To understand the security problems that can plague a database management system (DBMS), a basic knowledge of database systems is required. A brief discussion of database systems, including an introduction to database terminology, is presented.

Two key parts of a database management system are (1) the user defined data (data tables) and (2) the operations defined to manipulate the data [11.5]. The data tables, often called entities or touples, contain the database information. The tables are composed of constituent characteristics, or attributes [11.5]. For example, the employee data table in Figure 11.1 has four attributes: employee name, address, phone number, and department. In a similar manner, the department data table in Figure 11.1 consists of three attributes: department name, manager name, and location. The data contained in tables such as these are manipulated with operations provided by the database management system (DBMS).

EMPLOYEE TABLE

NAME	ADDRESS	PHONE	DEPT.
Fred	1234 Main Street	555-1234	Testing
Barney	6529 West Avenue	555-6529	Sales
Wilma	7320 Lincoln Court	555-7320	Testing
Betty	6343 Braddock Road	555-6343	Design

DEPARTMENT TABLE

DEPT.	Location	Manager
Design	BLDG. 210	Anne
Payroll	BLDG. 209	Michael
Sales	BLDG. 236	Edith
Testing	BLDG. 229	Andrew

Figure 11.1. Example database tables.

Manipulation of the data tables is accomplished with operations that add new data, update existing data, delete existing data, and list data with certain attributes [11.5]. The specific functions that perform these operations depend upon the requirements of the system. For example, a query could request a list of all employees in a given department. Depending on the design and scope of the DBMS, a query such as this may not be possible.

In some database environments the actions available to the users are limited. The limitations can either be the result of the environment or a restriction in a user's capabilities [11.6]. Environmental limitations prevent users from performing actions on data not related to the relevant environment. For example, environmental limitations would prevent a user from modifying their bank records from within an airline reservation system. Unlike environmental limitations, capability limitations restrict the actions a user can perform on relevant data. An example of a capability-based limitation would be an airline reservation system that allows the travel agent to change a traveler's reservation but not alter an airplane's flight schedule. Capability-based limitations such as this are often implemented with the use of multi-leveled security [11.16, 11.18].

Multi-leveled DBMSs attempt to control access to the system with the use of relative security classifications [11.1, 11.12, 11.21]. Commonly used security labels are top-secret, secret, confidential, restricted, and unrestricted. Security classifications such as these are used to determine whether a user can both access data and perform a given database operation. This is accomplished by applying the security classification labels to the system data, operations, and users. Users with a security label lower than that of an operation are prevented from performing the operation. Users with a security label lower than that of the data are not permitted to read the data. The ability to write information to the database will depend on the access rules enforced by the system. For a user to manipulate data, the user must obtain the authorizations to access the data and perform the desired operation. For example, a user wishing to read a name from an on-line phone book must have the security classification that allows the user to read information from the phone book. The permission to access information in a given manner, such as reading from, or writing to, a phone book is called a role. Roles are discussed in detail below.

11.2 DBMS Vulnerabilities and Responses

DBMSs may suffer from any of four different types of vulnerabilities [11.3, 11.13]. These vulnerabilities are: (1) inference, (2) aggregation, (3) data integrity, and (4) Trojan Horses. The presence of inference or aggregation vulnerabilities leads to the undesired release of normally secure, or hidden, information contained in the database. Data integrity vulnerabilities undermine the correctness of the information within the database. Trojan Horse vulnerabilities allow hidden operations to perform unauthorized actions in, and to, the DBMS. Removing these vulnerabilities often involves reorganizing the data tables, reclassifying the data, or improving the access controls and general security of the system.

11.2.1 Inference

Inference vulnerabilities in a DBMS allow a user to deduce the contents of inaccessible parts of a database [11.3, 11.12, 11.13]. For example, a database system indicates that a certain jet fighter with a maximum payload of 800 pounds will be flying a mission where it will carry a certain type of bomb. The database system, however, does not state how many of the bombs will be carried. Since it is general knowledge that each of the bombs weighs 100 pounds, it can be inferred that the fighter will carry 8 bombs. This example shows how common sense knowledge may be used to deduce the contents of the database. Inference vulnerabilities, however, may be made with the assistance of not just common sense, but other data within the database or external information [11.3, 11.5, 11.13]. The fact that information used to make inferences comes from uncontrollable sources hinders the protection required to prevent inference attacks.

Properly protecting a DBMS from inference attacks is a difficult task. This is because attackers do not need to perform any overtly malicious actions to determine the contents of the database and an attacker's presence and activities may go unnoticed. To determine what can be inferred from the system and create an optimal defense, a knowledge of an attacker's source of information is required [11.9]. Since this knowledge is often unattainable, the DBMS must be maintained such that external knowledge provides little assistance to the attacker. Modifying a database so that little can be inferred first requires identifying the information that must be protected and then adjusting the security classification of the data, the appropriate data relations, and operations |11.3|. Naturally, this is an application specific solution and modifications such as these must be made on a case by case basis.

11.2.2 Aggregation

Like inference, the damages that result from aggregation are only information dissemination, not database modification. Aggregation is the process of combining multiple database objects into one object with a higher security label than the constituent parts |11.11|. Combining two objects of similar types, such as two addresses, is called inference aggregation |11.9|. When the combined objects are of different types, such as a name and salary, the process is called cardinal aggregation |11.9|. While the two types of aggregation are similar in nature, they each require different means of prevention.

11.2.2.1 Inference Aggregation

As previously mentioned, inference aggregation is the result of combining the knowledge gained from multiple database objects |11.9, 11.21|. For example, knowing the information contained in any one of the tables in Figure 11.2 provides little information by itself. Knowing the contents of all three tables, however, results in the dissemination of what would otherwise be considered hidden, or private, information.

Inference aggregation can be prevented, by raising the security labels associated with any one or more of the tables involved in the aggregation |11.7|. For example, raising the security label of any single table in Figure 11.2 prevents an authorized user from aggregating the data. This results in requiring a DBMS user to have a higher security label to make the aggregation inference. Raising the security labels of the DBMS tables, however, may result in reducing the operations available to users with lower security labels. The information in a newly labeled data table will no longer be available to lower labeled users who require access. This side effect can be reduced by relabeling only the less frequently used data tables.

PHONE BOOK TABLE

NAME	MAIL STOP	PHONE	DEPT.
Fred	229-234	3-1234	Testing
Barney	236-652	6-2112	Sales
Wilma	229-176	6-3442	Testing
Betty	210-234	3-1242	Design

EMPLOYEE TABLE

NAME	EMPLOYEE NUMBER	HOME ADDRESS	HOME PHONE
Fred	143324	1234 Main Street	555-1234
Barney	135631	8709 West Avenue	555-8709
Wilma	114356	2607 Lincoln Court	555-2607
Betty	113542	6579 Braddock Road	555-6579

SALARY TABLE

EMPLOYEE NUMBER	SALARY	RETIREMENT FUND
143324	82,200	44,000
135631	45,400	22,100
114356	66,100	33,870
113542	52,100	10,790

Figure 11.2. Example of inference aggregation.

11.2.2.2 Cardinal Aggregation

Cardinal aggregation is the combining of like information in a manner that yields information not readily available or apparent to a user [11.9, 11.21]. A commonly used example of cardinal aggregation is a phone book. One phone number provides little information besides a name and phone number. A complete phone book, however, can provide information no single phone number can. It is unusual for dissimilar businesses to share a phone number. If a phone book were examined, and a list created of all businesses that share a single phone number, it could be inferred that the listed businesses may be either store-fronts or involved in unusual business practices. Another common example concerns military troop placement information. It may be of little value to know the location of one army troop. Knowing the location of every troop in the army, however, will be of significantly more value.

This type of aggregation, unlike inference aggregation, is difficult to prevent. Two generally accepted solutions are to: (1) lower the security label assigned to the data and restrict access and (2) raise the security label assigned to the individual data so that it equals that which can be aggregated [11.7]. Unfortunately, neither of these solutions provides a complete solution to the problem [11.21].

The first means of preventing aggregation is the downgrading of information labels and restriction of access. This solution requires a knowledge of both how the data can be exploited and the amount of data necessary to perform an accurate aggregation. It may be difficult, however, to determine the minimal number of touples needed to provide additional information by aggregation. Furthermore, attempting to limit the amount of data any user may access at any one time does not resolve the problem as a user may make multiple, smaller database accesses and build a complete database. For example, if a user is limited to requesting only 10 entries from a phone book at one time, the user need only make numerous 10 entry requests until the desired aggregation effect is possible. Clearly this solution does not completely prevent cardinal aggregation, rather it slows down the process by requiring a user to apply more effort to obtain the necessary data for aggregation.

The second cardinal aggregation solution is to raise the security label of each individual data record. Again using the phone book example, each name and phone number would be given a security label equal to that of the aggregated information. Thus, the information gained through aggregation is readily available to a user without aggregation. This solution, however, has two complications. First, it artificially inflates the security labels of the DBMS information. This is evident by the higher security label a user would need to access a phone number in the example above. Second, the highest security level of all possible aggregations must be determined so that the appropriate label can be applied to the data. This requires the ability to determine every possible aggregation from the data so that the proper label can be determined and applied. Determining every possible aggregation is often impossible, making it difficult to guarantee that the appropriate security label is applied [11.7, 11.12].

Unlike inference aggregation, there is no perfect solution to cardinal aggregation. With each solution comes unwanted side effects that make interaction with the database difficult. While some mechanism should be in place to reduce the possibility of aggregation, the security administrator should be aware that any protection will be incomplete.

11.2.3 Data Integrity

Data integrity vulnerabilities allow the unauthorized or inappropriate modification, addition, or deletion of database information. Data integrity vulnerabilities can be prevented with the implementation of an integrity policy. Many policies have been proposed. Some of these policies include the Bell-LaPadula policy [11.1], the Biba policy [11.2], and the Schell-Denning strict integrity policy [11.15]. The basic concept behind these policies, and others, is the same: reduce the privileges any user has at any given time and group related DBMS privileges [11.10, 11.19].

The goal of privilege reduction is to limit the operations that any one user has at any given time [11.10, 11.19]. For example, it is unnecessary to give a technician and personnel manager the same DBMS capabilities. A technician need not be able to add new employees or change an employee's personal data. Likewise, a personnel manager does not need the ability to modify any technical information. Therefore, DBMSs employ privilege reduction; they only grant each employee access to the data and operations that are required for an employee to perform his job.

Privilege reduction is not limited to one dependency. That is, the privileges granted to a user may depend not just upon their department, but upon their current task as well. For example, one personnel employee may only be able to add employees while another personnel employee may only be able to adjust the position and salary of an employee. This is shown in Figure 11.3. It should also be noted that more than one user may be assigned the same privileges; many users often have the same privileges. For this and other security reasons, DBMSs often employ a means of grouping related privileges called roles.

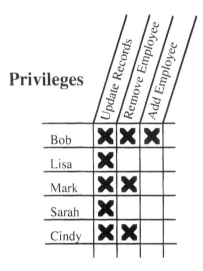

Figure 11.3. An example of user privilege mapping.

Grouping related DBMS privileges into a single representation (a role) allows system administrators to better control and represent the activities permissible by a user [11.17]. By creating roles that represent the activities of the different types of users, the DBMS can more clearly and accurately delineate the functions available to a user [11.10, 11.14]. For example, a personnel department worker can be assigned the corresponding role as opposed to listing each privilege individually. Since the reduced amount of authorized privilege combinations is represented by roles, the unauthorized addition of privileges to a user account becomes more noticeable. Furthermore, the use of roles allows a database administrator to adjust multiple user privileges by adjusting a single role. Figure 11.4, below, shows a role-based representation of the information in Figure 11.3.

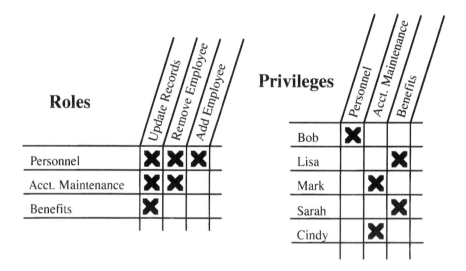

Figure 11.4. An example of role-based access control.

11.2.4 Trojan Horses

A Trojan Horse is a program that performs a task that a user does not expect and does not want completed [11.20]. The name, Trojan Horse, stems from the concept that the real functionality of the program is hidden from a user, only rarely making its true purpose apparent after its execution. A detailed discussion of Trojan Horses in general can be found in Chapter 13. In terms of DBMSs, Trojan Horses either modify the database, security labels, or user roles. For example, a user may execute a DBMS command that creates a backup of a confidential database, but has been altered to make a second copy available for every user to examine. In this example, the backup process functions properly, but the user is unaware of the activity of the Trojan Horse. While Trojan Horse programs may go unnoticed to the casual DBMS user, they are preventable [11.4].

The nature of Trojan Horse programs lends itself to prevention and possibly detection. Because their presence in a DBMS is an abnormality, they can often be found. This is accomplished by searching for the unusual activity and side effects of a Trojan Horse. Searching transaction logs for unusual activity or searching for unexplainable function modifications will often identify the presence of a Trojan Horse. This may not be enough, however, as they may have performed their intended task before they are noticed. Nonetheless, a system should take a few preventative measures. These measures are (1) restrict users from introducing additional functionality to the system and (2) frequent examination of existing system operations [11.13, 11.20]. Prohibiting users from adding functionality to the system will prevent the introduction of a Trojan Horse. In the event that users cannot or are not prevented from modifying the DBMS, frequent examination of the database operations may locate modified and unauthorized operations.

11.3 Summary

Security in a database management system (DBMS) refers to the promotion of data and operation availability, integrity, and privacy. These concepts are threatened by aggregation vulnerabilities, inference vulnerabilities, and Trojan Horses. Both aggregation and inference vulnerabilities allow a user, either authorized or unauthorized, to learn information that is otherwise unavailable to them. Aggregation is accomplished by combining select information from multiple data tables to identify information that is not otherwise accessible. Inference vulnerabilities allow an intruder to deduce the contents of a database without performing any overtly dangerous or suspicious behavior. Unlike aggregation and inference, Trojan Horses attack the DBMS operations as well as the data.

Prevention of these vulnerabilities begins with flow controls, inference controls, and basic system security mechanisms. Flow controls, such as multilevel security mechanisms, prevent unauthorized users from accessing or modifying information that an administrator has previously identified as inaccessible. Inference controls, such as data table reorganization, can reduce the possibility of inference. This process is often difficult, however, as every possible inference is not necessarily removed, let alone detected. Basic system security mechanisms are most useful in preventing Trojan Horse attacks. These mechanisms are often similar to those employed by non-database specific operating systems.

11.4 Exercises

11.1   When does the data aggregation problem coincide with the data inference
        problem? How can such a situation be prevented?

11.2   Why is it important to understand the purpose of a specific DBMS when
        implementing security in the system? What is the value of knowing which
        information within a DBMS should be visible to a user and which should be
        hidden?

11.3   Some researchers suggest encrypting the data in a DBMS to prevent
        aggregation, inference, and Trojan Horse attacks. Can encryption prevent
        these types of attacks? If so, how?

11.4   Some Trojan Horse programs attempt to bypass the DBMS operations by
        performing their tasks at an operating system level. Other Trojan horses,
        however, attempt to modify database information through a DBMS's native
        operations. What effect will a multilevel security system have on this type of
        attack?

11.5 References

11.1   Bell, D. E. and LaPadula, L. J., "Secure Computer Systems: Unified
        Exposition and MULTICS Interpretation", *MITRE Technical Report MTR-
        2997*, The MITRE Corporation, Bedford, Massachusetts, April 1974.

11.2   Biba, K. J., "Integrity Considerations for Secure Computer Systems, ESD-
        TR-76-372", *USAF Electronic Systems Division*, United State Air Force,
        Bedford, Massachusetts, March 1976.

11.3   Buckowski, L. J., "Database Inference Controller", *Database Security III*, D.
        L. Spooner and C. Landwehr editors, North-Holland Publishers, Stockholm,
        Sweden, Amsterdam, 1989, pp. 311-322.

11.4   Cohen, F., "Computational Aspects of Computer Viruses ", *Rogue Programs: Viruses, Worms, and Trojan Horses*, Lance J. Hoffman editor, Van Nostrand Reinhold, New York, New York, 1990, pp. 324-355.

11.5   Date, C. J., *An Introduction to Database Systems*, fourth edition, Addison-Wesley, Reading, Massachusetts, Vol. 1, 1986.

11.6   Ferraiolo, D. and Kuhn, R., "Role-Based Access Controls", *15th Annual National Computer Security Conference*, Baltimore, Maryland, October, 1992, pp. 554-563.

11.7   Fite, P. and Kratz, M. P. J., *Information Systems Security: A Practitioner's Reference*, Van Nostrand Reinhold, New York, New York, 1993.

11.8   Fugini, M., "Secure Database Development Methodologies ", *Database Security: Status and Prospects*, C. E. Landwehr editor, North-Holland Publishers, Stockholm, Sweden, Amsterdam, 1988, pp. 103-130.

11.9   Hinke, T. H. and Schaefer, M., "Secure Data Management System", *Rome Labratories Technical Report RADC-TR-266*, Rome Air Development Center, Griffiss AFB, New York, November 1975.

11.10   Lochovsky, F. H. and Woo, C. C., "Role-Based Security in Database Management Systems", *Database Security: Status and Prospects*, C. E. Landwehr editor North-Holland Publishers, Stockholm, Sweden, Amsterdam, 1988, pp. 209-222.

11.11   Lunt, T. F., "A summary of the RADC Database Security Workshop", *Proceedings of the 11th National Computer Security Conference*, Gaithersburg, Maryland, October 1988, pp. 188-193.

11.12   Meadows, C. and Jajodia, S., "Integrity Versus Security in Multilevel Secure Databases", *Database Security: Status and Prospects*, C. E. Landwehr editor, North-Holland Publishers, Stockholm, Sweden, Amsterdam, 1988, pp. 89-102.

11.13   Reymont Reports, "Detecting and Preventing Misuse of Data Processing Systems", Reymont Associates, New York, New York, 1978.

11.14   Sandhu, R. and Feinstein, H., "A Three Tier Architecture for Role-Based Access Control", *17th Annual National Computer Security Conference*, Baltimore, Maryland, October 1994, pp. 34-46.

11.15   Schell, R. and Denning, D., "Integrity in Trusted Database Systems", *9th Annual National Computer Security Conference*, Gaithersburg, Maryland, September 1986, pp. 30-36.

11.16   Smith, G. W., "Solving Multileveled Database Security Problems: Teaching is not Enough", *Database Security III*, D. L. Spooner and C. Landwehr editors, North-Holland Publishers, Stockholm, Sweden, Amsterdam, 1989, pp. 115-125.

11.17   Smith-Thomas, B., Chao-Yeuh, W., and Yung-Sheng, W., "Implementing Role Based, Clark-Wilson Enforcement Rules in a B1 On-Line Transaction Processing System", *17th Annual National Computer Security Conference*, Baltimore, Maryland, October 1994, pp. 56-65.

11.18   Su, T.-A. and Osoyoglu, G., "Multivalued Dependency Inferences in Multilevel Relational Database Systems", *Database Security III*, D. L. Spooner and C. Landwehr editors, North-Holland Publishers, Stockholm, Sweden, Amsterdam, 1989, pp. 293-300.

11.19   Ting, T. C., "A User-Role Based Data Security Approach", *Database Security: Status and Prospects*, C. E. Landwehr editor, North-Holland Publishers, Stockholm, Sweden, Amsterdam, 1988, pp. 187-208.

11.20   White, S. R. and Chess, D. M., "Coping with Computer and Related Problem", *Rogue Programs: Viruses, Worms, and Trojan Horses*, Lance J. Hoffman editor, Van Nostrand Reinhold, New York, New York, 1990, pp. 7-28.

11.21   Wiseman, S. R., "On the Problem of Security in Data Bases", *Database Security III*, D. L. Spooner and C. Landwehr editors, North-Holland Publishers, Stockholm, Sweden, Amsterdam, 1989, pp. 301-310.

11.6 Extended Bibliography

11.22   Elmasri, R. and Navathe, S. B., *Fundamentals of Database Systems*, Benjamin Cummings Publishing Company, Redwood City, California, 1989.

11.23   Fisch, A. M., "Oracle Data Security", *UNIX Review*, Miller Freeman Publications, San Francisco, California, Vol. 9, No. 6, June 1991, pp. 38-41.

11.24   Henning, R. R. and Walker, S. A., "Data Integrity vs. Data Security: A Workable Compromise", *Proceedings of the 10th National Computer Security Conference*, Gaithersburg, Maryland, September 1987, pp. 334-339.

11.25   O'Conner, J. P. and Gray III, J. W., "A Distributed Architecture for Multilevel Database Security", Gaithersburg, Maryland, *Proceedings of the 11th National Computer Security Conference*, October 1988, pp. 179-187.

11.26   Shockley, W. R. and Warren, D. F., "Description of Multiple Secure Entity-Relationship DBMS Demonstration", Gaithersburg, Maryland, *Proceedings of the 11th National Computer Security Conference*, October 1988, pp. 171-178.

11.27   Ullman, J. D., *Principles of Database and Knowledge-Base Systems*, Computer Science Press, Stanford, California, Vol. 1, 1988.

12

CRYPTOGRAPHY

Cryptography comes from the Greek words *kryptos* meaning hidden or secret and *graphos* meaning writing. Once the concern of diplomats and military officers, today cryptography is much more widespread. From the automated teller machines used by banks to private subscription television transmissions, cryptography is part of everyone's life. What was once a topic discussed only behind locked doors of organizations such as the National Security Agency now is a major academic topic, an active area of research, and a common aspect of business and industry.

The discipline relating to the use and development of techniques to encrypt and decrypt messages is called **cryptography**. An attempt to break a specific cryptographic technique is called **cryptanalysis**. Usually it is assumed that an individual only has a copy of an encrypted message when trying to break a specific technique in order to read the message. The process is often made easier if the cryptanalyst can obtain the encrypted version of some known message. The field that covers both cryptography and cryptanalysis is known as **cryptology**.

The process of **encryption** entails taking a message (often referred to as **plaintext** or **cleartext**) and changing it to hide the original meaning from everybody but the intended recipient(s). **Decryption** is the process that takes the encrypted message (now referred to as **ciphertext**) and restores it to the original message.

Figure 12.1. The encryption and decryption processes.

This process of changing plaintext to ciphertext and back again requires that a pair of transformations takes place. These transformations use mathematical functions which incorporate an additional piece of data, known as the **key**, to perform the required transformations. The key is kept secret so that only the intended recipient(s) can decrypt the message. These transformations can be represented as follows:

```
Ciphertext = Encrypt[key](Plaintext)
Plaintext = Decrypt[key](Ciphertext)
```

The desire to keep information and messages hidden from others is not a new phenomenon that has appeared with the advent of computers. Governments, the military, and businesses have used cryptography for centuries to hide their secrets from potential or actual adversaries or competitors. One of the first encryption methods was a simple substitution technique, which disguised each individual character.

12.1   Substitution Ciphers

Substitution Ciphers are based on the principle of replacing each character with another character in order to hide the actual meaning of the message. Substitution by itself is not new nor is it always used to hide the meaning of a message. A well known example of substitution is Morse code, which was created not to keep a message secret but rather to facilitate transmission of messages via various media. Another substitution is the Braille alphabet, which is used by those who cannot see normal printed characters.

12.1.1   Caesar Cipher

The famous Caesar Cipher was a simple substitution cipher which replaced each letter with one three to the right in alphabetical order. Using this technique, A would become D, B would become E, and so forth. The last three characters of the alphabet would wrap so that X becomes A, Y becomes B, and Z would become C. Using this technique, the word "computer" would become

```
A B C D E F G H I J K L M N O P Q R S T U V W X Y Z
D E F G H I J K L M N O P Q R S T U V W X Y Z A B C


    Cleartext ==>      C O M P U T E R
    Ciphertext ==>     F R P S X W H U
```

 The decryption process is a simple matter of replacing all characters in the ciphertext with the character three to the left (with the characters A, B, and C now wrapping around to X, Y, and Z, respectively).

12.1.2 ROT13

A common simple cipher, which can be found on some UNIX systems, is ROT13. Like the Caesar Cipher, ROT13 simply replaces each plaintext character with its equivalent, this time 13 spaces to the right instead of just the three spaces used by the Caesar Cipher. This technique has the advantage that the same transformation function can be used for both encryption and decryption since, with 26 characters in the alphabet, shifting 13 characters to the right is equivalent to shifting 13 characters to the left (with appropriate wrap-around). The C code for ROT13 is as follows [12.10]:

```
#include <stdio.h>

    /* if character >= 'a' or 'A' and <= 'm' or 'M'
     *    then add 13.  If another letter of alphabet
     *    then subtract 13.
     */
main ()
 {
   int chr;

   while (( chr = getchar()) != EOF)
     {
       if (chr >= 97 && chr <= 109) chr=chr+13;
         else if (chr >= 110 && chr <= 122 ) chr=chr-13;
           else if (chr >= 65 && chr <= 77 ) chr=chr+13;
             else if (chr >= 78 && chr <= 90 ) chr=chr-13;
       putchar(chr);
     }  /* end of while */
 } /* end of ROT13 */
```

12.1.3 Substitution Cipher Variations

An alternative method to the previous, very simple substitution techniques is to create a random sequence of letters and use this sequence to guide the transformation. For example, if the following sequence was chosen:

```
zxcvbnmasdfghjklqwertyuiop
```

the ciphertext could be obtained by lining the regular sequence above the key and making the appropriate substitution.

```
ABCDEFGHIJKLMNOPQRSTUVWXYZ
zxcvbnmasdfghjklqwertyuiop
```

Using this method, the message

```
Now is the time for all good men
```

becomes

```
Jku se rab rshb nkw zgg mkkv hbj
```

This message can be made a bit more unreadable by removing the spaces between the words and then grouping the message into blocks of characters as follows:

```
Jkuse rabrs hbnkw zggmk kvhbj
```

The weakness in all substitution techniques is that some letters are more frequently used than others. This allows an individual, by simply calculating the number of occurrences for each character in the ciphertext, to determine the substitutions that were made. In English text, the expected frequency of specific letters for a 1,000 character document can be seen in Table 12.1. From this table we can see that the most commonly occurring letter in English is E. In a 1,000 character document we would thus expect to find approximately 125 E's.

Simply substituting another character merely changes the frequency for specific characters but maintains the relative frequency that characters are used. Another problem with substitution techniques is that certain pairs of letters are more often used than others. This allows the cryptanalyst to search for commonly found patterns. This is especially true for characters that are repeated in a word. In our example above, the doubles 'gg' and 'kk' both appear in the ciphertext. Only certain letters are commonly found repeated in words (e.g. 'oo', 'mm', and 'll'). This characteristic of the language further helps the analyst to break the ciphertext.

Table 12.1 Expected number of occurrences for each letter of the alphabet in a 1,000 word English text document [12.11]

Letter	Times it Occurs	Letter	Times it Occurs	Letter	Times it Occurs
E	125	L	36	W	15
T	90	H	34	V	14
R	83	C	33	B	12
N	75	F	29	K	5
I	74	U	28	X	4
O	73	M	26	Q	4
A	71	P	25	J	2
S	58	Y	22	Z	2
D	40	G	20		

12.1.4 Vigenere Ciphers

The goal of a substitution cipher should be to break up the natural frequency of occurrence for letters and groups of letters. One way to accomplish this is to change the substitution key during the message. For example, if we chose the numeric key

```
3  5  7  9  11
```

we would shift the first letter three characters, the second five, the third seven, and so forth with the sixth letter starting the sequence over. This yields the following ciphertext for our earlier message:

```
Now is the time for all good men
Qtd rd wml ctpj mxc dqs pzri tny
```

This method starts to eliminate some of the problems associated with simple substitution ciphers and uses what is known as a Vigenere Table. A full Vigenere Table is shown in Table 12.2.

When using a Vigenere Table, the key may be a word which both parties know and which indicates the row of the table to use. If, for example, the word "computer" were chosen for the key, the row of the table to use could be selected several ways. One method is to repeatedly write the key over the plaintext. The specific row to use for the substitution is the one that starts with that letter of the alphabet. This will yield the following ciphertext for our previous example:

```
COM PU TER COMP UTE RCO MPUT ERC        (repeated key)
Now is the time for all good men        (plaintext)
Pci xm mlv vwyt zhv rnz sdiw qvp        (ciphertext)
```

Another method that can be used is to base the row selected on the sorted order of the letters in the key. In our example, the letter C is the first letter (alphabetically), E is the second, M the third, and so forth. Our earlier example would then be encrypted as follows:

```
C O M P U T E R                          (key)
1 4 3 5 8 7 2 6                          (sorted order)
143 58 726 1435 872 614 3587 261         (repeated key)
Now is the time for all good men         (plaintext)
Osz na ajk umpj nvt gmp jtwk oko         (ciphertext)
```

Notice that these two methods resulted in different ciphertexts even though the same key was used. Obviously, both sides of the encryption process must use the same method for a transmitted message to be correctly decrypted.

Using a word such as "computer" as a key, instead of a random selection of numbers, makes it easier to remember. While the methods shown have made it more difficult to determine the correct substitutions, they are still not perfect. Continuing with our plaintext example we can obtain the following additional ciphertext:

```
43 5872 61 435 872 61 43587 2614358726
to come to the aid of their countrymen
xr hwtg zp xkj ipf ug xkjqy euvrwwgtgt
```

If we were to examine the ciphertext we would first notice that the frequency in which letters occur does not match the expected frequency. We therefore know that a simple substitution has not occurred. If we were to further examine the ciphertext, however, we would notice that several groups of letters occur in the same sequence on more than one occasion. The pair 'tg' appears three times while the pair 'mp' appears twice as do the pairs 'gt' and the triplet 'xkj'. The pair 'mp' occurs 7 characters apart, the pair 'tg' occurs 15 and 24 characters apart, 'gt' 2 characters, and 'xkj' 8. This gives us a clue as to what length the key might be. Three of the pairs have two as a factor and two have eight as a factor. If we were to then group the letters into groups of two (assuming the key is two

Table 12.2 Vignere Table

```
 0 A B C D E F G H I J K L M N O P Q R S T U V W X Y Z
 1 B C D E F G H I J K L M N O P Q R S T U V W X Y Z A
 2 C D E F G H I J K L M N O P Q R S T U V W X Y Z A B
 3 D E F G H I J K L M N O P Q R S T U V W X Y Z A B C
 4 E F G H I J K L M N O P Q R S T U V W X Y Z A B C D
 5 F G H I J K L M N O P Q R S T U V W X Y Z A B C D E
 6 G H I J K L M N O P Q R S T U V W X Y Z A B C D E F
 7 H I J K L M N O P Q R S T U V W X Y Z A B C D E F G
 8 I J K L M N O P Q R S T U V W X Y Z A B C D E F G H
 9 J K L M N O P Q R S T U V W X Y Z A B C D E F G H I
10 K L M N O P Q R S T U V W X Y Z A B C D E F G H I J
11 L M N O P Q R S T U V W X Y Z A B C D E F G H I J K
12 M N O P Q R S T U V W X Y Z A B C D E F G H I J K L
13 N O P Q R S T U V W X Y Z A B C D E F G H I J K L M
14 O P Q R S T U V W X Y Z A B C D E F G H I J K L M N
15 P Q R S T U V W X Y Z A B C D E F G H I J K L M N O
16 Q R S T U V W X Y Z A B C D E F G H I J K L M N O P
17 R S T U V W X Y Z A B C D E F G H I J K L M N O P Q
18 S T U V W X Y Z A B C D E F G H I J K L M N O P Q R
19 T U V W X Y Z A B C D E F G H I J K L M N O P Q R S
20 U V W X Y Z A B C D E F G H I J K L M N O P Q R S T
21 V W X Y Z A B C D E F G H I J K L M N O P Q R S T U
22 W X Y Z A B C D E F G H I J K L M N O P Q R S T U V
23 X Y Z A B C D E F G H I J K L M N O P Q R S T U V W
24 Y Z A B C D E F G H I J K L M N O P Q R S T U V W X
25 Z A B C D E F G H I J K L M N O P Q R S T U V W X Y
```

letters long) and then eight (which assumes an eight character key) we get

```
O s                    O s z n a a j k
z n                    u m p j n v t g
a a                    m p j t w k o k
j k                    o x r h w t g z
u m                    p x k j i p f u
p j                    g x k j q y e u
  •
  •
  •
```

We could now check to see if the resulting groupings yielded the correct character occurrence frequency for each of the columns. If we found one that did, it might indicate the length of the key and allow us to break the cryptosystem. It should be obvious that the longer the captured ciphertext is, the easier it will be to break. It should also be obvious that the closer the key size is to the size of the plaintext, the harder it will be to break.

12.1.5 One Time Pads

Several techniques have been described to make breaking a cryptosystem difficult but there is one method, invented in the early part of this century, that results in an unbreakable code. This method consists of what is known as one time pads. Each pad contains several pages, each consisting of a large number of characters in random order. Each page of the pad is used only once to encrypt a message and is then discarded. Messages longer than the length of a single page use multiple pages so that the sequence is not repeated. The intended recipient of the ciphertext must have an identical pad as the sender. Since any key sequence from the pad is equally as likely, there is no way, given the ciphertext alone, to determine what the original plaintext message was. Consider the following plaintext message:

```
One if by land
```

If the key consisted of the letter sequence

```
thxysiesgdw
```

then, by using the key to determine which line of a Vigenere Table to use, the substituted ciphertext we would obtain is

```
hub gx jc dgqz
```

For the cryptanalyst who is trying to decipher this message, if the key

```
oynysielcqh
```

was guessed, the ciphertext would be decrypted as

```
Two if by seas
```

which is just as likely, from the cryptanalyst's perspective, as the original plaintext. In fact, any message of the same length is equally as likely with no way of determining which is correct.

Since the one time pad provides such secure communication it might at first appear as the solution to all cryptographic problems. In actuality, however, the one time pad suffers from one very big disadvantage, the pad itself. Pads must be distributed in a secure manner to all parties involved. This same problem exists for all symmetric cryptosystems and is known as the **key distribution** problem. In addition, the pads must contain random sequences longer than the plaintext message. With the increasing size and amount of encrypted communication seen today, one time pads do not offer a practical solution.

12.2   Transposition Ciphers

Transposition ciphers differ from substitution ciphers in that they do not change the characters themselves but rather the order in which they appear in the message. A simple example, using our previous message, is as follows:

```
won si eht emit rof lla doog nem
```

In this extremely simple example, the order of the characters has been reversed in each word while each character maintains its original identity. This means that the frequency of occurrence for each letter will not change and provides a clue that a transposition cipher is being used. While the above example is easily read, using other methods to transpose the character positions yields significantly more difficult ciphertext. The plaintext can be arranged, for example, in two vertical columns, then taken in horizontal pairs and placed into groups of five characters yielding

```
N o
o r
w a
i l
s l
t g        Noorw ailsl tghoe otdim meenf
h o
e o
t d
i m
m e
e n
f
```

Various numbers of columns can be used for the transposition process. Breaking this method of encryption consists of repeatedly using a different number of columns. Another transposition method consists of using various geometric patterns to transcribe the message. If we group the text into a square, we obtain:

```
N  o  w  i  s
t  h  e  t  i
m  e  f  o  r
a  l  l  g  o
o  d  m  e  n
```

We can then transcribe the message by taking the characters in any of several different patterns. We could, for example, start at the top and follow a spiral pattern in a counter-clockwise direction yielding:

```
N  t  m  a  o  d  m  e  n  o  r  i  s  i  w  o  h  e  l  l  g  o  t  e  f
```

Another approach would be to transcribe the message in a diagonal pattern. Starting at the top right and proceeding down and to the left would yield:

```
s  i  i  w  t  r  o  e  o  o  N  h  f  g  n  t  e  l  e  m  l  m  a  d  o
```

Should the plaintext message not be of the correct size, extra characters can be added to reach the required number for the desired block.

12.3   Encrypting Digital Communication

When considering the seven-layer Open Systems Interface (OSI) network model, encryption can take place at any of the layers. In practice there are two different approaches that are commonly seen: **Link Encryption**, which takes place at the physical layer; and **End-to-End Encryption**, which occurs between the network layer and the transport layer (or any of the other higher level layers).

At the physical layer, encryption devices ("black boxes") can be easily attached where the physical media exits each node. Decryption takes place at the other end of the media as it enters a node. This effectively encrypts all transmissions across the media. One particular advantage to this form of encryption is that it protects against **traffic-flow analysis**. Since everything that is sent along the media is encrypted, an individual who taps into the media would not even be able to determine the destination of the messages. A drawback to link encryption, however, is that it requires a large number of encryption devices and even one unencrypted link jeopardizes the security of the whole network. In addition, each node must be protected since all traffic is decrypted at each node. All users of the nodes must be trusted because all traffic is decrypted at each node, allowing anybody to read all traffic transmitted across the media.

In end-to-end encryption the ciphertext remains encrypted as it travels through each node until it reaches its final destination. The destination is not encrypted so traffic-flow analysis can take place but the message remains encrypted at each node; so, the individual nodes need not be secure nor do all of the users need to be trusted individuals.

Another characteristic of digital encryption techniques is whether the encryption is done in a block or stream. **Stream ciphers** convert the plaintext one bit at a time. Stream ciphers are not normally implemented at the software but at the hardware level. **Block ciphers**, on the other hand, work on blocks of either plain or ciphertext. The largest difference between the two is in error propagation. An error in a stream cipher will corrupt a single bit while errors in block ciphers will corrupt an entire block. Historically blocks tend to be 64, or multiples of 64, bits in length.

A **symmetric** cryptosystem is one that uses the same key for both the encryption and decryption processes. If two individuals wish to communicate they obtain a data value to be used as the key (how they obtain the same value will be discussed later). This value is kept secret from all other individuals, which allows the two parties to protect the contents of a message encrypted using this key from all others. The symmetric cryptosystem has three main problems:

1) If a third party determines the key, the messages sent between the two original parties would be compromised. In addition, the third party could send encrypted messages to fool the other parties.
2) The key must be distributed in a secret manner. In the past, this often has been accomplished by using couriers to distribute the keys.
3) A large number of keys is required to enable individual pairs of users to secretly communicate. The number of keys necessary is in fact $(n^2-n)/2$. Thus, if there were 10 users only 45 keys would be needed, but if there were 100 users 4950 keys would be required, and if there were 10,000 users 49,995,000 keys would be necessary.

12.3.1   DES

The Data Encryption Standard (DES) has been in use worldwide as a standard for more than a decade. It arose during a period when several companies were producing cryptographic equipment that wasn't compatible and whose algorithm's strength and security was unknown. The National Bureau of Standards (NBS, now called the National Institute of Standards and Technology or NIST) initiated an effort in 1972 and 1973 to

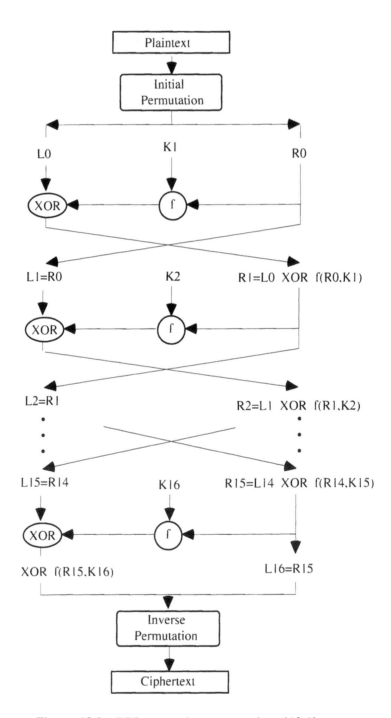

Figure 12.2. DES encryption computations [12.4].

develop a standard algorithm to protect digital data via a formal request for proposals. IBM answered this request with an algorithm based on an earlier one called LUCIFER (it is interesting to note that the original LUCIFER key was 112 bits long but after the National Security Agency was asked to help with the evaluation of the algorithm it was shortened to the current 56 bits).   The resulting algorithm was officially adopted as a federal standard in 1976 and authorized for all federal government unclassified communications. The NBS issued an official description of the algorithm in the Federal Information Processing Standards Publication 46 (FIPS PUB 46) in 1977 [12.4].

The DES algorithm is designed to encrypt or decrypt blocks of data consisting of 64 bits using a 64-bit key. The same key is used for both the encryption and decryption processes.   The block is first subject to an initial permutation (see Figure 12.2) as follows:

```
58 50 42 34 26 18 10 2
60 52 44 36 28 20 12 4
62 54 46 38 30 22 14 6
64 56 48 40 32 24 16 8
57 49 41 33 25 17  9 1
59 51 43 35 27 19 11 3
61 53 45 37 29 21 13 5
63 55 47 39 31 23 15 7
```

This means that the block after the initial permutation will have the 58th bit of the plaintext block as its first bit, the 50th bit as its second bit, and so forth.   After the initial permutation, the block is then subjected to a series of key-dependent computations. Finally, the block permutes once more via the inverse of the original permutation.

Following the initial permutation, the block of data is split into two halves consisting of 32 bits each.   These halves are combined with the key and processed through a function "f" sixteen times.   After the final iteration, the two halves are combined again and sent through the inverse permutation operation.   The DES key consists of 64 bits, 56 of which are used by the algorithm with 8 bits used for error detection. The function "f" consists of four operations:

1) the key is shifted and 48 bits are selected,
2) the right half of the data consisting of 32 bits is expanded to 48 and then an exclusive-or operation is performed on it and the 48-bit key,
3) 32 bits of this new value are selected using what has been called the "S-boxes", and
4) a final permutation on these last 32 bits is performed [12.4, 12.10].

One benefit of this algorithm is that the same process can be used for both encryption and decryption (with the exception of the key, which must be used in reverse order for decryption). The algorithm also has the advantage that it only uses logical operations resulting in a fast process whether implemented in hardware or software.

The S-Boxes play a crucial role in both the algorithm itself and the debate that surrounds its development. The cryptosystem must take the 48 bits that have been generated in the previous operation and select only 32 bits from it. Which 32 bits should be chosen and why? The answer to this is shrouded in some mystery since NSA has not allowed IBM to release why certain bits are chosen. Some speculate that this is because there may exist a quick way to decipher the message. As long as the reasons are not known, the cipher is reasonably secure from all; except NSA.

An ongoing debate has been exactly how secure is DES? There has been much suspicion that when NSA got involved, a "trap door" was inserted so they could decrypt any DES encrypted messages (the mysterious "S-Boxes"). A special U.S. Senate committee investigated this matter and, while the full transcript of their findings is classified, an unclassified summary cleared NSA of any improper manipulation of the algorithm. Debate also surrounds the issue of the DES key length. Some have speculated that there exist certain governments and organizations which may have built specialized DES breaking machines that utilize a brute-force attack. A longer key, some argue, would have made this option prohibitively expensive.

One known weakness in DES surrounds the selection of the initial key. If the key consists of all 0's or all 1's, then the shifting of the key at each step accomplishes nothing as the key will remain the same throughout the 16 step process. Another weakness, also associated with the key, is that there exist pairs of keys that will yield identical ciphertext. This means that a different key can be used to decrypt a message from the one that had originally been used. Even with these weaknesses, since there are more than 10^{16} different keys, DES still provides an excellent level of security.

12.3.2   IDEA

DES may be reaching a point where it will soon be at the end of its useful life. As a result, there have been several other efforts to develop a new encryption standard. One of these, first developed in 1990 and called the Proposed Encryption Standard (PES), is the International Data Encryption Algorithm (IDEA) [12.10].

IDEA, like DES, is a block cipher operating on 64-bit blocks of plaintext which uses the same algorithm for both encryption and decryption. Unlike DES, however, IDEA uses a 128-bit key. The algorithm itself splits the plaintext into four 16-bit sub-blocks. Each of these blocks then goes through a series of operations which include exclusive-or's, modulo 2^{16} addition, and modulo $2^{16}+1$ multiplication. The blocks do not, however, go through any complicated permutations. Another difference between

IDEA and DES is that IDEA only goes through eight iterations as opposed to DES's sixteen iterations. The key is split into eight 16-bit sub-blocks (K$_1$ through K$_8$). Six of these key sub-blocks are used each iteration; any that are left over are then used in the next block. After all key sub-blocks are used, the key is shifted 25 bits to the left, and then split up into 8 new sub-blocks. After the initial decomposition of the plaintext into four separate blocks (B$_1$ through B$_4$), the operations depicted in Figure 12.3 take place during each of the eight iterations [12.10].

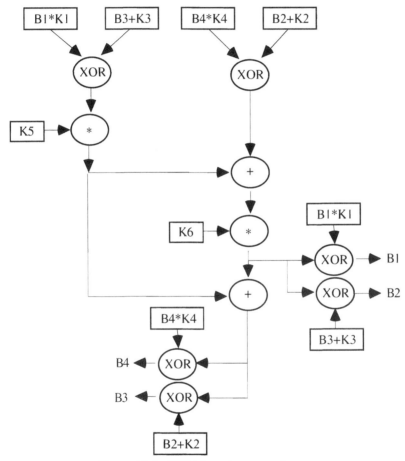

Figure 12.3. IDEA iterative operations.

The final four steps of each iteration (Steps 11 through 14) produce the four sub-blocks B$_1$ through B$_4$ of the next iteration. After the last iteration, the first four operations are performed again and then the four sub-blocks are joined together to form the 64-bit ciphertext. Decryption is done using the same operations except the key sub-blocks are changed to be either the additive or multiplicative inverses of the original encryption key sub-blocks and are then taken in reverse order.

Analysis of IDEA has shown it to be as fast as DES but, because of its larger key size, a brute force attack will take considerably longer than DES (perhaps greater than 10^{13} years) [12.10]. Another analysis showed that IDEA is also subject to weak key problems. In this case, however, the weak key is one which, if used, can be identified given a **chosen-plaintext** attack (an attack in which the cryptanalyst chooses the text to be encrypted).

12.3.3   Key Escrow

The White House announced the Escrowed Encryption Initiative in April of 1993. Despite a storm of criticism, NIST announced the Escrowed Encryption Standard less than a year later. The standard, and initiative, were designed to improve the security and privacy of electronic communication while still meeting the needs of law enforcement agencies. At the heart of the debate over Key Escrow are two conflicting desires. The first is the desire of private citizens to protect their electronic communications from eavesdropping. The second is the desire by law enforcement agencies to be able to, after having obtained the appropriate legal permissions, listen in on conversations of those suspected of involvement in illegal activities. Without debating the appropriateness of the initiative, it is informative to understand what is involved in the key escrow process.

Key escrow involves the use of a special encryption chip. Each chip has designed into it a special "backdoor" which will allow a third party to decrypt the transmission. The procedure for utilizing this backdoor entails the use of two unique keys. With only one of the keys the backdoor can't be opened; it requires both keys. The plan then is to store the two keys at separate "escrow" locations. A law enforcement agency would then have to obtain the appropriate legal permission to perform a wiretap before the keys would be released.

The original chip proposed to implement the key escrow plan was called the **Clipper Chip**. Each chip employs the NSA developed Skipjack algorithm and includes an 80-bit family key **F** (common to all chips), a serial number **S** (originally 30 bits), and an 80-bit secret key **U**, which can be used to unlock all messages encrypted by this specific chip [12.1]. Two individuals wishing to use the chip for encryption must also select an 80-bit session key **K**. The transmitted message consists of two values:

1) the encrypted message using the calculation

$$\mathtt{ciphertext} \ = \ \mathtt{Encrypt}_{[K]}\,\mathtt{(message)}$$

2) the law enforcement field using the calculation

$$\texttt{LE\_field = Encrypt}_{[F]}\texttt{(Encrypt}_{[U]}\texttt{(K) + S)}$$

The receiver can decrypt the message by simply performing

$$\texttt{message = Decrypt}_{[K]}\texttt{(ciphertext)}$$

The law enforcement field consists of two parts: an encrypted version of the session key (using the secret key) and the serial number for the chip. A law enforcement agency that has obtained the appropriate legal permissions to perform a wiretap can decrypt the original message in a five step process.

1) The law enforcement field is decrypted using the family key to obtain the encrypted session key and the serial number. The calculation is

$$\texttt{Encrypted\_K\_Key + S = Decrypt}_{[F]}\texttt{(LE\_field)}$$

2) The law enforcement agency provides the serial number for this chip, along with proof of its legal permissions to decrypt the transmission, to the two escrow agents.

3) The two escrow agents provide **U1** and **U2**, their parts of the secret key for this chip. These two parts are then XORed to obtain **U**, the unlocking secret key.

4) The law enforcement agency can then determine the session key by performing:

$$\texttt{K = Decrypt}_{[U]}\texttt{(Encrypted\_K\_Key)}$$

5) Now knowing the session key used, the law enforcement agency can decrypt the message by simply performing the same calculation as the receiver:

$$\texttt{message = Decrypt}_{[K]}\texttt{(ciphertext)}$$

One of the most controversial issues surrounding the key escrow scheme involved the key escrow agents. Obviously the organizations that hold the keys that are used to calculate the unlocking secret key must be trustworthy and reliable. The original intent was to have at least one of these organizations not be part of the federal government. For some, however, there is no organization that they would trust with this tremendous responsibility.

12.3.4   Public Key Cryptography

Public Key or asymmetric cryptosystems differ from symmetric cryptosystems in that they use different keys for decryption and encryption. The concept of public key cryptography was introduced by Whitfield Diffie and Martin Hellman in 1976 [12.2]. The public key process can be expressed as follows:

```
Ciphertext = Encrypt[key1](Plaintext)
Plaintext = Decrypt[key2](Ciphertext)
```

There are two modes of public-key system operation. The public key can be used to encrypt the Plaintext, or it can be used to decrypt the Ciphertext. A system that works in only one or the other of these modes is   known as an *irreversible public-key* cryptosystem. One that works in both directions is known as a *reversible public-key cryptosystem*.   The reason one might use a public-key for decryption is if data origin authentication is desired.

12.3.4.1   Diffie-Hellman   Algorithm

The original algorithm presented in "New Directions in Cryptography" [12.2] described a method two individuals could use to generate and distribute a secret key in a public environment.   The security of the technique comes from the difficulty of calculating logarithms mod q as compared to multiplication's mod q (where q is a prime number). In their technique, Diffie and Hellman describe how each user must generate an independent random number X_i from the set of integers $\{1,2, \bullet \bullet \bullet, \quad q\text{ -}1\}$ [12.2]. Their explanation is as follows: Each user keeps this chosen value, X_i, secret but stores

$$Y_i = a^{\lambda_i} \bmod(q) \qquad \text{where a is a large integer, and a} < \text{q}$$

in a public location. When two users, i and j, wish to communicate securely, they generate a key for their own private use as follows:

$$K_{ij} = a^{x_i x_j} \bmod(q)$$

but since neither knows the other's private key X, they must calculate it.   User i can calculate K_{ij} by using the public key Y_j and calculating

$$K_{\eta} = (Y_j)^{x_i} \bmod(q)$$

$$K_{\eta} = (a^{x_j})^{x_i} \bmod(q)$$

$$K_{\eta} = a^{x_i x_j} \bmod(q)$$

User j can obtain the key in a similar manner. For another user to determine the key, however, the following, much more labor intensive, calculation would be required:

$$K_{\eta} = Y_i^{((Log(a))Y_j)} \bmod(q)$$

Diffie and Hellman described how a cryptanalyst would require $2^{b/2}$ operations to determine the key if q were chosen so that it was slightly less than 2^b. For a b value of 200 this would result in approximately 10^{30} operations. The Diffie-Hellman algorithm is patented in the United States and Canada until April of 1997.

12.3.4.2   Knapsack Algorithms

A rather interesting algorithm was proposed by Ralph Merkle and Martin Hellman which utilized a famous NP-complete problem for its security [12.3]. The Knapsack problem, simply stated, is: given a collection of objects with different weights, determine which of the items should be placed in the knapsack so that it will weigh a specified amount. The time required to solve this problem grows exponentially with the number of objects in the collection to choose from. The way that Merkle and Hellman utilized this problem for cryptography was to encrypt a message as a solution to a series of knapsack problems. For example, if the objects had weights of 1, 3, 4, 8, 11, and 15, then the cleartext would be grouped into 6-bit blocks and the weights for each of these calculated as follows [12.10]:

```
Cleartext:     1 1 0 1  0  0    1 0 0 0  1  1    0 0 1 0  1  1
Weights:       1 3 4 8 11 15    1 3 4 8 11 15    1 3 4 8 11 15
Calculation:   1+3+0+8+ 0+ 0    1+0+0+0+11+15    0+0+4+0+11+15
Ciphertext:    =12              =27              =30
```

The public/private key aspect of this approach lies in the fact that there are actually two different knapsack problems — referred to as the easy and hard knapsack. The easy knapsack approach has been proven to be solvable in O(n) time. It is created as described above with one exception. The sequence of weights must be a **superincreasing sequence**. A superincreasing sequence is one in which each element is greater than the sum of all previous elements in the sequence. An example would be {1, 2, 4, 8, 16, 32}. A hard knapsack sequence is not superincreasing. The hard knapsack sequence is not solvable in O(n) but rather is the NP-complete problem described previously. It is this sequence that is put into the public sector as the public key. The private key will be the easy knapsack sequence and is kept secret. The public key can be generated from the private key by multiplying each element of the easy knapsack sequence by $a \mod b$, where b is an integer greater than the sum of all numbers in the sequence, and a is an integer that has no factors in common with any value in the sequence. If the easy knapsack sequence were {2, 4, 8, 16, 32} and if a is chosen to be 23 and b to be 65, then the hard knapsack sequence (the public key) would be calculated as follows:

```
 2 x 23 mod 65 = 46
 4 x 23 mod 65 = 27
 8 x 23 mod 65 = 54
16 x 23 mod 65 = 43
32 x 23 mod 65 = 21
```

The resulting hard knapsack sequence would be {46, 27, 54, 43, 21}. Using this public key sequence, we can encrypt the following 10-bit message as follows:

```
Cleartext:     1  0  0  1  1          0  0  1  0  1
Public key:  {46 27 54 43 21}       {46 27 54 43 21}
Calculation:  46+ 0+ 0+43+21=110     0+ 0+54+21+ 0=75
Ciphertext:  110,75
```

The message can then be decrypted using the private key. The first step of this decryption is to determine a^{-1} so that $a \times a^{-1} = 1 \mod b$. With $a = 23$ and $b = 65$, $a^{-1} = 17$. Each value in the ciphertext is then multiplied by this number mod b which will yield the plaintext values.

```
Ciphertext:    110,75
Private Key: {2, 4, 8, 16, 32}

        110 x 17 mod 65 = 50 = 10011 (2+0+0+16+32)
         75 x 17 mod 65 = 40 = 00101 (0+0+8+ 0+32)

Plaintext: 10011 00101
```

In practice, the value of b is chosen to be very long as is each value in the knapsack (approximately 200 to 400 bits). The knapsacks themselves should contain about 200 items [12.10]. Even with values of this length, this knapsack algorithm has been broken (a method was shown that allowed the private key to be determined from the public key). Many other proposed knapsack algorithms have arisen but the wisest course of action is to probably stay away from using them.

12.3.4.3　RSA

Named after its inventors, Ron Rivest, Adi Shamir, and Leonard Adleman, RSA has proven to be an extremely reliable algorithm used for both public key encryption and digital signatures (discussed in the next section).　The security of RSA is derived from the problem associated with the factoring of large numbers [12.8].　The keys used are calculated from a pair of large prime numbers p and q. These prime numbers may exceed 200 digits in length.　The public key consists of a pair of numbers, n and e, where $n = p \times q$. The value for e, which is the encryption key, is chosen randomly and should be relatively prime to $(p - 1) \times (q - 1)$.　The decryption key, d, is then computed as $d = e^{-1}(\mod (p - 1) \times (q - 1))$ [12.10].　The two prime numbers chosen earlier, p and q, are no longer needed and can be discarded but should be kept secret.

To encrypt a message m using the RSA algorithm, the message should be partitioned into blocks of characters (or bits for binary data) no larger than the number of characters or bits in n. Each of these blocks will be encrypted into ciphertext blocks, c_i (of the same size), using the encryption key (public key) and the following formula [12.8, 12.10]:

$$c_i = Encrypt(m_i) = m_i^e (\mod(n))$$

Decryption uses the decryption (private) key as follows:

$$m_i = Decrypt(c_i) = c_i^d (\mod(n))$$

In actuality the values for d and e are interchangeable so that encryption could take place with d and decryption with e.　An example will help to illustrate the RSA encryption and decryption processes.　If $p = 31$ and $q = 53$, then $n = 1643$.　The encryption key e must be relatively prime, i.e., have no factors in common with $(p - 1) \times (q - 1) = 30 \times 52 = 1560$.　We can randomly select e to be 71.　The public key is thus the pair {71, 1643}. The decryption key is:

```
d = 71⁻¹(mod 1560) = 791
```

Remember that the inverse function here is a modulo inverse, which means that

```
71 x 791 = 1 (mod 1560)
```

To encrypt

```
m = 34511228919
```

the message must first be broken into blocks of less than four characters since n has four characters (we must insure that there is a unique value for each block mod n). The corresponding m_i blocks and their encrypted forms would then be

$$m_1 = 345 \qquad c_1 = 345^{71}(\text{mod } 1643) = 190$$
$$m_2 = 112 \qquad c_2 = 112^{71}(\text{mod } 1643) = 196$$
$$m_3 = 289 \qquad c_3 = 289^{71}(\text{mod } 1643) = 81$$
$$m_4 = 19 \qquad c_4 = 19^{71}(\text{mod } 1643) = 475$$

The ciphertext is thus {190 196 81 475}. The process to decrypt the ciphertext as explained before would produce

$$m_1 = 190^{791}(\text{mod } 1643) = 345$$
$$m_2 = 196^{791}(\text{mod } 1643) = 112$$
$$m_3 = 81^{791}(\text{mod } 1643) = 289$$
$$m_4 = 475^{791}(\text{mod } 1643) = 19$$

RSA works because there is no current way known to solve the factorization problem in polynomial time. If there were, then RSA would not be secure. RSA has been tested and considerably researched with no serious flaws found. This does not guarantee its security but rather provides a certain level of trust in it. One known problem with RSA is illustrated below. It has been shown that for every key combination there exists a message such that

$$m^e = m \ (\text{mod } n)$$

which would mean the encrypted message and the original message are equivalent [12.9]. For example, using the values for e and n obtained before, if the message was {159}, the ciphertext would be:

$$c = 159^{71}(\text{mod } 1643) = 159$$

The encryption process returned the same value as the original message, as does the decryption process as is illustrated below:

$$m = 159^{791} (\bmod\ 1643) = 159$$

Another problem with RSA is that it is considerably slower than DES for large quantities of data. Despite these problems, RSA is a *de facto* standard for much of the world. The International Organization of Standards has even selected RSA as the standard to be used for digital signatures.

12.3.5 Digital Signatures

A digital signature is completely analogous to a handwritten signature used for centuries to authenticate documents. The reason that signatures have been used is that, generally speaking, everyone's signature is unique and hard to forge and a document that has been signed would be hard to later repudiate. These same assurances are desirable for computer generated and transmitted documents. We would like to be able to prove that a document sent to us by somebody was indeed sent to us by that individual (authentication) and we would also like to later be able to prove that it had been sent to us by that individual (nonrepudiation). A digital signature is designed to provide these assurances.

One method to implement digital signatures is to use encryption with pairs of known and secret keys and a trusted arbitrator. Two individuals who want to communicate each share a different secret key with the arbitrator. The sender encrypts the message and sends it to the arbitrator who then decrypts it using the key known only to it and the sender. The arbitrator then encrypts the cleartext message with the secret key known only to it and the receiver and sends the new ciphertext on. The receiver can then decrypt the message using its key. Obviously the arbitrator plays a key role and all parties must implicitly trust this third party. There are a number of drawbacks to this approach. First, there is the obvious need for a trusted third party. In addition there is a considerable amount of overhead since each message must be encrypted, decrypted, and transmitted twice. An alternative approach is to instead use a public key system, such as RSA, with senders using their private key to encrypt the message and receivers using the public key to decrypt. Obviously, since only the senders would know their private key, this assures the receiver that the sender did in fact author the message. Often, since encryption takes a considerable amount of time, a sender may not want to encrypt the entire document but rather provide just a signature authentication. Often digital signature algorithms simply encrypt the signature with an additional time stamp and hash value for authentication purposes.

12.3.5.1   The Digital Signature Standard (DSS)

In 1991, NIST proposed that their Digital Signature Algorithm (DSA) be accepted as the Digital Signature Standard (DSS) for the United States [12.6]. This proposal was immediately met with opposition, mostly from proponents of RSA. DSA is a variation of two earlier signature algorithms by Schnorr and ElGamal [12.10]. In DSA the public key is a set of four values $\{p, q, r, t\}$ and the private key is a single value x (for a full description of DSA see [12.6, 12.10]). If the sender wants to provide a signature for a message m, the entire message is not used as part of the signature. Instead, the Secure Hash Algorithm [12.5] is used to create a 160-bit output referred to as the "message digest". If the message is altered, the message digest of this new copy will not match the message digest of the original. Thus, attaching the original message digest provides a comparable level of assurance as attaching the entire message but without the extra overhead. Obviously, since we are talking about a hashing function, two different messages may hash to the same message digest. The 160-bit size of the output, however, makes it computationally unfeasible to find two messages with the same message digest. As was mentioned, DSA has received much criticism, most of which comes from the RSA community. One valid criticism of DSA, however, is that it is slower than RSA. Otherwise, it provides a reasonable level of security for authentication.

12.3.5.2   ESIGN

Another digital signature algorithm is ESIGN. This algorithm is reported to be both faster than RSA and DSA with comparable key and signature lengths, and at an equivalent level of security [12.7, 12.10]. ESIGN uses a pair of large prime numbers, p and q, for its secret key and a public key, n, which is computed to be p^2q. Like DSA, ESIGN uses a hash function, H(m), on the message, m, to provide an equivalent block to the message digest. To compute the signature, the sender first selects a value x such that $x < pq$, and determines w which is the smallest integer that is larger than (H(m) - x^k mod n)/pq [12.10]. The value for k, as recommended by the developers of the algorithm, should be a power of 2 between 8 and 1024. The signature, s, is then calculated as follows [12.10]:

$$s = x + \left(\left(w / kx^{k-1}\right) \bmod \ p\right) pq$$

The receiver can verify this signature by first computing s^k mod n and a, which is the smallest integer that is larger than the number of bits in n divided by 3. The signature is considered authentic if both of the following conditions hold true [12.10]:

$H(m) \le s^k \bmod n$

$s^k \bmod n < H(m) + 2^a$

When ESIGN was first developed, the value for k = 2 and k = 3 was quickly broken. When the current recommended values (a power of 2 greater than 4) have been used, the algorithm has not been broken. In addition, the size of p and q are recommended to be at least 192 bits long which will result in a value of n with at least 576 bits (192 x 3). This seems to provide adequate security for the algorithm.

12.4   Summary

Cryptography is as valuable in today's highly technical society to help secure our communication as it was for the past several thousand years. It entails the disguising of messages so that only the originator and the intended recipient(s) will be able to understand the contents. Two basic techniques used in cryptography are substitutions and transpositions. In substitutions, each character is replaced by another so that the message is obscured. In transpositions, the characters remain the same but their order is changed to accomplish the obscuring. Encryption schemes usually employ some sort of key, known only to the sender and receiver, to describe what substitutions and transpositions to perform.

Modern day algorithms used to encrypt our digital communications use a combination of these techniques. The Data Encryption Standard (DES), for example, uses logical operations such as XORs to change the characters (bits) and at the same time divides the blocks up, shuffling them around and thus transposing their positions. DES suffers from a number of criticisms and many individuals are suspicious of its origins and ability to provide security. Other algorithms, such as IDEA, have been developed which use larger keys to increase the complexity of breaking the scheme.

In public-key algorithms, each individual uses two separate keys. The public key is published openly and is used by those wishing to send a message to the individual whose public key was used. The individual whose public key was used has a second key, known as the private key, which is secret and is used to decrypt the message. Variations of public-key systems are also used to provide digital signatures for authentication and non-repudiation purposes.

12.5   Exercises

12.1   Using Table 12.1, decrypt the following ciphertext, which was encrypted
          using a simple substitution scheme:
                BXFMM SFHVM BUFEN JMJUJ BCFJO HOFDF
                TTBSZ UPUIF TFDVS JUZPG BGSFF TUBUF
                UIFSJ HIUPG UIFQF PQMFU PLFFQ BOECF
                BSBSN TTIBM MOPUC FJOGS JOHFE
          What effect did grouping the letters have on your decryption?

12.2   Given the key SECRET and the following ciphertext:
                YSCZV YGVEV FXSX CUQR
          determine what method was used to encrypt the message and decrypt it.

12.3   Given the following ciphertext

                ASDFGHJKLQWERTYUIOZXCV

          find a key to be used with the Vigenere Table that will yield the following
          plaintext:
                FOUR SCORE AND SEVEN YEARS

          Find a key that, given the same ciphertext, will decrypt to

                MARES EAT OATS AND DOES EAT

          What are the implications, in terms of security, of ciphertext that is no longer
          than the key used to encrypt it?

12.4   An interesting problem, similar to the famous "Dining Philosophers
          Problem" in texts on operating systems, is the "Dining Cryptographers
          Problem" by David Chaum (see "The Dining Cryptographers Problem:
          Unconditional Sender and Recipient Untraceability", *Journal of Cryptology*,
          Vol. 1, No. 1, 1988, pp. 65-75). The problem begins at a restaurant in
          which three cryptographers are dining. The waiter shows up and announces
          that the bill has been paid for, anonymously. The diners talk among
          themselves and the question is raised as to whether it is one of them that is
          paying for the meal or somebody else. Develop an algorithm that will allow

them to determine whether one of the cryptographers paid the bill or if somebody else did. Should the generous individual be one of the cryptographers, the algorithm should not indicate who it is (i.e., the generous cryptographer must remain anonymous). The answer should not involve writing anything down (they would recognize each other's handwriting) nor should it involve a fourth party (you just can't trust somebody else to remain silent).

12.5   A common problem in cryptography is the distribution of keys. Obviously one way to distribute them is to have a courier deliver them by hand. This is expensive and time consuming so an electronic means is much more desirable. How can public-key schemes be used to help solve the key distribution problem?

12.6   Given a knapsack problem with the following collection of weights {14, 27, 32, 41, 57, 61, 74, 91, 107, 118}, which items are actually in the knapsack if its total weight is 254?

12.7   A number of newspapers and periodicals provide a daily crypto problem for their readers enjoyment. The problem generally employs a simple substitution method. Develop a computer program to help an individual solve one of these simple crypto problems. The program should allow the user to make various substitutions, and should provide suggestions, based on letter frequency, when requested.

12.6   References

12.1   Alexander, M., "Controversy Clouds New Clipper Chip", *InfoSecurity News*, July/August 1993, pp. 40-42.

12.2   Diffie, W. and Hellman, M., "New Directions in Cryptography", *IEEE Transactions on Information Theory*, Vol. 22, No. 6, November 1976, pp. 644-654.

12.3   Merkle, R.C. and Hellman, M.E., "Hiding Information and Signatures in Trapdoor Knapsacks", *IEEE Transactions on Information Theory*, Vol. 24, No. 5, September 1978, pp. 525-530.

12.4   National Bureau of Standards, "Data Encryption Standard", *FIPS PUB 46*,
            January 15, 1977.

12.5   National Institute of Standards and Technology, "Secure Hash Standard", *FIPS
            PUB 180*, May 11, 1993.

12.6   National Institute of Standards and Technology, "Digital Signature Standard",
            FIPS PUB 186, May 19, 1994.

12.7   Okamoto, T., "A Fast Signature Scheme Based on Congruential Polynomial
            Operations", *IEEE Transactions on Information Theory*, Vol. 36, No. 1,
            1990, pp. 47-53.

12.8   Rivest, R.C., Shamir, A., and Adelman, L., "A Method for Obtaining
            Digital Signatures and Public-Key Cryptosystems", *Communications of the
            ACM*, Vol. 21, No. 2, February 1978, pp. 120-126.

12.9   Sauder, T. and Ho, C.Y., "An Analysis of Modern Cryptosystems",
            Technical Report CSC-93-11, Department of Computer Science, University
            of Missouri - Rolla, 1993.

12.10   Schneier, B., *Applied Cryptography*, John Wiley & Sons, Inc.,
            New York, New York, 1994.

12.11   Stallings, W., *Network and Internetwork Security Principles and Practice*,
            Prentice Hall, Englewood Cliffs, New Jersey, 1995.

12.7 Extended Bibliography

12.12   Akl, S., "Digital Signatures: A Tutorial Survey", *Computer*, Vol. 16, No.2,
            February 1983.

12.13   Anderson, R. J., "Why Cryptosystems Fail", *Communications of the ACM*,
            Vol. 37, No. 11, November 1994, pp. 32-40.

12.14   Blackburn, S., Murphy, S., and Stern, J., "Weaknesses of a public-key
            cryptosystem based on factorizations of finite groups", *EUROCRYPT 93*,
            May 1993, pp. 50-54.

12.15　　Campbell, C.M., "The Design and Specification of Cryptographic Capabilities", *IEEE Computer Society Magazine*, Vol. 16, No. 6, November 1978, pp. 15-19.

12.16　　Chaum, D., "The Dining Cryptographers Problem: Unconditional Sender and Receiver Untraceability", *Journal of Cryptology*, Vol 1., No. 1, January 1988, pp. 65-75.

12.17　　Coppersmith, D., "The Data Encryption Standard (DES) and Its Strength Against Attacks", *IBM Journal of Research and Development*, Vol. 38, No. 3, May 1994, pp. 243-250.

12.18　　d'Agapeyeff, A., *Codes and Ciphers*, Oxford University Press, New York, New York, 1939.

12.19　　Demillo, R. and Merritt, M., "Protocols for Data Security", *Computer*, Vol. 16, No. 2, February 1983, pp. 39-50.

12.20　　Denning, D., *Cryptography and Data Security*, Addison-Wesley, Reading, Massachusetts, 1982.

12.21　　Denning, D., "The Clipper Encryption System", *American Scientist*, Vol. 81, No. 4, July/August 1993, pp. 319-324.

12.22　　Diffie, W. and Hellman, M.E., "Privacy and Authentication: An Introduction to Cryptography", *Proceedings of the IEEE*, Vol. 67, No. 3, March 1979, pp. 397-427.

12.23　　Fahn, P., "Answers to Frequently Asked Questions about Today's Cryptography", RSA Laboratories, September, 1992, available via anonymous *ftp* at *csrc.nist.gov*, pub/secpub/faq-k.ps.

12.24　　Fisher, S., "Encryption Policy Spurs Concern", *Communications Week*, April 26, 1993, pg. 8.

12.25　　Fisher, S., "Who'll Hold Clipper Keys?", *Communications Week*, September 27, 1993, pp. 35-36.

12.26   Ford, W., *Computer Communications Security*, Prentice Hall, Englewood Cliffs, New Jersey, 1994.

12.27   Gasser, M., *Building A Secure Computer System*, Van Nostrand Reinhold, New York, New York, 1988.

12.28   Glover, D. B., *Secret Ciphers of the 1876 Presidential Election*, Aegean Park Press, Laguna Hills, California, 1991.

12.29   Gong, L., "Authentication, Key Distribution, and Secure Broadcast in Computer Networks Using No Encryption or Decryption", SRI International Report SRI-CSL-94-08, May 1994.

12.30   Hart, G. W., "To Decode Short Cryptograms", *Communications of the ACM*, Vol. 37, No. 9, September 1994.

12.31   Hellman, M.E., "The Mathematics of Public-Key Cryptography", *Scientific American*, Vol. 241, No. 8, August 1979, pp. 146-157.

12.32   Hoffman, L. and Faraz, A., "Cryptography Policy", *Communications of the ACM*, Vol. 37, No. 9, September 1994.

12.33   Landau, S., Kent, S., Brooks, C., Charney, S., Denning, D., Diffie, W., Lauck, A., Miller, D., Neumann, P., and Sobel, D., "Crypto Policy Perspectives", *Communications of the ACM*, Vol. 37, No. 8, August 1994, pp. 115-121.

12.34   Nechvatal, J., Public-Key Cryptography, NIST Special Publication 800-2, April 1991.

12.35   Okamoto, T. and Shiraishi, A., "A Fast Signature Scheme Based on Quadratic Inequalities", *Proceedings of the 1985 Symposium on Security and Privacy*, IEEE, April 1985, pp. 123-132.

12.36   Patterson, W., *Mathematical Cryptology for Computer Scientists and Mathematicians*, Rowman & Littlefield, Pub., Totowa, New Jersey, 1987.

12.37   Schneier, B., "The Blowfish Encryption Algorithm", *Dr. Dobb's Journal*, Vol. 19, No. 4, April 1994, pp. 38-40.

12.38   Schneier, B., "The Cambridge Algorithms Workshop", *Dr. Dobb's Journal*,
         Vol. 19, No. 4, April 1994, pp. 18-24.

12.39   Schneier, B., "The IDEA Encryption Algorithm", *Dr. Dobb's Journal*, Vol.
         18, No. 12, December 1993, pp. 50-56.

12.40   Selmer, E., "From the Memoirs of a Norwegian Cryptologist",
         EUROCRYPT 93, Lofthus, Norway, May 1993, pp. 142-150.

12.41   Simmons, G., "Subliminal Communication is Easy Using the DSA",
         EUROCRYPT 93, Lofthus, Norway, May 1993, pp. 218-232.

12.42   Simmons, G. J., "Cryptanalysis and Protocol Failures", *Communications of
         the ACM*, Vol 37, No. 11, November 1994, pp. 56-65.

12.43   Smith, L. D., *Cryptography: The Science of Secret Writing*, W.W. Norton
         & Company, Inc., New York, New York, 1943.

12.44   Smith, P., "Cryptography Without Exponentiation", *Dr. Dobb's Journal*,
         Vol. 19, No. 4, April 1994, pp. 26-30.

12.45   Stallings, W., "SHA: The Secure Hash Algorithm", *Dr. Dobb's Journal*,
         Vol. 19, No. 4, April 1994, pp. 32-34.

12.46   Stinson, D. R., *Cryptography: Theory and Practice*, CRC Press, Boca
         Raton, Florida, 1995.

12.47   Tsudik, G. and Van Herreweghen, E., "On Simple and Secure Key
         Distribution", IBM Research Report RZ 2512 (#82820), September 1993.

13

MALICIOUS CODE

It's March 14, 11:55 PM. A group of business partners are putting the finishing touches on an important presentation. After celebrating the completion of their efforts they identify a previously unnoticed typo. At 12:05 AM they turn the computer back on only to be greeted with a message saying "Beware the Ides of March" — their project was deleted by a computer virus.

Computer viruses are just one example of what is commonly referred to as *malicious code*, or *malicious programs*. Malicious programs are created to perform a series of harmful actions on a computer system. Examples of some actions include file deletion, file corruption, and data theft. These programs often remain dormant and hidden until an activation event occurs. Examples of activation events are program execution and specific access dates, such as March 15 or Friday the 13th. When the predetermined activation event occurs, the malicious program begins its task. In the example above, this task was the deletion of all files in the computer system.

As mentioned above, this type of malicious behavior is not limited to computer viruses. Other types of malicious programs are worms and Trojan Horses. The difference between each of these programs is primarily seen in how they are introduced, or *infect*, a computer system. This chapter discusses viruses, worms, and Trojan Horses; and further explores their differences and similarities.

13.1   Viruses

One of the more well known types of malicious code are viruses. Named after their biological counterparts, viruses are segments of code that attach themselves to existing programs and perform some predetermined actions when the host program is executed. These actions include both further infection and modification of a system. The additional modification most often takes the form of a malicious action such as file alteration or disk erasure. For these actions to take place, the virus code must be activated. As viruses are not stand alone programs, they require a host application or operating system for activation. Once activated, they search the local computer system for other programs to infect. It should be noted that viruses only infect executable programs and not data as a virus requires a means of activation which a data file cannot provide.

13.1.1   Infection

Before infection from a virus can become wide spread, a virus must first be created, and then introduced to a system. The creation of a virus is easily accomplished by any person familiar with the target operating system [13.3]. Depending on the operating system, this may require a knowledge of program execution techniques, file system management and storage, and operating system-program interaction and communications [13.8, 13.9]. Once created, the author must determine a means of spreading the newly created virus.

For a computer system to become infected with a virus, it must come into contact with a carrier of the virus. Contact can come from many possible locations. For example, a co-worker can bring an infected disk from home, or a student can bring home a disk that was infected at a school lab. Obviously, any communal computing environment is prone to infection. The possibly large number of uncontrolled users, many of whom are careless, promotes the infection and spread of a computer virus. For these environments to become infected, however, the virus must be introduced to the system.

For a virus to have a wide spread effect on the computing community, the virus must be strategically placed. It must be placed in a location that is guaranteed to be accessed by numerous people — preferably a location that will promote world wide distribution. Some very popular locations to place applications that are infected with the virus are public and private computer bulletin boards, on-line computer services, and file repositories (i.e., public *FTP* sites) [13.3]. On occasion, authors have been able to place their viruses in commercially available programs before they were shipped for sale to the public [13.7]. Thus, when the new program was installed by the user, they became infected. An otherwise isolated system would then become infected without the computer operator either knowing or considering the system susceptible to infection. Viruses are not limited to placement on officially licensed software. Not surprisingly, viruses are often found on software that has been pirated — illegally copied without permission by the publisher [13.7]. As many pirated copies of software packages, particularly games, are easily found and widely distributed, they make excellent programs to infect [13.3].

After a system, or program, is infected, it becomes a carrier that can infect other systems. To do this, an uninfected system must come into contact with the infected system, or program. This is accomplished by executing an infected program while the uninfected system is on-line. Thus, a user can take an infected program from one location and infect another system by executing the program at a second location. In situations where the media carries a copy operating system, simply accessing the media will result in infection. One such system is the Disk Operating System employed by the Apple 2 series of computers. These particular systems initialized a disk with operating system information that was executed whenever the disk was accessed. Thus, simply requesting a listing of a disk's contents would result in the execution of a disk-stored operating system program, and infection of the system. It was therefore possible to install viruses that would do something as simple as initialize a disk after a specific number of accesses.

13.1.2   Theory behind Viruses

To better understand what a virus can do, it is helpful to understand how a virus performs its task. Figure 13.1 has been provided for this purpose. Figure 13.1 contains a flowchart describing the actions of a virus. Each action identified in the figure is numerically labeled for explanatory purpose only. The order in which these actions are to be performed is indicated both pictorially, in Figure 13.1, and in the discussion that follows. While the order of these actions may vary slightly with each virus, the general process remains unchanged — perform an undesirable task and infect other programs and operating systems.

For this discussion two terms are defined: virus activation and virus execution. Virus activation will refer to the initiation of the virus. Virus execution, however, will refer to the initiation of the portion of the virus that performs the possibly harmful activity, the code not directly concerned with infecting a system. Thus, virus execution must be preceded by activation, but activation may not necessarily lead to execution.

Once an infected program is executed or an infected operating system performs a task, the virus is activated. The virus will first determine whether it should be activated. In the event that it should not be executed, it will attempt to locate and identify other susceptible programs, disks, or systems. Any such item will then be infected. After determining that all susceptible items carry a copy of the virus, the virus will stop and allow normal computations to proceed. If the virus meets all of its internal conditions to execute, it will do so. Upon completion of execution, the virus may either reset its conditions or remove itself. After the virus has adjusted its execution conditions, it will complete and allow normal computation to continue. With the assistance of Figure 13.1, the steps involved in this process are discussed on the following pages.

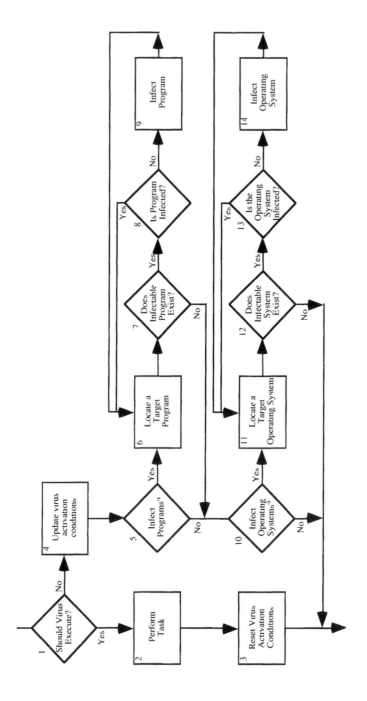

Figure 13.1. Flowchart showing the actions of a virus program.

Step 1: Following activation, the virus will determine if it should execute — if it should carry out its primary purpose. This purpose will be defined by the author of the virus however, it is usually file or disk erasure. If the necessary conditions exist for the virus to execute, it will do so and proceed to Step 2. If the necessary conditions do not exist, the virus will not execute, but rather adjust the conditions that lead to execution as described in Step 4. This would occur, for example, if the virus were to execute on a certain date or after a certain number of disk accesses.

Step 2: After determining that it should begin execution, the virus will proceed to carry out its primary purpose. As previously mentioned, this may be disk erasure or file modification. Other possible activities include temporarily displaying a message or picture, or transmitting information to a networked computer. Once the activity has been completed, the activation conditions of the virus will need to be changed.

Step 3: Once the virus has executed, it may need to rest itself for future execution. If the program or disk was not erased and the virus still exists, it may reset the conditions that initiate its execution. In some cases, the virus may remove itself. After the virus has either reset its execution conditions or removed itself, the virus stops and normal execution begins.

Step 4: As the virus cannot execute, it will update its execution conditions so that future execution will be possible. Examples of information that may be updated are access counts or the number of days since the item was infected. This will depend upon the author's desired effect.

Step 5: After the virus execution conditions are updated in Step 4, the virus will attempt to infect other items. If the virus infects other programs, it will attempt to locate a vulnerable target program (Step 6). If the virus does not effect programs, but rather operating systems, it will proceed to Step 10.

Steps 6 and 7: The virus will attempt to locate a potentially vulnerable program in the system. When a vulnerable program is identified, it is examined to determine if it is already infected (Step 8).

Step 8: After a program has been identified as being vulnerable, it must be examined for an existing virus. This is accomplished by looking for a unique identifier in the program. The identifier is selected by the author as some word or value that will only exist if the program is infected. If the identifier is found, the virus assumes the program is infected and will search for another program to infect (Step 6). In the event that the program is not infected, the virus attaches itself to the program so that it will be activated when the program is started (Step 9).

Step 9: Viruses infect programs by attaching themselves to the target program and inserting a command that executes the virus. Simple viruses append their code to the end of the program and insert a command at the very beginning of the program that causes the computer to execute the code. For those familiar with assembly language, this would be a command akin to the jump-to-subroutine command. As the presence of a virus can be detected by an unexplained increase in a program's size, the more intelligent viruses attempt to replace unused parts of a program with the virus code. Thus, the length of the program does not change and the program still becomes infected. This requires a significant understanding of system architecture and program design. In addition to the virus code, a virus identifier must be installed. In many cases, these are one in the same. Some virus authors, however, prefer to use a separate unique identifier to ensure the accuracy of testing for a virus's presence. This is also useful for the advanced virus whose specific location in a program is not quickly identifiable. Following the installation of the code and identifier, the virus will look for another program to infect (Step 6).

Step 10: This step is much like Step 5. If the virus infects operating systems, it will proceed to determine if any available operating system, or fragment thereof, is infected. If the virus only infects programs, the virus will halt its operation and allow the system to continue its operations.

Steps 11 and 12: As the virus infects operating systems, it will attempt to locate a susceptible operating system. In many environments, the complete operating system is not infected; rather, portions of the operating system are infected. For example, the previously mentioned Apple 2 virus only infected the operating system's file manager. In addition, some computers provide the ability to have more than one operating system on-line: one active system and multiple backup, or alternate, systems. These alternate systems may also be vulnerable to a virus. Thus, a virus may search for multiple operating systems to infect. Once the virus finds a susceptible operating system, it must determine if it has already been infected (Step 13).

Step 13: After an operating system has been identified as being susceptible, the virus will examine it for an existing virus. Like the activity of a virus in Step 8, the virus will look for identifiers that the operating system has already been infected. In the event that the operating system has already been infected, the virus will search for another system to infect (Step 10).

Step 14: Immediately proceeding the identification of an uninfected operating system, the virus will place a copy of itself within the system. The exact location will depend on the author's objectives of distributing the virus. It may attach itself to the file management routines, the user authentication routines, or possibly the system accounting routines. In addition to attaching the virus code and patching the existing files to activate the code, an additional virus identifier may be added to mark the presence of the identifier. This will be used to identify the existence of the virus so that infected systems are not continuously reinfected. As will be discussed below, this can also increase the chance of the virus being found and removed.

The exact steps that a virus undertakes to infect and harm a system will vary with both the author's intentions and capabilities. Nonetheless, the general algorithm presented above provides an accurate representation of the activity of a virus. Understanding the concepts employed by this algorithm will assist in understanding the general concepts associated with viruses as well as the actions that should be taken to detect, prevent, and remove a virus.

13.1.3 Prevention, Detection, and Removal

The prevalence of malicious code such as viruses requires user and system administrators to both protect against becoming infected and to quickly remove any virus that enters the system. Many software products have recently been released to detect, prevent, and remove viruses. These packages, however, are not enough. Because virus detection and prevention often relies on another user's confrontation and identification of a virus, it is possible that existing detection and prevention mechanisms will not identify new viruses. Furthermore, removal is often performed in response to the known presence of a virus thus, the virus may have already caused unrecoverable damage. Additional action is therefore required to better protect a system and reduce the need for virus removal. In the event that virus eradication and system recovery are required, steps should be taken to prevent future infection.

13.1.3.1   Prevention and Detection

The first step in protecting a system from a virus is preventing infection. As infection can come from many places, a comprehensive set of protective policies should be established and adhered to. These policies should indicate the acceptable sources of software, a list of programs acceptable for use, and a list of actions to perform in the event the presence of a virus is suspected. Some widely accepted policies are listed in Table 13.1 [13.5, 13.6].

These techniques will go far in preventing viruses from infecting a system. This is often not enough, however, as viruses are often unknowingly introduced into a system. For example, a co-worker could unknowingly bring a virus into work that their child brought home from school. In this type of situation, quick detection of a virus is the best means of reducing the possibility of harm or damage. Detection is accomplished using any one or more of the following four techniques: (1) identifying symptoms, (2) checksum verification, (3) access monitors, and (4) virus signature identification [13.3, 13.6]. A fifth detection technique would be identifying the aftermath of a virus; hopefully, this technique will rarely be employed.

The first means of suspecting or detecting a virus will most likely be through identifying symptoms of viral infection — for example, slower processing, a change in the system time, or altered file attributes. Many viruses make their presence known by exhibiting at least one of these side effects. One of the more common side effects is an increase in the actual size of a program [13.3]. Some of the more knowledgeable virus authors are aware of these, and other, symptoms and program as to avoid them. They are able to write code that does not modify the length of a program, does not negatively impact processing speed, and does not cause excessive disk accesses. Preventing these types of symptoms, however, will not keep a knowledgeable and perceptive user from detecting a virus's presence.

If a user suspects a virus has infected the system, but no single symptom seems to confirm this, a commercial virus detection program may provide some assistance. These programs will scan the system and search for known viruses. In most cases, this will be

Table 13.1 Suggested virus prevention policies

- Use only sealed software that is purchased from a reputable vendor.
- Make backup copies of all new software before they are used, and possibly infected.
- Purchase and use programs that actively search for viruses and remove them.
- Use checksum programs that can be used to identify changes to programs.
- Keep logs of all software that is installed and used in the system.
- Avoid programs that come from untrustworthy sources such as computer bulletin boards or other on-line services.
- Always test new software for viruses before they are used or installed.
- Educate users about the danger of viruses and how to prevent infection.
- Do not use or install illegally copied software.

sufficient to identify the presence of a well-documented virus. As not all viruses are well documented and known to these programs, a new virus may go unnoticed. To prevent this, a user can employ checksum calculating programs. These programs examine a program and calculate a hash value, or checksum. When compared to a checksum taken from the program at installation, this value should match. In the event that the two checksum values do not match, the program has been modified. If modification has not been authorized, this may indicate that the file has been infected.

The third technique often used in detecting viruses is access monitors. Access monitors are programs that examine all disk access looking for suspicious behavior. Suspicious behavior includes modification to normally unaltered system files of programs. This process is improved when the access patterns of known viruses are used in identifying malicious behavior. These patterns are unnecessary, however, as the undesired modifications will still be identified by the monitor. In addition to identifying the unwanted accesses, most monitors inform the user of the activity and prevent it from completing. This is quite useful as the user is able to identify both the presence and location of a virus, and then prevent the infection before it can harm the system.

The fourth method of identifying the presence of viruses is to search for the virus identifiers used to indicate that a program or operating system has been infected. Recall that these signatures are selected by a virus author to uniquely identify a virus's presence.

This fact can also be used in the detection of a virus. Once a virus identifier has been uniquely distinguished, it can be used to positively identify the presence of a virus. This process may be made generic by examining files for code sequences that would indicate the presence of a possibly unknown virus. These sequences might include disk accesses file or directory searches. Clearly, these types of activities are not unique to viruses. Thus, they may provide little assistance in identifying a virus. Furthermore, both the generic search as well as the specific signature search are often slow processes that cannot be performed as a background task. This does not invalidate their value, however, as they are very accurate in identifying the presence of known viruses.

13.1.3.2   Disinfection

Once the presence of a virus has been confirmed, the entire system must be disinfected; the virus must be removed. Disinfection does not just mean that a new copy of an infected program should be installed; other infected files will simply reinfect the program. Proper virus removal should include a comprehensive virus search and removal of both on-line media (i.e., hard drives) and removable media such as floppy disks and backup tapes. Examination of all on-line media at one time will work to ensure that the virus is completely removed from the system. Examination of all removable and backup media will prevent a user from reinfecting an otherwise uninfected system and beginning the infection process anew. Many commercially available programs assist in the detection and removal process. It is suggested that these programs be used to remove viruses as they will be able to both locate every copy of the virus, and completely remove any trace of the virus [13.9]. Furthermore, a virus may be too well imbedded into a program or operating system for manual removal to be either complete or accurate.

Automated virus removal programs will scan all programs and operating systems for virus signatures or other virus identifying code. Once found, these programs modify the virus carrier by removing the virus code and activation statements. Upon completion of this process all known viruses will be removed from the system. Great care must be taken during this process so as not to reinfect the programs or systems. It is not unusual for people to perform the disinfection process with an infected disinfection program. While all traces of the virus will appear to have been found and removed, the disinfection program will reinfect the system. This can be prevented by storing the disinfection program in an isolated, write-protected environment such as a floppy disk.

Commercially available disinfectant programs are not the only means of removing a virus. Another, more drastic, method is to completely erase all media and reinstall the system software and programs from their originals. This method is time consuming and often impractical or impossible. Furthermore, if the replacement software is also infected, reinfection is almost certain. Before this process begins, all data files should be backed up. As the data files cannot support a virus, concern of recontamination from them is unnecessary.

13.2   Worms

A worm is very much like a virus in that it replicates itself and attacks a system with the potential to do irrecoverable damage. Unlike a virus, a worm is a stand-alone program that infects a computer system and infects other computers only through network connections [13.1, 13.5]. Once a worm infects a system, it actively seeks out connections to other computers and copies itself onto these systems. In addition to propagating from computer system to computer system, worms often perform malicious action. This malicious activity is not limited to just deletion of files. Since the computers are connected via a computer network, the worm can communicate information back to the author regarding such things as user passwords, network service information, and even proprietary research or information. Furthermore, a worm may be able to completely disrupt normal operations on a computer, thus causing a denial of service attack. This often occurs when a worm does not check a system to see if it has already been infected and multiple worm programs execute on one computer system. To understand how this could happen, it is useful to know how a worm infects a system.

13.2.1   Infection

Before a system can become infected with a worm, the worm must be created. Unlike creating a virus, creating a worm is a more difficult task. For a worm to properly function, the author must be knowledgeable with communication protocols, network system vulnerabilities, and operating system details such as file locations, file contents, and file manipulation [13.3, 13.5]. Once a worm has been created and tested, it can be released.

For an operating system to become infected, a worm must either be initially released into the computer, or have migrated over a computer network [13.5]. While these are the only methods of infection, the many possible network sources of a worm make them difficult to fend off. One means of preventing infection is to identify and control any security vulnerabilities or holes in a system. This too is difficult, as many administrators are not aware of security vulnerabilities until they have been exploited. Because many of these security deficiencies involve either easily determined user passwords or uncontrolled network services worms are capable of easily infecting a system [13.1].

Once a worm has gained access to a single system, it is quite easy to gain access to other systems. By taking advantage of trusted host lists (e.g., UNIX .rhosts files), a worm would be capable of quickly infecting numerous systems without painstakingly searching for a system's security holes. In the event that trusted host lists are unavailable, many worms will attempt to penetrate a system by guessing user passwords [13.1]. Previous experience has demonstrated the high success rate of guessing passwords [13.2, 13.7]. When both password guessing and trusted host accessing fails, a worm may attempt to exploit (widely) known security holes. This technique requires a worm's author to be very familiar with the inner-workings of a computer's network services; a programmer must understand both how network services work and how they may be exploited to install a worm. An example of one such incident where this knowledge was used is the widely known Internet Worm.[1] Details about how this and other system penetration methods are used in distributing a worm are discussed below.

13.2.2   Theory of Worms

The process a worm undergoes when infecting and attacking a system is identified in Figure 13.2. The flowchart in Figure 13.2 lists the logical actions a worm takes to achieve its goals. Again, the numeric labels attached to each step of the process do not indicate the order in which the steps are undertaken; they are provided only as a means of providing detailed descriptions.

> **Step 1**:   Following the introduction of the worm to a computer system, the worm will first determine if the system is already infected. In the event that the worm currently resides in the system, the new worm should terminate. Note that this stage is for a worm installation that does not occur through network communication channels. This step will be performed for all initial placement of the worm by a user as opposed to a networked computer system. Before a worm is installed by network communication means, Step 5 will ensure that a duplicate virus is not installed.

> **Step 2**:   Once a worm has determined that the system in question is not infected, the worm will install a permanent copy of itself. A worm is a stand alone program; it does not need to attach itself to another program. After the worm has copied itself into the system, it will begin its execution (Step 3). To reduce the chance of the worm being noticed and removed, it may attempt to hide its presence by masquerading as a system task.

---

[1] This incident is discussed in detail in Chapter 15.

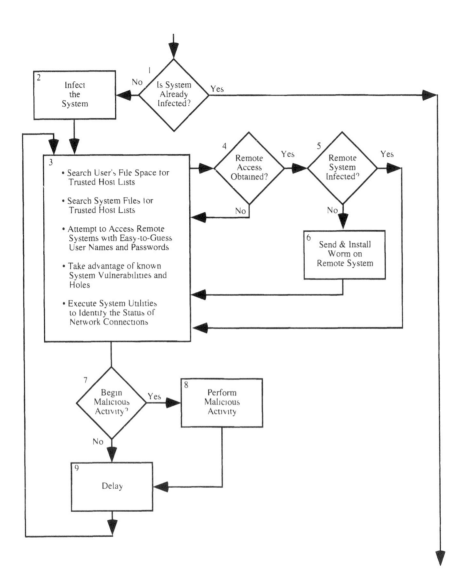

Figure 13.2. A flowchart identifying the actions a worm undertakes.

Step 3: When the task is firmly installed into the system, it will begin its attempt at compromising other computer systems. One method worms use to enter and infect other systems is to exploit files that allow users to enter other systems without authentication (e.g., the UNIX .rhosts file). These files allow worms, as well as users, to enter other systems without being challenged for further identification. A second method of gaining access to remote systems is by guessing user passwords. As many users have passwords that are easy to guess, this can often provide the necessary means to enter a system. This is also effective because many administrators do not remove, or otherwise secure, system default passwords, thus allowing anyone to gain administrative privileges. A third means of gaining access to another system is by exploiting known security holes. One well known worm, for example, exploited holes in a computer's network services that allowed the worm to execute programs on the remote system. In a similar manner, some poorly administered systems provide utilities that outright allow remote systems to execute programs. Regardless of how a worm is capable of executing programs on remote systems, the end result will be the installation of the worm.

Step 4: Once a system and means of attack have been selected, the worm will begin its attack on the system. If the worm is unsuccessful at accessing the system, it will select another means of attack (Step 3). In the event the worm is successful, it will attempt to determine if the newly accessed system is already infected (Step 5).

Step 5: After a worm gains access to another computer system, it will attempt to ascertain whether the system is already infected. If the system is not infected, it will install itself on the system (Step 6). If the system was previously infected, the worm will attempt to gain access to another system (Step 3). In the event that the worm infects the remote system before determining if it was previously infected, multiple copies of the worm will infect the system. This will eventually lead to a denial of service attack as the system will be too busy supporting the worms to perform its normal operations.[2] Clearly, this will be noticeable to the system's users and administrators.

Step 6: Upon determining that a system has not been infected, the worm will send itself to the remote system and then install itself. Once the worm is installed it will begin to seek out additional systems to infect (Step 3). The installation process will be similar to that described in Step 2 — the worm will attempt to conceal its presence by

---

[2] This mistake led the Internet community to identify the presence of the Internet Worm (see Chapter 15).

masquerading as a system program and then begin its attack on other systems.

Step 7: After a given number of access attempts (as selected by the worm's author) the worm will determine if it should perform its intended action. This action may be performed immediately after a worm has gained access to a system, after a certain event occurs, or possibly after a specific amount of time has elapsed. Again, the exact triggering conditions will be programmed by the worm's author. For example, if the author desires the worm to steal user passwords, it may be programmed to wait until a certain number of passwords are captured before it sends them to the author. If the worm's purpose is to display a New Year's greeting, the worm may be programmed to activate on January 1.

Step 8: Not every worm has a malicious goal or purpose. Those that do, however, will want to perform that activity. Possible activities include stealing user passwords, stealing proprietary information, displaying a simple message, erasing files, or bringing a computer system to a halt. The final action in this step may be for the worm to remove itself. For example, a worm programmed to display a New Year's message may be programmed to remove itself on January 2. If this is the case, the worm may terminate its processing and no longer attempt to infect other systems.

Step 9: A worm that continuously processes will raise suspicion among system administrators and users. To reduce its chances of being noticed, a worm may periodically become dormant and delay its operations. After it has completed its sleep cycle, it will continue to search for susceptible systems (Step 3).

The exact execution steps that a worm will follow may vary slightly from those described above. Regardless of the minor differences that may exist, the means by which an infection is prevented and a worm is removed will be similar. This similarity stems from the fact that a worm's communications channels, regardless of their format, must be closed.

13.2.3   Prevention and Removal

After the presence of a worm has been detected in a system, the administrator will work to remove it. This can be a difficult endeavor as the worm may be successfully reinstalled by a neighboring computer.

13.2.3.1   Preventing Worm Attacks

Preventing the infection of a computer system from worms is similar to protecting a system from an intruder. Both types of attacks attempt to exploit the same system vulnerabilities to gain access. The primary difference between the two types of attacks is the deterministic methodology employed by a worm. As a worm can only perform the actions selected by its author, in the manner in which they are programmed, its modus operandi is unlikely to change. Knowing the methods employed by a worm, as well as the vulnerabilities the worm attempts to exploit, an administrator can protect a system from infection. Furthermore, this information will be required when worm eradication is performed.

As with intrusion prevention, methods such as firewalls and access control can significantly reduce the means by which a worm can enter a system. Two additional steps an administrator can take towards preventing infection are: (1) periodic examination of user account passwords to ensure their strength under attack, and (2) disallowing the use of system files that grant trusted remote access without the proper authentication. Additional protection mechanisms that are similar, if not identical, to those used on a site-by-site basis for intrusion prevention should also be employed to prevent infection.

13.2.3.2   Worm Removal and System Recovery

Worm removal is a difficult task. Neighboring computer systems will immediately work to reinfect a clean, or uninfected, system. There are three possible techniques for preventing a system from becoming reinfected: simultaneous wide-spread removal, system isolation, and infection prevention coupled with local worm removal. Each of these techniques will allow a worm to be removed from a system without being reinfected; however, the viability, advantages, and disadvantages of each technique vary greatly.

The first technique, simultaneous wide-spread removal, is the process of removing the worm from every system at approximately the same time. The times at which each copy of the worm is removed do not need to be exact; it needs only to be close enough to prevent a worm on one system from completing a processing cycle and successfully accessing and infecting another system. In a small network, such as a network with ten computers, this may be possible. When a network has a larger number of computers or is attached to a larger network, this process is no longer viable. Because the removal activity of a smaller network can be more greatly controlled, every system can be cleaned simultaneously. Larger networks, such as the Internet, do not provide this type of control. If just one infected computer on the network is not cleaned at the same time as the others, the worm will reinfect the network. In the event it were possible to clean every system at the same time, network propagation delays would work against this process and the system may still remain infected. Simply cleansing every infected computer simultaneously is not a reasonable solution for every computing environment.

The second technique for preventing reinfection is system isolation. By either physically or logically separating a system from a larger network, the isolated system may be easier to cleanse without reinfection. This solution has received much debate [13.2, 13.4]. Some researchers argue that isolation will allow a site to cleanse itself without fear of reinfection. They further suggest that this will prevent a local worm from infecting other systems [13.4]. Other analyses of this technique indicate that remaining attached to other networks provides significant advantages. Isolation may prevent the timely exchange of security information and patches. Furthermore, systems that isolate themselves and act as a mail relay for other systems will delay the timely flow of information to the other system.

The third, and most successful, technique in preventing reinfection is to apply local worm removal methods. That is, patch all of the holes exploited by a worm and then remove any existing copies. Because the worm will be unable to utilize any previously identified security holes, it will have to either use another security hole or not fail to propagate. As a worm's actions are limited to only those included by the author, there will be a point at which every security hole utilized by a worm will be patched. Once this occurs, the worm can be removed without fear of reinfection. This process may require administrators to remove some of the functionality of their system or lock accounts with easily guessed passwords. These actions, however, are both temporary and easily worked around.

13.3 Trojan Horses

Trojan Horse programs were named because of their functional similarity to the mythical horse of Troy. Trojan Horse programs are advertised to perform one function while, in fact, they perform a different function. This alternate, or secondary, function usually performs a covert action such as stealing user passwords. While the secondary function always executes in some manner, the advertised functionality may not necessarily exist. For example, a program may be advertised as the greatest game ever, but merely erase a disk and halt. Trojan Horse programs that wish to function in a concealed manner, however, will perform their advertised task so as not to arouse suspicion. A common example of this is a system's user login program that not only authenticates users, but records a user's plain text password for use in future, unauthorized access.

As will become increasingly obvious throughout this section, Trojan Horses are very similar to viruses; both infect programs or operating systems; both hide their presence behind another program; both hide their activity behind another program. This similarity has often caused confusion concerning the relationship between Trojan Horses and viruses and the appropriate classification of malicious code [13.6, 13.8]. While the two are similar, their differences are significant. The differences between Trojan Horses and viruses are twofold: (1) Trojan Horses actively advertise an alternate functionality to bait the unsuspecting user, and (2) viruses attempt to attach themselves to multiply to existing programs. These differences are enough to warrant somewhat different approaches to detection, prevention, and recovery.

13.3.1 Receiving Trojan Horses

The means by which a Trojan Horse can enter a system are not as great as that of either worms or viruses. As Trojan Horses are neither self-replicating nor self-propagating, user assistance is required for infection. This occurs by users installing and executing programs that are infected with a Trojan Horse. These programs may come from many possible locations. Three popular locations for programs infected with Trojan Horses are bulletin board systems, public access file servers, and computer labs such as those found at universities [13.6]. These locations are often used because they provide a great opportunity for wide spread release of a Trojan Horse. Furthermore, the files found on these systems — public domain, shareware, and possibly pirated software — come with little or no guaranty of any sort. That is, the downloader or user of this software does so at their own risk.

The placement of Trojan Horses in public domain software, shareware, or pirated software is very strategic. These types of software are popular to the public as they are available for little or no money, albeit some illegal. Regardless of their legality, this popularity makes them excellent candidates for achieving the desired effect of wide spread distribution. The additional benefit of using public domain software or shareware is that the Trojan Horse can be interwoven directly into a program as opposed to being added to an existing program. The perceived benefit of infecting pirated software is that it may reach the many unethical users who traffic pirated software. Attaching a Trojan Horse to pirated software, however, is different from adding it to incomplete versions of public domain software or shareware. The Trojan Horse, like its virus counterpart, must first be appended to a host program, then marked for execution by the host. This is not necessarily difficult to implement; rather, the changes may be easily observed by a user.

After a Trojan Horse has infected a system, it will remain dormant until it is activated. Upon activation, a Trojan Horse will perform its programmed task. As previously mentioned this task can be as trivial as adding bogus files to a system, or as severe as stealing passwords or erasing data. Trojan Horses do not, however, replicate themselves and infect other programs — this type of program would be a virus.

13.3.2　Theory of Trojan Horses

The similarity between Trojan Horses and viruses will again be noticeable when comparing the algorithms of the two. The Trojan Horse algorithm depicted in Figure 13.3 is nearly identical to the algorithm for viruses in Figure 13.1. The key difference between the two is that Trojan Horses do not perform the steps that lead to infecting other programs or systems.

Like a virus, once a Trojan Horse infected program is executed or an infected operating system performs a task the Trojan Horse is activated. The Trojan Horse will first determine whether it should be activated. If the Trojan Horse meets all of its internal conditions to execute, it will do so. Following completion of the task, the Trojan Horse may either reset its conditions or remove itself. After the Trojan Horse has adjusted its execution conditions, it will complete and allow normal computation to continue. With the assistance of Figure 13.3, the steps involved in this process are detailed below.

Step 1: Upon activation, the Trojan Horse will determine if it should execute — if it should carry out its primary purpose. This purpose will be defined by the author of the Trojan Horse. If the necessary conditions exist for execution, the Trojan Horse will do so and proceed to Step 2. If the necessary conditions do not exist, the Trojan Horse will not execute, but rather adjust the conditions that lead to execution as described in Step 4.

Step 2: Upon determining that it should begin execution, the Trojan Horse will proceed to carry out its primary task. This is often unauthorized password or file theft. Once the activity has completed, the activation conditions of the Trojan Horse may need to be changed.

Step 3: Once the Trojan Horse has executed, it may need to reset itself for future execution. After the Trojan Horse has reset its execution conditions, the Trojan Horse stops and normal program execution begins.

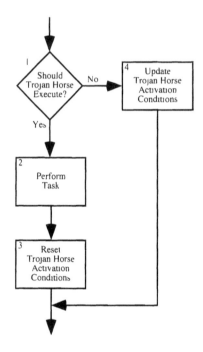

Figure 13.3. A flowchart identifying the actions a Trojan Horse undertakes.

Step 4: As the Trojan Horse does not meet the necessary conditions to execute, it will only update its execution conditions for future execution. Examples of information that may be updated are access counts or the date a file or password was last stolen. Again, like viruses, this will depend upon the author's desired effect.

The precise execution steps of any given Trojan Horse will most likely vary from those presented here. This variation, however, will be minimal and the general algorithm presented above accurately represents the activity of a Trojan Horse. Furthermore, this difference will not effect the means by which a Trojan Horse is detected and removed.

13.3.3   Prevention, Detection, and Removal

Unlike viruses or worms, the prevention and detection of Trojan Horses can be largely accomplished by educating the users. Because Trojan Horses neither propagate nor replicate, they must come from programs that a user introduces to a system. If the users can be educated to carefully screen and examine programs before they are used, the introduction of a Trojan Horse can be severely reduced. Not every Trojan Horse, however, will be identified before it has entered a system. Simple methods do exist to reduce this threat and eventually lead to the removal of a Trojan Horse [13.6].

13.3.3.1   Trojan Horse Prevention and Detection

As with virus prevention, Trojan Horse prevention can be largely accomplished by enforcing a strict software installation policy and educating users. By preventing users from installing untrusted and unauthorized software, the possibility of infection is greatly reduced. By installing only new and original copies of commercially available software, the paths of Trojan Horse infection are blocked. As it is difficult to control every system user and prevent them from installing unauthorized software, users must also be educated in the dangers of Trojan Horses. Because users often underestimate the possibility of infection and dangers that come with Trojan Horses, they ignore security policies. Education should reduce this problem and prevent users from carelessly installing software. In the event education does little to stem the installation of unauthorized software, prevention can be enforced through hardware means.

One hardware means of preventing Trojan Horses, or any other infection, is through the use of read-only storage devices such as ROM drives. While this is a severe response to the problem of unauthorized software installation, it does prevent infection. Unfortunately, this process may result in an increase in the amount of administrative assistance required to maintain a system. That is, any authorized modification of the system may require construction of a new ROM tape or medium.

As infection prevention is not always successful, Trojan Horse detection techniques should be prepared and used. Three techniques available to detect Trojan Horses are observation, checksums, and audit trail analysis. Observation, the most commonly used technique, is performed by administrators in an informal manner. That is, many administrators do not actively search for Trojan Horses; rather, daily system use, modification, and examination are used to detect Trojan Horses. As observation is not the most scientific or exacting means of detecting Trojan Horses, other methods such as checksums and audit trails must be used.

Checksums can be used to detect the presence of Trojan Horses by providing a means of file comparison. When checksum values of suspicious programs are compared to the checksum values of the program in an unmolested state, Trojan Horses, or any other modification to a program, can be detected. That is, if the two checksum values are in agreement, a Trojan Horse has not infected the program. If the checksums do not agree, the file has been modified and should be replaced with a new copy. As current checksum technology severely reduces the possibility that a file has been modified and has the old checksum values, this can be considered a reliable means of Trojan Horse detection. An issue of concern, however, is the availability and trust of the original file checksums. In the event that these checksums are either unavailable or possibly modified by an intruder or Trojan Horse, they cannot be trusted.   Because the checksum values cannot be trusted, the checksum comparison process is of little value.   The next best means of detecting the presence of a Trojan Horse is by examining audit trails.

As was discussed in previous chapters, audit trails can be used to identify the activity taken by intruders and possibly Trojan Horses.   Under most circumstances, a Trojan Horse's activity will not be recorded by the audit trails.   If, however, the trails do identify the unusual activities of a Trojan Horse, the presence of a Trojan Horse can be detected.   This will require a detailed analysis of the audit trails to identify the program infected with a Trojan Horse.   Assuming this process locates the Trojan Horse, the Trojan Horse can be removed.   Because the audit trails may not be detailed enough to identify the infected program, a security administrator may not be able to locate the Trojan Horse.   If the presence of a Trojan Horse is suspected, but it cannot be located, an administrator will have to either rely on observation and checksums or laboriously search for the infected file.

13.3.3.2   Trojan Horse Removal

Removal of Trojan Horses is much like removal of viruses.   Trojan Horse removal, however, is easier as viruses propagate, thus necessitating extensive system examination and eradication.   The first step of the Trojan Horse removal process is locating the Trojan Horse.   That is, the detection mechanisms employed by the system must have not only identified the presence of a Trojan Horse, but located it as well.   In the event that the presence of a Trojan Horse has been confirmed, but its location is unknown, system administrators will have to track it down.   One of the easiest ways to accomplish this is with the use of checksum comparisons.   This, of course, requires the availability of trusted checksum values for the unmolested system.   In the event that checksum comparison is not possible and the infected program cannot be identified, complete system restoration may be required.   Assuming that an infected program can be identified, removal simply requires replacing the file with an unaltered, trusted copy of the program.   This replacement, however, should not be the primary concern of an administrator.   Of greater importance is the ramifications of the activation of the Trojan Horse.   For example, removing a Trojan Horse that captures user passwords is important.   Responding to the fact that numerous accounts have been compromised, however, is of greater importance.   Thus, future system security relies upon determining the Trojan Horse's actions before it is completely removed.   After an administrator has determined the purpose of a Trojan Horse, damage response can, and should, begin.   Chapter 8 provides insight into the possible responses an administrator can perform.

13.4 Summary

Programs that intentionally modify or destroy system and user files are called malicious programs, or malicious code. Three examples of malicious code are viruses, worms, and Trojan Horses. The programs propagate from one computer system to another by either attaching themselves to executable programs that are copied onto another system or by migrating over a computer network. Once inside a computer system they corrupt data, erase files, or record sensitive information for use by their author.

The probability of being victimized by malicious code can be largely reduced through the enforcement of a software installation policy and by user education. The software installation policy should indicate the means by which a user can install software into a system. This policy should also dictate the acceptable sources for software packages and how software should be examined and tested before it is permanently installed. User education will also assist in preventing attack as informed users will understand the ramifications of installing malicious code.

In addition to a software installation policy and user education, specialized tools are available to prevent and detect the presence of malicious code. These programs periodically examine systems and files for the signs of malicious code and report their findings to a system administrator. This is often not enough to completely obstruct an attack. Thus, administrators must attempt to remove the offending code. After the program has been removed, its actions and intentions should be identified so that the necessary actions can be taken to nullify its effects.

13.5 Exercises

13.1   What would be the motivation for an individual to write malicious code?

13.2   In addition to erasing or changing files, what activities may a virus perform?

13.3   A possible means of preventing viral infection is to install the unique virus identifiers throughout the system without installing the associated virus. What are the advantages and disadvantages of this technique? Is this a technique that could be widely used?

13.4   Some researchers have proposed the use of a benevolent worm — a worm that performs a desirable activity. How could a benevolent worm be used? Is this a dangerous proposition? Why, or why not?

13.5   Assuming that an individual decides to write malicious code, what
            characteristics should be evaluated when choosing to author either a virus,
            worm, or Trojan Horse?

13.6   References

13.1   Curry, D., *UNIX System Security*, Addison-Wesley Publishing Co.,
            Reading, Massachusetts, 1992.

13.2   Eichin, M. W. and Rochlis, J. A., "With Microscope and Tweezers: An
            Analysis of the Internet Virus of November 1988", *Massachusetts Institute
            of Technology Technical Report*, Massachusetts Institute of Technology,
            February 1989.

13.3   Fites, P., Johnston, P., and Kratz, M., *The Computer Virus Crisis*, Van
            Nostrand Reinhold, New York, New York, 1989.

13.4   Garfinkel, S. and Spafford, G., *Practical UNIX Security*, O'Reilly &
            Associates Inc., Sebastopol, California, 1992.

13.5   Russell, D. and Gangemi Sr., G. T., *Computer Security Basics*, O'Reilly &
            Associates Inc., Sebastopol, California, 1991.

13.6   Shaffer, S. L. and Simon, A. R., *Network Security*, Academic Press, Inc.,
            Cambridge Massachusetts, 1994.

13.7   Stallings, W., *Network and Internetwork Security: Principles and
            Practices*, Prentice Hall, Englewood Cliffs, New Jersey, 1995.

13.8   Stubb, B. and Hoffman, L. J., "Mapping the Virus Battlefield: An Overview
            of Personal Computer Vulnerabilities to Virus Attack", *Institute for
            Information Science and Technology Report GWU-IIST-89-23*, George
            Washington University, August 1989.

13.9   Wack, J. P. and Carnahan, L. J., "Computer Viruses and Related Threats: A
            Management Guide", *NIST Special Publication 500-166*, National Institute
            of Standards and Technology, August 1989.

13.7   Extended Bibliography

13.10   Foster, E., "Virus Stories Can Sell Papers But May Contain a Trojan
            Horse", *InfoWorld*, International Data Group Publishers, Vol. 12, No. 14,
            April 2, 1990, p. 41.

13.11   Gibson, S., "Computer Viruses Follow Clever Paths to Evade Detection",
            InfoWorld, International Data Group, Vol. 13, No. 8, February 18, 1991, p.
            28.

13.12   Robertson, W., "The Best Defense Against Viruses May Be Sheer Luck",
            Network World, International Data Group, Vol. 7, No. 34, August 13,
            1990, p. 28.

13.13   Stephenson, P., "A Reality Check on Virus Vulnerability", *Lan Times*, Vol.
            5, No. 6, March 22, 1993, p. 57.

13.14   Stoll, C., "An Epidemology of Viruses & Network Worms", *Proceedings of
            the 12th Annual National Computer Security Conference*, Baltimore,
            Maryland, October 1989, pp. 369-377.

14

GOVERNMENT-BASED SECURITY STANDARDS

Several governments have established their own computer security standards in an attempt to attain a consistently high level of computer security. These standards identify the security criteria that a software or hardware product must follow in order to be considered for use by the various governmental departments. The requirements are used to determine the security classification that is assigned to each product. This classification is based upon the security features implemented in a product and is used in the selection of adopted products. Naturally, each government can be expected to have their own security needs and therefore their own security standards. Until a universal criteria is released, this will be true; there are at least three major standards developed and used by seven governments. These standards are: the United State's Department of Defense Trusted Computer System Evaluation Criteria (TCSEC), the Communications Security Establishment's (formerly known as the Canadian System Security Centre) Canadian Trusted Computer Product Evaluation Criteria (CTCPEC), and the joint France, Germany, Netherlands, and United Kingdom Information Technology Security Evaluation Criteria (ITSEC). There are less formal standards that are employed by other governments. Some of these standards, however, have become outdated and replaced with one of the aforementioned standards, thus reducing the number of existing standards to a small handful.

In an effort to further reduce the number of existing security standards, a single unified standard is being developed. This standard is called the Common Criteria (CC). The CC encompasses all of the requirements of the previous standards without invalidating the security classifications of existing products. The CC, as well as each of the standards that are going into the creation of the CC, is discussed below. Before this discussion is presented, however, a brief history of the various standards is in order. Figure 14.1 provides a pictorial summation of the relationships, in both time and content, of the standards.

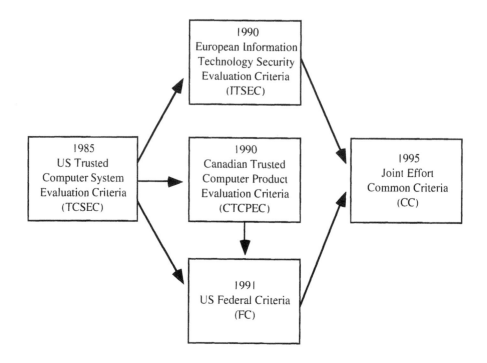

Figure 14.1. The evolution of security criteria.

14.1 The History of Security Standards

The United States Defense Science Board published a report in 1970 containing technical recommendations on reducing the threat of compromise of classified information processed on remote-access computer systems |14.8|. Work stemming from this report led to the creation of the Department of Defense's first computer security standard, the Trusted Computer System Evaluation Criteria (TCSEC). This criteria was first published in December 1985 in accordance with DoD Directive 5200.28, "Security Requirements for Automatic Data Processing (ADP) Systems" |14.8|. The purpose of this document was to provide technical security criteria and evaluation methodologies for the support of an ADP system security policy. The value of this policy was not only seen in the United States, but overseas as well.

In 1990, a group of four governments from France, Germany, the Netherlands, and the United Kingdom gathered to create the first draft of the Information Technology Security Evaluation Criteria (ITSEC). The ITSEC builds upon concepts in the TCSEC but approaches some issues in a different manner. While differences do exist between the ITSEC and the TCSEC, approximate security classification equivalencies can be made. The comparison is not exact, however, as these differences are sufficient enough to require a product to be re-evaluated with the TCSEC. More details regarding these differences are provided in the ITSEC discussion below.

Like the ITSEC, the Canadian Trusted Computer Product Evaluation Criteria (CTCPEC) also has its beginnings rooted in the TCSEC. Unlike the TCSEC, its fundamental premise is the separation of functionality and assurance. This has not, however, greatly affected the CTCPEC's intentionally close relationship with the TCSEC. This relationship has enabled much of the evaluation and classifications to be somewhat similar. A direct result of this harmonization was the updating of the TCSEC with the Federal Criteria; a joint venture in the computer security standardization process.

In February 1991, six years after the original introduction of the TCSEC, the Federal Criteria (FC) was released [14.1, 14.11]. The FC builds upon the TCSEC by recognizing and addressing new technology such as operating environments that include multi-window capable workstations [14.1]. These updates were made with the Communications Security Establishment in an attempt to promote international harmonization in the development and use of security criteria. Its great success instigated a joint venture which included the authors of the ITSEC as well as the CTCPEC. The result of these efforts is known as the Common Criteria.

14.2 The Trusted Computer System Evaluation Criteria

The criteria defined in the TCSEC primarily concern trusted commercially available automated data processing (ADP) systems [14.8]. The criteria state the minimal required security features and assurance measures associated with each of the various security classifications. The feature requirements are intended for information processing systems that rely upon general purpose operating systems. The security feature requirements, however, can also be applied to systems with special environments, such as communications processors or process control computers. Unlike the feature requirements, the assurance requirements are applicable to all types of computing systems and environments.

The purpose of these requirements, and the criteria itself, are threefold [14.8]: (1) to provide a security standard for manufacturers, (2) to provide the Department of Defense (DoD) with a security metric to evaluate the degree of trust that can be placed on a system, and (3) to provide a basis for specifying security requirements in product specifications.

The first purpose, to provide a security standard for manufacturers, is intended to give manufacturers the necessary information to implement security features in their existing or planned products. This enables manufacturers to know and meet the security needs of the DoD before a product is released and classified. This also reduces any confusion associated with the evaluation criteria and process as the standards are specifically detailed in advance of product evaluations.

The second purpose, to provide the DoD with a security metric for the evaluation process, allows the DoD to fairly and accurately evaluate any two products by the same standards. This reduces any question that may arise concerning the process. Evaluations must be defined for both systems as there is more than one type: those that are computing environment independent and those that are environment specific. The evaluation of a product for an environment independent system is performed by the National Security Center by means of the Commercial Product Evaluation Process [14.8]. Evaluation of a product's trust and security attributes in terms of a specific operating environment is known as a certification evaluation. It should be noted that this process is only an evaluation, not an accreditation. Once a product has been evaluated and given a security classification, it must still be accredited for use in the handling of any classified information.

The third purpose, to provide a basis for specifying security requirements in product specifications, concerns the customer's determination of the security level required for a given situation. That is, the customer must evaluate their environment and determine the minimal security classification an employed product must attain. This forces customers, usually groups within the DoD, to evaluate their system and maintain their current level of security.

The criteria from which these purposes were based are divided into four divisions: A, B, C, and D; the highest, or most comprehensive security division, is A; the lowest is D. Each division represents a major difference in a product's confidence rating. Within each of these divisions are numbered subdivisions called *classes*. These classes provide a more granular rating of products in each division. The classification of a product into one of these divisions and classes is based upon four criteria: (1) security policy, (2) accountability, (3) assurance, and (4) documentation [14.8]. While the classification process is quite detailed and relies upon many characteristics, a general description of each division and class is provided in Table 14.1 [14.8].

The TCSEC includes the detailed requirements for meeting each of the possible security classifications as well as the rationale and guidelines for its use. This includes information concerning the first three security criteria (the security policy, accountability, and assurance), a rationale for the division of the classes, information about covert channels, and guidelines for security testing. Further supporting information and rationale are provided in the DoD's Rainbow series — a series of documents with multicolored covers that contain detailed explanations and background information for the TCSEC.

Table 14.1 TCSEC security classification criteria descriptions

Security Classification	General Criteria Description
D	This classification is for those systems that have been evaluated and failed to meet the requirements of the A through C classifications.
C1	This classification indicates that a product provides need to know (discretionary) protection. This is accomplished with a separation of users and data.
C2	Products with this classification provide a more granular access control than those in C1. This is accomplished with login procedures, audit trails, and resource isolation.
B1	In addition to requiring the C2 features, this classification requires data labeling, mandatory access control over named subjects and objects, and an informal statement of the security policy model.
B2	This protection builds upon B1 by requiring a formal declaration of the security policy, and a more encompassing discretionary and mandatory access control enforcement. Authentication mechanisms must be strengthened for this classification. Covert channels are also addressed in this classification. In general, a B2 system is relatively resistant to unauthorized access.
B3	This classification begins with the B2 requirements and adds that all user actions be mediated, the system be tamperproof, and the security features be extremely robust and streamline. No additional code or information should be included in the security package. The system must also provide administrator support, auditing, and backup and recovery procedures. In general, a B3 system must be highly resistant to unauthorized access.
A1	A1 classification is functionally equivalent to B3. The A1, however, has gone thorough a more formal analysis that was derived from a formal design and verification of the security features. This analysis must provide a high level of assurance that the system is correctly implemented.

14.3 The Information Technology Security Evaluation Criteria

The ITSEC was created in an attempt to consolidate the many European security evaluation methodologies of information technology products. The ITSEC was a joint security standardization effort that intended to address the needs of both commercial and governmental security products. This standardization is intended as a super-set of the TCSEC, with ratings mappable to those of the TCSEC [14.7].

To achieve the super-set status, the ITSEC separates the concepts of security functionality and functionality assessment. Each product is given at least two ratings, one (or more) that indicates the implemented security functionality and one that indicates the correctness of the implementation.

The functionality criteria are measured on a rating scale from Fl to Fl0, with Fl being the lowest rating [14.2, 14.7]. An ITSEC rating of Fl roughly corresponds to a TCSEC rating of Cl, with each successive rating of the ITSEC corresponding to the successive ratings in the TCSEC. The F6 through F10 functionality ratings add the following concepts: data and program integrity (F6), system availability (F7), data communication integrity (F8), data communication confidentiality (F9), and network security including confidentiality and integrity (F10) [14.7]. Each of these ratings are appropriately given to a product in addition to a base rating of Fl through F5. For example, a product may be functionally rated at Fl, F4, and F5. The detailed requirements to receive a given functionality rating are provided in the formal ITSEC standards.

The correctness criteria are used to evaluate the level of assurance to which a product has been tested. An assurance rating corresponds to the amount and type of correctness testing a product has received. The ratings, from lowest to highest, are: testing (El), configuration control and controlled distribution (E2), access to detailed design and source code (E3), extensive vulnerability analysis (E4), demonstrable correspondence between design and source code (E5), and formal models and descriptions with formal correspondences between the two (E6). These assurance ratings are cumulative. That is, a product with an E3 correctness evaluation has also passed an El and E2 evaluation.

Table 14.2 Mappings of ITSEC classifications to TCSEC classifications

| ITSEC Classifications | | TCSEC |
Functional	Assurance	Classifications
	E0	D
Fl	E2	Cl
F2	E2	C2
F3	E3	Bl
F4	E4	B2
F5	E5	B3
F5	E6	Al

The two ratings, functionality and assurance, compose an ITSEC security classification that can be roughly mapped to a TCSEC classification. This mapping is provided in Table 14.2. Because the TCSEC classifications do not provide any direct correspondence to the ITSEC's F6-F10 classifications, they are not included in the mapping table. It should also be noted that these mapping are not bi-directional. Because of the additional granularity in security classifications resulting from the separation of functionality and assurance, a TCSEC security classification does not uniquely map to a ITSEC classification.

The existence of the mappings in Table 14.2 does not mean that the TCSEC evaluation process can be bypassed. It is simply a means of approximating the associated classification. The approximated classification, however, should be easily attained through the proper TCSEC evaluation process.

14.4   The Canadian Trusted Computer Product Evaluation Criteria

In May 1989, the Canadian System Security Centre (now known as the Communications Security Establishment) released the CTCPEC in response to the Canadian Treasury Board's Government Security Policy [14.3]. Like the other security evaluation metrics, the CTCPEC evaluates the effectiveness of a product's security services. This criteria was designed for governmental use without the intention of providing a direction of growth for commercial products. Because the criteria provide information concerning the Canadian government's evaluation process, however, it is still of value to a developer.

The CTCPEC metric, like the ITSEC, divides the security requirements into two groups: functional requirements and assurance requirements [14.3]. The functionality requirements are further divided into four policy categories: (1) confidentiality, (2) integrity, (3) availability, and (4) accountability. Each category consists of security requirements that should prevent specific system threats. Each security requirement is further divided into a pre-defined set of rating levels that indicate a product's effective security. These ratings range from zero to five — in most cases, only four — where zero indicates a failure to meet a requirement. These functional requirements and the associate rating levels are listed in Table 14.3.

The functional security requirements listed in Table 14.3 are not necessarily independent of each other [14.3, 14.4]. That is, some requirement ratings are dependent upon other requirement ratings. This was intentionally planned and included in the design of the CTCPEC as the proper implementation of many security features requires the presence of other security features. For example, a product that successfully meets the requirements of a CD-1 rating must first have met the WI-1 requirements. Additional constraints are made more apparent in the CTCPEC document.

Table 14.3 The CTCPEC functional requirements and their rating ranges

Accountability	Range	Availability	Range
Audit	WA-0 to WA-5	Containment	AC-0 to AC-3
Identification and Authentication	WI-0 to WI-3	Fault Tolerance	AF-0 to AF-2
Trusted Path	WT-0 to WT-3	Robustness	AR-0 to AR-3
		Recovery	AY-0 to AY-3

Confidentiality	Range	Integrity	Range
Covert Channels	CC-0 to CC-3	Domain Integrity	IB-0 to IB-2
Discretionary Confidentiality	CD-0 to CD-4	Discretionary Integrity	ID-0 to ID-4
Mandatory Confidentiality	CM-0 to CM-4	Mandatory Integrity	IM-0 to IM-4
Object Reuse	CR-0 to CR-1	Physical Integrity	IP-0 to IP-4
		Rollback	IR-0 to IR-2
		Separation of Duties	IS-0 to IS-3
		Self Testing	IT-0 to IT-3

The second part of the evaluation process is the evaluation of a product's assurance requirements. A product will receive an assurance rating, from a low of T-0 to a high of T-7, based upon meeting the assurance requirements dictated in the CTCPEC. These assurance requirements within the CTCPEC concern the following: architecture requirements, development environment requirements, development evidence requirements, operational environment requirements, documentation requirements, and testing requirements [14.3]. These requirements dictate how a product is to be designed, how a product is to be prepared for evaluation, how a product is to be provided to a customer, and how a developer is to indicate that a product's trust has been sufficiently tested. The assurance rating resulting from this evaluation, in addition to a functional rating, completes a product's security rating.

Like the ITSEC rating, the CTCPEC ratings can be mapped to equivalent TCSEC ratings. Approximate TCSEC equivalencies are indicated in Table 14.4 [14.3, 14.6]. Because of the more granular ratings of the CTCPEC, this mapping is neither exact nor bi-directional.

Table 14.4 Mapping a CTCPEC rating onto a TCSEC rating

CTCPEC rating	TCSEC rating
WA-1, WI-1, CD-2, CR-1, ID-1, IS-1, IT-1	C2
WA-1, WI-1, CD-2, CM-2, CR-1, ID-1 or IM-1, IS-1, IT-1	B1
WA-1, WI-1, WT-1, CC-1, CD-2, CM-3, CR-1, ID-1 or IM-1, IS-2, IT-1	B2
WA-2, WI-1, WT-2, AY-1, CC-1, CD-3, CM-3, CR-1, ID-1 or IM-1, IS-2, IT-1	B3

14.5 The Federal Criteria

The Federal Criteria for Information Technology (FC) was created in an attempt to update the TCSEC [14.9]. The original goal of the Federal Criteria was to create a U.S. national security standard that protects the existing investment in security technology, improves the existing security evaluation process, plans for the changing needs of the customer, and promotes international harmonization in security evaluation. The FC is generally considered to be a successful improvement to the TCSEC; however, it is not without faults [14.9, 14.10]. After several modifications since its initial release in December 1992, the FC has been adopted by the security community and initiated efforts to create the Common Criteria.

The FC addresses its goals with the introduction of a protection profile. A protection profile is a set of criteria that define a specific level of security and trust for a given product. This allows new profiles to be created as technology progresses and the security community's needs change. Profiles are stored in a central location, a registry, so that developers, evaluators, and consumers can easily obtain new profiles that are guaranteed to be accurate and up to date. A profile consists of a functional component, a development assurance component, and an evaluation component. The functional component identified the features that a product must support to meet the profile. Possible functional components include features like auditing, access controls, and trusted paths. As the design of the FC is highly dependent upon both the TCSEC and the

CTCPEC, the functionality discussed in each of these criteria was included in the various FC profiles. The development assurance components dictate the degree to which a product must support its design, control, and use. This is similar to the assurance controls used in the CTCPEC. The evaluation assurance components of a profile are the assurance measures a product has undergone to verify the trust and security it claims to provide. Some evaluation assurance components include such items as security testing and covert channel analysis. This separation of evaluation assurance and development assurance is similar to the T-level provided by the CTCPEC, but the inclusion of evaluator assurance is more closely related to the ITSEC. Unfortunately, the increased combinations of possible assurances have resulted in numerous similar profiles. This has resulted in overly complicating the evaluation and rating process.

While the rating process is difficult, it is possible to create a rough mapping of the FC's assurance ratings to those of the TCSEC and the CTCPEC. Not surprisingly, they are quite similar to the T-levels of the CTCPEC. Table 14.5 shows this relationship.

Table 14.5 Approximate assurance rating mapping of
the TCSEC, FC, CTCPEC, and the ITSEC

TCSEC	FC	CTCPEC	ITSEC
D			E0
C1			E1
C2	T-1	T-1	E2
B1	T-2	T-2	E3
	T-3	T-3	
	T-4		
B2	T-5	T-4	E4
B3	T-6	T-5	E5
A1	T-7	T-6	E6
		T-7	

The attempt to harmonize the trust evaluation process between the TCSEC and the CTCPEC produced what many consider to be an improved, but flawed criteria. The greatest benefit of this collaboration is not the resulting FC, but rather the decision to begin the collaboration process anew with input from the creators of the European ITSEC. This collaboration resulted in the creation of the CC.

14.6 The Common Criteria

The CC is an attempt to combine the many existing security criteria into a unified standard [14.5]. This process began in 1993 and, as of May 1995, was still early in the developmental stages. The first version of the CC is intended to be released for review by 1996. Wide acceptance of the CC will depend largely on the various security organization's evaluation of the final product. As most of these organizations are involved with the design of the criteria, this process should be a relatively quick process.

The current draft version of the CC incorporates many of the design features of the FC and the ITSEC [14.5]. The CC borrows its concept of protection profiles from the FC. Additionally, the CC's trust evaluation process separates the examination and rating of a product's functionality and assurance, as do both the FC and the ITSEC. As the concept of building upon the ideas found in the other criteria was fundamental to the design of the CC, additional similarities exist.

Table 14.6 The functional classes of the Common Criteria

Functional Class Name	Number of Family Members
Communication (FPE)	2
Identification and Authorization (FIA)	10
Privacy (FPR)	4
Protection of the Trusted Security Functions (FPT)	14
Resource Allocation (FRU)	3
Security Audit (FAU)	10
TOE Entry (FTE)	9
Trusted Path (FTP)	3
User Data Protection (FDP)	13

The CC also builds upon the functional ratings found in the other criteria, not necessarily by creating new functional trust attributes, but rather by combining many of the attributes of each of the existing criteria and extrapolating the rest. The end result of this process was the development of a hierarchical set of functional requirements. Similar functional requirements are separated into groups called *classes*. Each of nine different functional classes addresses a particular functional concept such as privacy or auditing. These classes are listed in Table 14.6 [14.5]. Within each class are the more specific functional requirement groups called families. For example, the privacy class has four families: unobservability, anonymity, pseudonymity, and unlinkablity. The 9 functional classes of the CC contain a total of 63 families. Within each of the families is a varying number of functional requirements. The number of functional requirements in a family depends upon what is termed a "necessary requirement". In addition to its constituent families, a class has information regarding its purpose and use. This information is provided at this level, as well as at each larger requirement grouping, to assist users in the application of the requirements. The assurance requirements of the CC are presented in a hierarchical structure similar to that of the functional requirement. The CC defines 7 assurance classes, each of which are further divided into a total of 29 assurance requirement families. Table 14.7 lists the assurance requirement classes of the CC [14.5]. Like functional requirements, the number of assurance requirements depends on what the criteria's creators identify as necessary. The design of the assurance classes and families also mimics the functional classes with the inclusion of supporting documentation.

Table 14.7 The assurance classes of the Common Criteria

Assurance Class Name	Number of Family Members
Configuration Management (ACM)	3
Delivery and Operation (ADO)	2
Development (ADV)	10
Guidance Documents (AGD)	2
Life Cycle Support (ALC)	4
Tests (ATE)	4
Vulnerability Measures (AVA)	4

Once the assurance requirements of a product are identified, an assurance rating can be assigned to the product. The CC identifies eight assurance levels, AL0 through AL7, AL0 being the lowest. These ratings are based upon the amount of assurance testing each of a product's features has undergone. That is, a product must meet a minimum assurance requirement in several areas to receive a given assurance rating. As can be expected, users of the CC will wish to map its rating system to that of the CTCPEC, ITSEC, FC, and TCSEC. Predicting this, the authors of the CC provide a comprehensive mapping of each of the 63 functional requirements to an appropriate rating in each of the CTCPEC, ITSEC, FC, and TCSEC.

While the assurance and functional requirements have been defined, as of May 1995, much of the 700+ page CC has yet to be completed. Because the criteria are still in a preliminary draft stage, many of the concepts are not complete and will therefore continue to change and evolve until the first formal release. Until then, many of the questions stemming from the CC will have to go unanswered.

14.7 Summary

Security standards such as the TCSEC were created with the intent of ensuring that trusted products achieve a measurably high degree of security. This has become increasingly necessary as organizations, such as a government, require products that can be trusted to maintain and secure confidential information. In response to this need, the CTCPEC, the ITSEC, and the FC as well as the TCSEC were created for the evaluation process. The various standards identify a definition of acceptable levels of security and trusted computer systems. The difficulty with evaluating a product with any one of these established security standards is that the potential customer may not acknowledge the same set of standards as the developer. In an attempt to reduce this possibility, the international security community has created the Common Criteria: a set of security evaluation standards that enforce a globally accepted level of trust. The long term success of the CC will not only depend on how it is accepted by developers, evaluators, and authors, but on its ability to adapt to an ever maturing technology.

14.8 Exercises

14.1 How does reducing the number of security standards affect a developer's burden in creating new trusted security products?

14.2 What are the negative impacts of combining the many existing trusted computer evaluation criteria into a single criteria?

14.3 In what respects do each of the CTCPEC, TCSEC, and ITSEC provide a more complete form of trusted product evaluation?

14.9 References

14.1 Bacic, E. M., "The Canadian Criteria, Version 3.0 & the U.S. Federal Criteria, Version 1.0", *Proceedings of the Fifth Annual Canadian Computer Security Symposium*, Ottawa, Canada, 1993, pp. 537-548.

14.2   Brouwer, A. Casey P., Herson, D., Pacault, J., Taal, F., and Van Essen, U., "Harmonized Criteria for the Security Evaluation of IT Systems and Product", *Proceedings of the 13th National Computer Security Conference*, Washington, DC, October 1990, pp. 394-403.

14.3   Canadian System Security Centre, *The Canadian Trusted Computer Product Evaluation Criteria*, Version 3.0e, January 1993.

14.4   Cohen, A. and Britton, K., "Comparison of CTCPEC and TCSEC Rated Products", *Proceedings of the Sixth Annual Canadian Computer Security Symposium*, Ottawa, Canada, 1994, pp. 457-469.

14.5   Common Criteria Evaluation Board-94/080, *Common Criteria for Information Technology Security Evaluation*, Version .9, October 1994.

14.6   Gibson, V. and Fowler, J., "Evolving Criteria for Evaluation: The Challenge for the International Integrator of The 90s", *Proceedings of the 15th National Computer Security Conference*, Baltimore, Maryland, October 1992, pp. 144-152.

14.7   Information Technology Security Evaluation Criteria, *Harmonized Criteria of France, Germany, the Netherlands, and the United Kingdom*, Draft Version 1, May 1990.

14.8   National Computer Security Center, *Department of Defense Trusted Computer System Evaluation Criteria*, DoD 5200.28-STD, December 1985.

14.9   National Institute of Standards and Technology and the National Security Agency, *Federal Criteria for Information Technology Security*, Vol. 1 and 2, December 1992.

14.10   Neumann, P. G., "Rainbows and Arrows: How the Security Criteria Address Computer Misuse", *Proceedings of the 13th National Computer Security Conference*, Washington, DC, October 1990, pp. 414-422.

14.11   Schwartau, W., "Orange Book II: The New Federal Criteria", *InfoSecurity News*, MTS Training Institute Press, Framingham, Massachusetts, Vol. 4, No. 4, July/August 1993, pg. 74.

14.10 Extended Bibliography

14.12　　　Branstad, M. A., Brewer, D., Jahl, C., Pfleeger, C. P. and Kurth, H.,
　　　　　　"Apparent Differences between the U.S. TCSEC and the European ITSEC",
　　　　　　Proceedings of the 14th National Computer Security Conference,
　　　　　　Washington, DC, October 1991, pp. 45-58.

14.13　　　Cohen, A., "Modeling the Government of Canada Security Policy",
　　　　　　Communications Security Establishment Technical Report, Ottawa, Canada,
　　　　　　May 1994.

14.14　　　Straw, J., "The Draft Federal Criteria and the ITSEC: Progress Toward
　　　　　　Alignment", *Proceedings of the 16th National Computer Security
　　　　　　Conference*, Baltimore, Maryland, October 1993, pp. 311-323.

15

CASE STUDIES

To better illustrate which computer system capabilities need protection, three specific system incidents are discussed. Each of the three incidents addresses a different aspect of computer security. The incidents are (1) the Hannover Hackers, (2) the Internet worm, and (3) an Evening with Berferd. The first incident, the Hannover Hackers, provides two valuable pieces of information: (1) intrusive activity has grown to global proportions, and (2) system vulnerability often results from uninformed or apathetic system administrators. The second incident, the Internet Worm, provides insight into the operations of a worm. This incident also shows that sophisticated techniques are not necessary for implementing and deploying wide spread system attacks. The third incident concerns a virtual jail that was created for the purposes of restricting and observing an intruder's actions. This was done with the intent to gain insight into the techniques employed by intruders.

It should be noted that this discussion is not intended to be a how-to guide. It is provided with the intent that the knowledge gained by learning and understanding previous system attacks will be useful in preventing future attacks.

15.1 The Hannover Hackers

It all started with a 75 cent accounting discrepancy.[†] Clifford Stoll was tasked with tracking down a computer accounting error at the Lawrence Berkeley Laboratory (LBL) computer facility — an unclassified research center at the University of California, Berkeley. This discrepancy was tracked to a new computer account that did not have the required billing information. LBL's initial belief that this was the work of an intruder was confirmed when the National Computer Security Center informed LBL that someone

---

[†] The following account is based on Cliff Stoll's recount of the incident in [15.12].

from their lab had attempted to break into the system. Even though the offending account was removed, unusual system activity made it clear that the intruder still had access to the system.

Unbeknownst to Stoll, LBL, and the other victims, the hacker had been using simple techniques to obtain access to the various systems. His methods focused on guessing passwords and taking advantage of holes in both the *sendmail*[1] and *emacs*[2] programs. Password guessing was most successful at gaining access to default accounts that were shipped with the system but never changed. Once an account was compromised, the attacker gained system administrator, or root,[3] capabilities by means of the *sendmail* and *emacs* holes.

Once inside a computer system, the intruder would hide his presence by appearing as an authorized user or root. The intruder would then search for interesting data and attack other systems by examining files for the presence of specific words or phrases. The process started with the disabling of audit trails that record a user's actions. The hacker would then plant a Trojan Horse[4] program to capture passwords. The hacker's next course of action would be to attack other systems. Successful attacks were made to at least eight U.S. military sites during the period in which the intruder had access to the LBL system. A more detailed picture of the intruder's means of access is provided in Figure 15.1.

In an attempt to both catch the intruder and learn more about the intruder's techniques and interests, LBL decided to track and observe him. Whenever the intruder logged into the system, LBL began to trace and record the line. This required special modifications to be made so that the intruder's presence would be immediately detected and recorded. Line printers and personal pagers were therefore connected to the system. The line printers recorded all network communications with the intruder and the modem called the pagers when the intruder logged on. These tools became very important for four reasons. First, unlike software, the hardware could neither be modified nor detected

---

[1] The *sendmail* program implements the SMTP protocol (see footnote 13). The DEBUG problems that exist in the SMTP protocol exist in the sendmail program as well. This security hole allows a user to execute commands on a remote computer system.

[2] The Gnu *emacs* editor is a widely used versatile text editing program. Its versatile design includes, among other things, its own mail system. The mail capability is shipped with portions operating with superuser privileges. This can be used to change file ownership and move files into reserved system areas as well as other user's directories.

[3]*Root*, or superuser, is the system administrator's account. This account has complete control over all aspects of the computer system [15.6].

[4] A *Trojan Horse* is a program that appears to perform one task, but either performs a different task or second task. The second task performs unwanted actions and often goes unnoticed until complete damage recovery is near impossible (see Chapter 13).

by the intruder. Second, detailed lists of other compromised sites and accounts were kept so that the appropriate security administrator could be informed. Third, the operators could immediately respond to the intruder's presence at any hour of the day. Fourth, the detailed activity logs would help to predict and react to the intruder actions. For the benefits of using these tools to be realized, however, the intruder would have to keep coming back. This, of course, was not a concern.

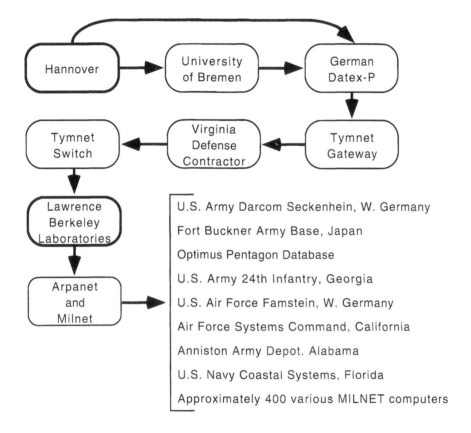

Figure 15.1. The Hannover Hacker's system access route and destinations.

As expected, the intruder returned many times. Unfortunately, he only remained connected for short periods of time approximately two minutes each time. Nonetheless, the intruder was traced to a TYMNET[5] port in Oakland, California. With the proper

---

[5] The *TYMNET* computer communications network was originally established for time sharing purposes. Since its inception in 1971, it has evolved from providing only service throughout the United States into a world wide network with connections to Europe and the Canadian Datapac network.

authorizations, the intruder was then traced from Oakland to a dial-up modem at a Virginia defense contractor. Close inspection of the contractor's phone records indicated that the intruder had been accessing the contractor's system months before he was detected at LBL. The contractor responded by restricting access to their system. While this did stop the intruder from accessing the contractor's connection, he was still able to exploit other access routes to LBL and his other victims. This did not matter, however, as the intruder's new route to LBL was then traced back to Hannover, Germany.

While the tracing enabled Stoll and the authorities to determine the city of origin, they could not be more precise. The brevity of the attacker's connections prevented the telephone companies from tracking his location any further. The German telephone company required establishment of a long connection so that they could check the older mechanical switches[6] that route phone calls. To achieve this, Stoll's group created volumes of fictitious data that would appeal to the hacker. Their hope was that the information would seem valuable enough to warrant a long connection. The data, therefore, contained key words that suggested that the information was about the U.S. Government's Strategic Defense Initiative (SDI). As hoped, the volumes of fake memos, personal e-mail, mailing lists, contact points, and general research was too much for the hacker to resist. The hacker spent over one hour skimming and gathering data. During this time, a trace was established back to the hacker's home. Shortly thereafter, the hacker and four others were arrested on charges related to the intrusions.

The German Government charged the five men involved with espionage — specifically, selling information to the Soviet KGB. The primary hacker and two other defendants were to each receive a maximum of two years in prison and fines up to $12,000. One of the remaining defendants cooperated with the state in exchange for immunity. The fifth defendant was found dead of mysterious causes before the trial began.

---

[6] Before small computers were implemented to automatically route telephone calls, large mechanical *switches* were used. Since there were no electronic means of determining the routing established by a telephone call connection, a person would have to manually locate the proper bank of switches and decipher the caller's phone number.

15.2 An Evening With Berferd

With the history of phone phreaks[7] attacking the American Telephone and Telegraph Company (AT&T), it should come as little surprise that the AT&T Bell Laboratories takes both phone and computer security seriously. In an attempt to reduce the number of incidents, they installed a secure Internet gateway and reduced the number of computer services supported by their system [15.2]. This did not deter one of their technical staff, Bill Cheswick, from wondering whether someone was attempting to gain unauthorized access. Cheswick wanted to determine who was trying to break in, where these people were coming from, and how they were trying to breach the existing security system.

To satisfy their curiosity, Bell Labs added some fake services to their system and wrote the necessary programs to scan the log files produced by the services. The additional services included the File Transfer Protocol[8] (FTP), *telnet* access[9], *rlogin*[10] and *rsh*[11] access, *finger*[12] capability, guest user accounts, and

---

[7] *Phone Phreaks* are people with more than a passing interest in the operations of the phone system. They have knowledge and capability to control every aspect of the telephone system. Their knowledge includes the ability to alter billing records, alter a customer's services, reroute telephone calls, and establish or disconnect service as they so desire [15.7].

[8] The *File Transfer Protocol* (FTP) is a method of copying files from one computer system to another. FTP requires the user to have an account on each of the systems. Some systems provide "anonymous", or "guest", accounts that allow anyone to access the system. The privileges given to anonymous accounts are normally restricted as there is limited control over their use [15.11].

[9] *Telnet* allows a user to log on to a computer system from across a computer network. Telnet may operate between two computers running different operating systems [15.11].

[10]*Rlogin* was initially intended for remote logins between two UNIX systems. Since its inception, however, it has been ported to include several non-UNIX systems. Rlogin requires the local user and system to be trusted by the remote system. That is, the remote system must have previously granted a user permission to access the system from their local computer. Since permission must be explicitly set, a user is often not prompted for a user name or password [15.6].

[11] The *rsh* (or rmsh) command executes a command on a remote computer system. The remote system executes the command as if it were requested locally and redirects any output back to the user. As with rlogin, rsh only executes on trusted systems [15.1, 15.3].

[12] The *finger* service allows a user to obtain information about other users. This information often includes the user's real name, their home directory, their last login time, and when the user last read and received mail. This service is under scrutiny for two reasons. First, its use may be an invasion of privacy as a user has limited control over the information returned by a finger command. Second, a bug in the service played a significant role in the deployment of the Internet Worm (see Section 15.3) [15.3].

SMTP DEBUG[13]. The FTP services were installed such that attempts to obtain the FTP password files were reported. In addition, the service would report attempts to exploit some older FTP bugs. Like the FTP services, all *telnet* and login attempts, either failed or successful, were reviewed. Since the gateway had limited access, locating unauthorized accesses would be simple. The *rsh* and *rlogin* services were completely disabled as they rely on a poor authentication system. Attempted use of these services, however, was reported. In a similar manner, the *finger* services were disabled as they can provide an intruder with useful information about the user. Guest accounts were modified and installed such that they made the system appear to be busy and also reported their activation. The final modification the group made was the introduction and alteration of an old *sendmail* hole that allowed outsiders to execute a shell script as root[14]. In the event that the *sendmail* DEBUG hole was exploited, the intruder's script would be sent to the group. In addition, each of these services attempted to locate the attacker by performing a finger to the attacker's computer. All that was left to do was wait for something to happen.

While many probes of the system did occur, it was not until seven months after the security setup had been installed that something of significance happened. On January 15, 1991 an intruder from Stanford University had located the sendmail hole and requested the AT&T system to mail back a copy of the systems password file. Having a bogus password file readily at hand, Cheswick mailed it to the intruder. The next mail he sent was to both Stanford and the Computer Emergency Response Team[15] (CERT), informing them of the evening's activities. Stanford replied that they were already aware of the problem and that the offending user account had been stolen. A few days later, Cheswick received mail that the password file had shown up in a user account in France. The intruder returned later that day.

The intruder's presence was signaled when he attempted to finger an account named 'berferd'. A few minutes later, the intruder attempted to make a new account, berferdd. Deciding that it would be worth the time to clean up after the intruder, Cheswick decided to set up the account and string the intruder along to see what he would do. This would require Cheswick to manually respond to the intruder's actions since many of the services to the system were disconnected or falsified.

---

[13] The *Simple Mail Transfer Protocol* (SMTP) is the means of communication used by computer systems to send mail back and forth. One of SMTP's few commands, DEBUG, puts the protocol into a debugging mode. This mode has the ability to allow a user to specify commands for the system to execute as opposed to performing mail related actions [15.11].

[14] *Root* — See footnote 3.

[15] The *Computer Emergency Response Team* (CERT) was established to respond to Internet-based intrusions and other security concerns. CERT attempts to analyze security vulnerabilities and distribute the necessary security patches [15.1].

For Cheswick to be able to masquerade as the system and maintain a level of consistency in his responses, he had to make a few decisions about the state and operation of the system. The first few decisions were simple, the most obvious one being that the bogus FTP password file had to be real. This led to the second decision; the password file and sendmail hole existed because general administration of this system was poor. The third decision was that the system was excruciatingly slow. Realizing that he could not respond to the attacker as fast as native services, Cheswick felt it was the most plausible reason for any delay.

Cheswick's delay in creating the berferdd account prompted the intruder (now referred to as Berferd by Cheswick) to attempt to create another account, bferd. While Cheswick installed the new account, Berferd's impatience got the best of him and he attempted to use the *talk*[16] command. Berferd's poor typing led Cheswick to decide that errors would not be reported when using the sendmail hole. Furthermore, errors in script files would halt the script. While this slowed the attacker down, he was persistent. Not wanting to support *talk*, Cheswick next decided that the system did not have the command. This led Berferd to create another account, bfrd, and attempt to rlogin into the system. After failing to talk and rlogin, Berferd requested a copy of the inetd.conf[17] file from the system. Cheswick, realizing the importance of this file, did not want to give it up nor did he want to spend the time creating a fake one. This led to the decision that the system was not deterministic. Thus, the file was never sent to Berferd. Following Berferd's next command, a failed attempt to see a list of all of the tasks the computer was performing, Cheswick decided to get CERT more involved. CERT got Cheswick in contact with the system administrators at Stanford and began to log and monitor everything. After another hour of watching Berferd poke around the system and modify the finger program, Cheswick decided to call it a night. He sent out warnings of possible disk errors and shut down the system. Approximately half an hour later, Cheswick brought the machine back on line so that mail could get through.

As expected, Berferd returned later that evening. Review of the log files revealed that Berferd decided to cover his tracks and execute the necessary command to erase all of the system files. He was unsuccessful. The next morning, Berferd returned and again tried to erase the system files. In an attempt to simulate a successful erasure of the files, Cheswick took the machine down, cleaned up the modified files and posted a general

---

[16] *Talk* allows two users to interactively communicate with each other in real-time. Each user's terminal is divided into an incoming and outgoing region. All incoming information from the remote user is displayed in one region, while everything a user types is sent and displayed in the outgoing region. The end result is the equivalent of a typed telephone call |15.6|.

[17] The inetd, or Internet services daemon, is responsible for overseeing most network operations. This is accomplished by managing several specialized services such as FTP, rlogin, and telnet. These services are listed in the inetd configuration file, inetd.conf. This file indicates the manner in which each of the services operates and how they are activated and possibly protected |15.5|.

login message that there was a disk crash. Berferd returned that afternoon, and a few more times over the next week. Cheswick's response time had dropped significantly, especially since he was often unable to respond more than once or twice a day. Berferd's persistence and patience clearly meant that he believed he had found a valuable system to penetrate.

With the help of others at AT&T Bell Laboratories, Cheswick set up a software version of a jail for Berferd. This jail would allow them to monitor Berferd's activities, learn Berferd's techniques, and warn any victims without the risk of losing valuable data. In an effort to hide the effects of being in a jail, they removed any software that would reveal the presence of the jail. They also prepared a believable, but fake, login script and file system that contained tempting files. Hopefully, Berferd would be interested enough in the files and system to spend enough time for a trace to be made.

As hoped, Berferd spent considerable time in the jail. Once inside, he was tracked to Stanford. Berferd was then traced from Stanford to a modem line. The next step was to obtain a phone trace. With much work, Stanford obtained a trace; the calls were coming from the Netherlands. Further tracing of Berferd was impossible, however, as Dutch law does not make computer hacking illegal. The tracing that did take place, however, did not stop Berferd from causing much grief at Stanford. He had compromised a large number of machines and continued to use Stanford for many months

Berferd's presence had become minimal in the AT&T Bell Lab's jail. His last login to the jail was on May 1, 1991. At that time he unsuccessfully attempted to break into a large number of other systems. Two days later, at the request of the management, the jail was shut down. Berferd failed to gain access to the system a few more times before he stopped trying.

While prosecution was not the end result of using the jail, the jail did serve to provide a reasonable means of containing an intruder and monitoring his actions. This does not mean, however, that creating a jail is the best solution to the hacker problem. As Cheswick points out, the security of the jail was far from convincing and they were somewhat surprised that the intruder seemed to either not care, or not know of its existence. Had either a more knowledgeable or determined intruder discovered that it was a jail, or find a way out, serious damage could have resulted. Had the circumstances of the Berferd attack been different, important data and network service may have been greatly affected. Before others begin to implement their own jail, the expected goals and benefits of using the jail must be carefully examined. While jails can be both interesting and entertaining, the knowledge gained from using a jail is often not worth the time and effort required to create and maintain them.

While realizing that the benefits of implementing a jail is often overshadowed by the risks, more important is the realization that once an intruder gets an account on a computer system, they will very likely gain root, or superuser, privileges shortly thereafter. Many existing operating systems and programs were never intended to employ security. Therefore, many of these same programs and operating systems contain bugs that offer an intruder the opportunity to gain unauthorized privileges. In addition, many of the security conscious programs that exist often contain little known bugs, or features, that allow obtrusive behavior to take place. It is in an organization's best interest to understand the components of their system and maintain a watchful eye over system activity.

15.3 The Internet Worm

On November 2, 1988 a Cornell graduate student released a computer worm that, within 48 hours, brought thousands of computers to a virtual standstill [15.8]. This worm began its journey from a Stanford Computer Laboratory and continuously duplicated itself onto connecting computers [15.8]. As it traveled across the Internet,[18] the worm not only reduced system performance but raised both concern that it may be malicious and confusion at its actions. Naturally, this led to widespread speculation and panic. Teams at places such as MIT and Berkeley set out to accomplish two goals: (1) determine how to stop the worm from spreading and (2) determine the actions performed by the worm to prevent them from successfully completing [15.8]. The final goal, of course, was to completely eradicate the worm from the numerous systems and fix any resulting damage.

As Berkeley and MIT were to realize, the worm was migrating from system to system by taking advantage of three holes in the Berkeley version of the UNIX operating system [15.8]. These holes allowed an infected system to send a small C program to an uninfected system and request the uninfected system to compile and run the program. Once executed, the uninfected system would download the worm from the infected system and become infected by executing it. This process was first attempted via holes in the *rsh*[19] and *rexec*[20] commands. In the event the first attempt was unsuccessful, the worm tried to exploit a hole in the *finger*[21] command, and finally a *sendmail* hole [15.8].

---

[18] The *Internet* is a large collection of computer networks and host computers globally connected to create a public network. The Internet was originally intended for academic and military pursuits. It is currently used by millions of people, including those not associated with the military nor academia.

[19] *Rsh* — See footnote 11.

[20] The *rexec* command functions much like the rsh command (see footnote 11). Rexec, however, requires the remote user to provide a password as it does not rely upon trusted hosts [15.5].

[21] *Finger* — See footnote 12.

The *rsh* and *rexec* commands allow users to gain trusted access to remote computer systems and user accounts [15.3, 15.5]. This requires both the local and remote system to be properly configured for the trusted connection. The worm's first approach at infecting a system started with an attempt to locate and utilize the trusted connections established for the *rsh* and *rexec* command. When a trusted *rexec* connection was established, the worm infected the system. In the event that the worm was unsuccessful at accessing systems via *rsh* and *rexec*, the *finger* program was attacked.

While the *finger* program exists to provide a user information concerning another user, it also had the undesirable bug of improperly interpreting its input as commands when certain conditions existed [15.3]. The worm would take advantage of this bug and force the uninfected system to open a communications channel to the attacking system. The necessary code was then transferred to the uninfected system and the machine became infected. The nature of this attack, however, was such that only VAX's running certain versions of the Berkeley UNIX operating system would be susceptible. Nonetheless, this did not deter the worm. Unsuccessful attacks against the *finger* program were followed by attacks against the *sendmail* command.

The hole exploited in the *sendmail*[22] program is similar to that exploited by Berferd on his attack of the AT&T Bell Labs computer system [15.2, 15.8]. When the debugging features of *sendmail* are turned on, a user can mail a program to the recipient with the instructions to execute the program. Unfortunately, early versions of the Berkeley UNIX and Sun Operating systems were shipped with the *sendmail* debugging features enabled. This hole, however, could be easily patched by turning *sendmail's* debugging features off.

While work was being done to find and plug the three holes exploited by the worm, teams were working to determine the ultimate purpose of the worm. Since most worms have malicious intent and this one already had put computers into a catatonic state, it was reasonable to assume this worm had a more maniacal purpose. In an attempt to determine this purpose, people began to decompile the worm program [15.9]. The decompilation of the worm, or any program for that matter, is a very arduous and time consuming process. The urgency to decompile the program grew as researchers found instructions for the worm to perform an unknown task, named "H_Clean", every twelve hours [15.6]. Fortunately, this task was only designed to clean up some of the worm's internal tables. While the worm itself was dangerous, the "H_Clean" procedure posed no direct threat.

Further decompilation of the worm revealed serious flaws in the communications between worms located on the same machine. The flaw led each instance of the worm to believe it was the first to infect a machine. This allowed each machine to get inundated with numerous copies of the worm. Thus, an infected machine would be too busy

---

[22] *Sendmail* — See footnote 1.

processing the worms to perform any meaningful task. Aside from putting machines into a catatonic state via faulty communication logic, the worm was harmless.

Once the worm had been stopped and normal system operation could return, two questions took center stage. The first was whether the worm's code should be released to the public. The second question concerned the severity of the punishment that would be placed upon the worm's author.

Once the worm was completely decompiled, debate grew over the safety of making the program listing, or source code, public. Many people, including those in the Department of Defense, believed it would only encourage others to improve and emulate the worm. Others, however, believed that release of the source code would be harmless as the holes exploited by the worm were already being patched. Furthermore, they claimed, it was not their position to dictate to the public how the source code should be used. In the end, details about the worm's operation were released; however, actual code was concealed.

Debate over an appropriate punishment for the worm's author was equal to, if not larger than, that concerning the release of the program listing. Many believed that the author should receive minimal or no punishment as there was no irreversible damage and the worm actually helped system security by identifying faults in the Internet system. Others argued that regardless of the increased awareness that resulted, the author's actions were deliberate and valuable computing time was lost. The only opinion that mattered, however, was that of the courts. On January 22, 1990 the court declared the worm's author guilty of committing a federal fraud by unleashing a worm on the Internet under 18 U.S.C. § 1030 (a)(5)(a) [15.13]. For his crimes, the author received a three year probation, a $10,000 fine, and 400 hours of community service.

15.4 Summary

This chapter presents three incidents in which computer security was breached. In each of these incidents, the principals responded differently and achieved different results. In one case, the system administrator attempted to track the intruder back to his point of origin. The administrator's success at this endeavor required as much patience, determination, and hard work as that shown by the intruder. In the second case, the administrator attempted to place the intruder into a virtual jail with the intent to monitor the intruder and learn from his actions. While this task became rather involved, it did meet with some success, albeit minimal. It is therefore suggested that this course of action be given much thought and involve much pre-planning before it is attempted. The third case did not involve chasing or tracking an intruder, but tracking the activity of a program. Fighting an inhuman opponent poses many different challenges not otherwise present in a human antagonist. For example, both the time and manner in which a computer reacts and responds is quite different from a person. Pre-programmed computer activity will be quick and consistent. These differences can be exploited in the protection and decomposition process. Regardless of whether the threat is human or not, it must be stopped.

15.5 Exercises

15.1   Many of the problems found in the Hannover Hackers incident were directly related to the inactivity of system administrators. What can an organization do to prevent such a problem in the future?

15.2   In regards to the electronic jail used to contain Berferd, what responsibility did the system administrator have to the authorized users of the system?

15.3   How would Berferd's escape from the electronic jail affect the system and its authorized users?

15.4   What would the ramifications of releasing the Internet worm code be on the computing community?

15.5   The incidents discussed in this chapter show that many computer systems are vulnerable. What responsibility does a system administrator or organization have to the users of their system? Are these responsibilities reasonable or does the user have to assume some risk in using the system?

15.6 References

15.1   Adam, J. A., "Threats and Countermeasures", *IEEE Spectrum*, IEEE/IEE Publications, Vol. 29, No. 8, August 1992, pp. 21-28.

15.2   Cheswick, W. R., and Bellovin, Steven M., *Firewalls and Internet Security*, Addison-Wesley Publishing Co., Reading, Massachusetts, 1994.

15.3   Curry, D., *UNIX System Security*, Addison-Wesley Publishing Co., Reading, Massachusetts, 1992.

15.4   Eichin, M. W. and Rochlis, J. A., "With Microscope and Tweezers: An analysis of the Internet Virus of November 1988", *MIT Technical Report*, Massachusetts Institute of Technology, February 1989.

15.5   Ferbrache, D. and Shearer, G., *UNIX Installation Security and Integrity*, Prentice Hall, Englewood Cliffs, New Jersey, 1993.

15.6   Frisch, Æ., *Essential System Administration*, O'Reilly & Associates, Sebastopol, California, 1991.

15.7   Hafner, K. and Markoff, J., *Cyberpunk: Outlaws and Hackers on the Computer Frontier*, Simon & Schuster Inc., New York, New York, 1991.

15.8   Seeley, D., "A Tour of the Worm", *University of Utah Technical Report*, The University of Utah, 1988.

15.9   Spafford, E. H., "The Internet Worm Program: An Analysis", *Purdue Technical Report CDS-TR-823*, Purdue University, November 1988.

15.10   Sterling, B., *The Hacker Crackdown: Law and Disorder on the Electric Frontier*, Bantam Books, New York, New York, 1992.

15.11   Stevens, R. W., *TCP/IP Illustrated, Volume 1*, Addison-Wesley Publishing Co., Reading, Massachusetts, 1994.

15.12   Stoll, C., "Stalking the Wily Hacker", *Communications of the ACM*, ACM Press, New York, New York, Vol. 31, No. 5, May 1988, pp. 484-496.

15.13   *West Federal Reporter Series*, 928f.2d 504 (2d Cir. 1991), West Publishing Company, Saint Paul, Minnesota, 1991.

15.7 Extended Bibliography

15.14   Denning, P. J. editor, *Computers Under Attack: Intruders, Worms, and Viruses*, Addison-Wesley, Reading, Massachusetts, 1990.

15.15   Hoffman, L. J., editor, *Rogue Programs: Viruses, Worms, and Trojan Horses*, Van Nostrand Reinhold, New York, New York, 1990.

15.16   Levin, R. B., *The Computer Virus Handbook*, McGraw-Hill, Berkeley, California, 1990.

15.17   Safford, D., Schales, D., and Hess, D., "The TAMU Security Package: An Ongoing Response to Internet Intruders in an Academic Environment", *Proceedings of the Fourth USENIX Security Symposium*, Santa Clara, California, October 1993, pp. 91-118.

15.18   Sterling, B., *The Hacker Crackdown*, Bantam Books, New York, New York, 1992.

15.19   Thompson, K., "Reflections on Trusting Trust", *Communications of the ACM*, ACM Press, Vol. 27, No. 8, August 1984, pp. 761-763.

Appendix ***A***

INFORMATION WARFARE

The term *Information Warfare* has become popular to describe what some believe to be the method for the next, or as a few believe, current, great global conflict. The battlefield for this conflict will not be found in the cities and countryside of any distant land but rather in the fields of silicon found in our computer systems. The weapons of choice will not be the bombs, bullets, tanks, and planes we have associated with warfare in this century but rather the keyboard, monitor, and telecommunication systems that permeate society. The assets being fought over will not be the lands, cities, factories, and natural resources of a country but simply information. Before one scoffs at the idea of information being both the object and means of warfare, remember that increasingly nations depend on computers and the information they process to operate not only their telecommunications and financial services but their aircraft, cars, hospitals, businesses, and homes as well. Computers store information about us ranging from medical records to our past and current financial status. Of immense importance is how closely our computer and telecommunications industries are now intertwined. Our telephone system cannot operate without computers. At the same time our modern computer networks rely on our telecommunications base to provide reliable and inexpensive connectivity throughout the world. Our society has arrived at a point that both our businesses and governments rely on the computer and telecommunications industries to the extent that we no longer can imagine effectively operating without the products and services they provide.

Two thousand years ago Sun Tzu stated in *The Art of War* that skillful warriors watched for vulnerabilities in their opponents [A.15]. Through the many centuries that followed, military strategists have endeavored to follow this sage advice. If our reliance on computers and telecommunication facilities has become so dramatic, then this is truly a vulnerability. If this is true, then the question is what exactly is the potential for the exploitation of this vulnerability? *Computers at Risk*, a 1991 report by the National Research Council, lists six trends that underlie the assessment that there is a growing potential for abuse of U.S. computer and communications systems [A.5]. The six trends listed are:

- Networks and the use of embedded computer systems are proliferating. This has greatly increased the number of individuals who now are dependent on computer systems, some without even realizing it.
- Computers have become an indispensable part of American business to the extent that computer risks can now also be considered general business risks (e.g., viruses).
- The proliferation of databases that contain highly personal information such as medical and credit records puts the privacy of every individual at risk.
- The increased use and dependence on computer systems in safety-critical applications increases the possibility that an attack on a computer system could result in the loss of human life.
- The ability of individuals to abuse computer systems is becoming more widespread and the attacks are often very sophisticated.
- The world political climate is unstable giving rise to the possibility of transnational attacks, especially at this time when the international nature of corporations and research is increasing [A.5].

These trends point to a number of vulnerabilities that we are becoming increasingly susceptible to. If we were to try and find a specific vulnerability, we have to look no further than the U.S. telecommunications network. Commercial carriers provide over 90% of the government's telecommunication services [A.1]. Since national security and emergency preparedness organizations in the U.S. rely so heavily on these telecommunication services, the government is greatly concerned with the possible threat to these public services [A.1]. During a time of national emergency, what additional damage would occur if these telecommunication services were also impaired? Intruders have already penetrated every element of these services including switching, transmission, and signaling systems as well as systems used for operation, administration, and maintenance of the public packet switched network. One example of how these systems can be manipulated came to light in 1991 with the arrest of Kevin Poulsen. Allegations against Poulsen included charges that he modified existing telephone services, monitored telephone conversations, obtained unlisted telephone numbers along with the customer's name and address, added new telephone services, and forwarded calls to other numbers at will [A.1]. This example serves to show the extent that our telecommunication services can be manipulated and how exposed they actually are.

A.1   Levels of Information Warfare

Information Warfare is not just an issue for governments to be concerned with. Just like any global conflict, this war will affect many more individuals than just the combatants themselves. In addition, just like other forms of warfare, there are several different levels on which this war may occur. Winn Schwartau has described three different levels of intensity with different goals, methods, and targets for each [A.9]. These three levels are (1) personal, (2) corporate, and (3) political.

At the Personal Level, the attack is against a specific individual. The attacker may be engaging in this warfare for a number of reasons: revenge, financial gain, mischief, or for some other dark motive. An attack at this level may be directed at the records that define who we are in society or it may be aimed at the lifelines that connect us to the world such as our phone or other utilities. An example of an attack at this level occurred in 1984 to Richard Sandza, a writer for *Newsweek* magazine. Sandza had written an article in *Newsweek* entitled "The Night of the Hackers". Some individuals didn't like what he wrote and Sandza subsequently found himself the target of a personal information attack. These individuals obtained some of his credit card account numbers and posted them along with his name and address on an electronic bulletin board [A.8]. He had not been physically attacked or harmed but information about him was used as a weapon against him.

Another example of an attack at the personal level occurred numerous times in the case of Kevin Mitnick. For a decade, Mitnick, a "hacker" and "phone-phreak", manipulated numerous computers and phone systems to gain access to information on still other systems. (For the story of Mitnick's early career in "hacking" and "phone phreaking", see [A.3].) When he became upset with an individual, they were likely to find their phone service disconnected or rerouted. He once, for example, manipulated the phone company's billing so that a hospital's $30,000 phone bill was attached to the account of an individual Mitnick disliked [A.3]. His ability to manipulate the phone system was so overwhelming that when he was arrested in 1988 for breaking into supposedly secure computer systems and stealing software, the judge in his case denied him bail and severely restricted his telephone access, allowing only numbers approved by the court. Mitnick later was convicted and spent a short time in jail. In 1995, only a few years after he was released, Mitnick was again in trouble with the law and arrested for breaking into computers, illegally using cellular telephone services, and stealing thousands of credit-card numbers from an Internet service.

The target of warfare at a corporate level is a business. The target may be information stored on corporate computer systems needed to perform daily operations or it may be the image or reputation of the company, which can be affected in numerous ways. In 1988, for example, Kevin Mitnick was turned down at the last minute for a job as a security consultant at the Security Pacific Bank in California when a tip to the bank revealed his previous criminal activities. Two weeks later a press release was sent over a news service wire to a news service in San Francisco stating that the bank had experienced a first quarter earning loss of $400 million dollars. Fortunately for the bank, a reporter called to confirm the report which was in fact totally false. The bank later estimated that the potential damage from falling stock prices and closed accounts could have easily exceeded the $400 million figure had the release become public [A.3]. Though it was never proven (in fact there was no way to prove it short of a confession by the culprit) Mitnick was the prime suspect in this incident.

Another example of corporate vulnerability to information warfare also occurred in 1988. In September of that year, Gene Burleson, a former employee of USPA & IRA, a Fort Worth-based insurance and investment company, was convicted of planting a "time bomb" program which destroyed 168,000 sales commission records [A.6]. Burleson had been having numerous conflicts with supervisors and was eventually fired from the company. A short while after his dismissal, the "time bomb" went off destroying the records. Though he tried to cover his tracks, he was discovered and arrested. While both of these examples involve a single individual attacking a company or institution, it is important to note that corporate warfare could easily involve two companies. The attacks may be similar to the ones described or they could involve one company attempting to gain knowledge of corporate secrets to gain a competitive edge. An example of corporate level information warfare between two corporations can be seen in a court case involving Borland International, Inc. and Symantec Corp. In this case, an employee of Borland was accused of sending sensitive corporate documents to Symantec via the Internet. The employee had allegedly done this after agreeing to work for Symantec [A.4].

Warfare at the political, or international, level involves a country as the victim. The attackers may be individuals acting on behalf of another country, or it may be a terrorist organization trying to gain publicity for their cause. The target may be government secrets, the military industrial complex, or the citizens. Probably the best known example of warfare at this level was the case of the West German spy ring which broke into U.S. computer systems and then sold the information they obtained to the KGB [A.3, A.12]. The ring, which was eventually broken in 1989 due mostly to the efforts of Clifford Stoll, an astronomer at the Lawrence Berkeley Labs, had gained access to numerous government computers throughout the world. It took Stoll several months to track the intruders due to the maze of systems they used to hide their trail. When finally caught, it was learned that the intruders had been selling the information obtained to the KGB for tens of thousands of dollars and small amounts of cocaine.

Another example of the potential harm that can occur to governments from *Information Warfare* occurred during the summer of 1994. A Scottish "hacker" was able to break into British Telecom databases gaining access to thousands of pages of confidential records [A.2]. The details of these records, which were subsequently published in London's newspapers, included the phone numbers for the Prime Minister and Royal Family, as well as the location of certain secret military installations and secret buildings used by the British intelligence services [A.2]. While the individual who perpetrated this break-in did not intend to cause any harm, the same information could have been obtained by a terrorist organization whose methods and goals are much more destructive.

A third example of the potential harm that a country can suffer should its information systems be targeted occurred in November of 1988. At that time a graduate student at Cornell University, Robert Morris, released what has come to be known as the **Internet Worm**. Though it appears that the resulting confusion was unintentional, the worm caused several thousand machines to grind to a halt [A.3, A.12, A.13]. Several days were spent attempting to rid the network of all traces of the worm, with numerous sites simply "unplugging" themselves from the network to avoid any possible harm. The loss in terms of the hours spent in cleaning up after the worm, as well as the lost hours of work, has been a subject of debate with some figures placing the figure well over a million dollars. The figure that was used in court during the trial of Morris was $160,000, a number which the public could more easily understand. While it appears that Morris' intentions were not to bring the Internet down, this was the result. What are the implications of this worm if we assume that there are organizations that may indeed want to disrupt the research efforts of numerous companies, universities, and government agencies? What would have been the result had a terrorist organization performed the act instead?

A.2 Weapons of Information Warfare

There are many weapons used in a conventional war. *Information Warfare* also may employ many different weapons. Obviously one of these weapons is the computer itself. An individual such as Kevin Mitnick or Robert Morris sitting at one of these tools can be the cause of much damage to computer systems and the data they process. Winn Schwartau has described a number of different weapons, which can be used to conduct information warfare [A.10]. Among these are:

- Malicious Software
- Sniffers
- Electromagnetic eavesdropping equipment
- Computer chips
- HERF Guns
- EMPT Bombs

We are already aware of the damage that can be caused by malicious software such as viruses, time bombs, worms, and Trojan Horses. Usually we think of this type of software as being developed by a disgruntled employee or college students with a bit too much time on his hands. Usually this type of software "announces" its presence when it performs its destructive action, leaving no doubt that the system and user have been the victim of some form of malicious attack. What if, instead, the malicious software was carefully designed by professionals with the intent of damaging a specific corporation? A virus could be written, for example, to only attach itself to a specific piece of software, such as a spreadsheet or database management system from a certain vendor. It could also be written in such a manner that it did not activate its destructive segment until a long latency period had elapsed allowing it time to infect a large number of systems. Then, when it did activate, instead of doing something extremely visible, such as reformatting a disk, it might just change a few bits here and there. Nothing major, just enough to cause the user to become frustrated with the software package. Eventually, the users of the software would become so disenchanted that they would stop using it and might instead purchase a rival vendor's package. Malicious software designed and engineered by professionals, instead of the unorganized activity of current "hobbyists", would have an even greater impact if its target was the software that controls our networks and computer systems themselves. We have only just begun to see the potential impact malicious software can have.

Sniffers are used to "sniff" or monitor a network. They listen to the traffic that is sent between systems in a network searching for specific packets or types of packets. They could also be used to garner unencrypted mail or files sent between users or even to grab and modify them before they are sent along their way. The widespread use of encryption can reduce the impact of this form of attack.

Electromagnetic eavesdropping, also known as TEMPEST (Transient Electromagnetic Pulse Emanation Standard), is designed to take advantage of the fact that electronic equipment emits signals that can be picked up with the appropriate equipment. This means that an individual can sit in one room and pick up the information being displayed on the terminal or printer in the next room. This type of information warfare can be used to collect data files as they are being displayed, or even passwords and userids to be exploited later. Shielding the computer equipment can help protect against this form of warfare. This type of attack has also been referred to as "van Eck phreaking" after Win van Eck, a scientist in the Netherlands, demonstrated its potential [A.4].

"Chipping" is the hardware version of malicious software. It involves designing computer chips that contain back doors or other hidden features not known to the users of the chips. They might even be designed to display a specific electromagnetic "footprint" or "signature" which would allow other equipment (or weapons) to locate (or home in on) them. (Some have speculated that this type of information warfare was employed by the United States against Iraq during the Gulf War [A.10].)

High Energy Radio-Frequency (HERF) guns are designed to exploit the same effect used by TEMPEST equipment except in an offensive manner. They are designed to emit a burst of high energy at high frequency in order to overload the circuits of computers and other electronic equipment. These devices have reportedly been able to disrupt the operation of computer systems at ranges up to 300 yards [A.4, A.10]. We have all probably seen this phenomenon in operation without realizing its information warfare potential. How often have we noticed that certain pieces of electrical equipment have interfered with our televisions, or how often have we had our radio station reception interfered with as we drove near high power cables? The same phenomenon, employed by terrorists in a van packed with this type of weapon, could be used to disrupt the operation of thousands of computer systems and consequently adversely affect numerous companies if the weapon was employed in an area such as Wall Street [A.4].

Electromagnetic Pulse Transformer (EMPT) bombs take advantage of technology learned in the design and testing of nuclear weapons. These bombs are designed to fuse the chips of our computer systems and other electronic equipment together with a high powered electromagnetic pulse. The possibility of this form of attack has been known for a number of years as is evidenced by the U.S. military's efforts to shield its most important equipment from the possible effects of a nuclear weapon.

A.3   Summary

The widespread use of computer systems and networks in our society has led us to a point where the information they contain, and the services they offer, can be used as weapons against us. This is not only true for us on a personal basis, but is true for corporations protecting their industrial and trade secrets, as well as countries with their military and diplomatic secrets. The weapons and warriors of this new type of warfare include programmers working on computer systems, terrorists with HERF guns, and nations employing EMPT bombs.

All of this leads us to the question of what is to be done about the possibility of information warfare? Should we be considering the establishment of what amounts to CyberCops as we expand the power of our law enforcement agencies in cyberspace [A.14] or instead should an awareness program be initiated to insure that the dangers of information warfare are known and understood by everyone? In reality, the answer is probably a little of both.

A.4   Exercises

A.1   Assume the role of an *Information Warrior*. List a number of targets that
       would be available to you in a Personal Level conflict.

A.2   Again assume the role of an *Information Warrior* but this time determine
       targets for a Corporate Level conflict.

A.3   Once again assume the role of an *Information Warrior* terrorist now intent
       on carrying out warfare on the International or Political Level. What are your
       targets now?

A.4   From a military perspective, what Information Warfare targets exist whose
       destruction or disruption could affect an enemy's fighting capabilities while
       enhancing yours (consider U.S. and Coalition Force examples during the Gulf
       War)?

A.5   How could "chipping" be used to insert covert channels into a computer
       system?

A.6   Consider the infamous bombing of the World Trade Center. Economic losses
       due to the disruption of business communication exceeded the actual physical
       damage to the building. What implications does this have for *Information
       Warfare* ?

A.5   References

A.1   Frizzell, J., Phillips, T., and Groover, T., "The Electronic Intrusion Threat
       To National Security & Emergency Preparedness Telecommunications: An
       Awareness Document", *Proceedings of the 17th National Computer Security
       Conference*, Baltimore, Maryland, October 1994, pp. 378-388.

A.2   Goldstein, E., "Inspiration", *2600 The Hacker Quarterly*, Winter 1994-95,
       Vol. 11, No. 4, pp. 4-5.

A.3   Hafner, K. and Markoff, J., *Cyberpunk: Outlaws and Hackers on the
       Computer Frontier*, Simon & Schuster, New York, New York, 1991.

A.4   Kabay, M.E., "Prepare Yourself for Information Warfare", *Computerworld*, Leadership Series, March 20, 1995, pp. 1-7.

A.5   National Research Council, *Computers at Risk: Safe Computing In the Information Age*, National Academy Press, Washington, DC, 1991.

A.6   Reese, L., "Computer Crime and Espionage: Similarities and Lessons Learned", *Proceedings of the 12th National Computer Security Conference*, Baltimore, Maryland, October 1989, pp. 389-395.

A.7   Sandberg, J., "Undetected Theft of Credit-Card Data Raises Concern About On-Line Security", *The Wall Street Journal*, February 17, 1995, pg. B2.

A.8   Sandza, R., "The Revenge of the Hackers", *Newsweek*, December 10, 1984, pg. 81.

A.9   Schwartau, W., "Information Warfare:™ Waging and Winning Conflict in Cyberspace, An Outline for a National Information Policy", *Proceedings of the IFIP Sec'94 Conference*, Curacao, June 1994.

A.10   Schwartau, W., "Information Warfare", Keynote Address, *IFIP Sec '94 Conference*, Curacao, June 27, 1994.

A.11   Seline, C. J., "Eavesdropping on the Electromagnetic Emanations of Digital Equipment: The Laws of Canada, England and the United States", 1990 Draft Document, available via anonymous *ftp* at *ftp.funet.fi, /pub/doc/security/pyrite.rutgers.edu/tempest.cjs*, March 24, 1995.

A.12   Stoll, C., *The Cuckoo's Egg*, Doubleday, New York, NY, 1989.

A.13   Stoll, C., "An Epidemiology of Viruses & Network Worms", *Proceedings of the 12th National Computer Security Conference*, Baltimore, Maryland, October 1989, pp. 369-377.

A.14   Sussman, V., "Policing Cyberspace", *U.S. News and World Report*, January 23, 1995, pp. 54-60.

A.15   Tzu, S., *The Art of War*, translated by Thomas Cleary, Boston, Massachusetts, 1988.

A.6   Extended Bibliography

A.16   Brewin, B. and Sikorovsky, E., "Information Warfare: DISA stings uncover
            computer security flaws", *Federal Computer Week*, February 6, 1995, pp.
            1, 45.

A.17   Denning, D., "Concerning Hackers Who Break into Computer Systems",
            Proceedings of the 13th National Computer Security Conference,
            Washington, DC, October 1990, pp. 653-664.

A.18   Green, J. and Sisson, P., "The 'Father Christmas Worm' ", *Proceedings of
            the 12th National Computer Security Conference*, Baltimore, Maryland,
            October 1989, pp. 359-368.

A.19   Grier, P., "Information Warfare", *Air Force Magazine*, March 1995,
            pp. 34-37.

A.20   Kabay, M., "Information Warfare Could Be More Than Fiction", *Network
            World*, September 6, 1993, pg.32.

A.21   McDonald, C., "Computer Security Bloopers, Bleeps, Blunders", *Summary of
            Papers Presented at the Tenth DOE Computer Security Group Conference*,
            Albuquerque, New Mexico, May 1987, pp. 35-45.

A.22   Schwartau, W., "Hackers Indicted for Infiltrating Corporate Networks",
            INFOWORLD, July 27, 1992, pg. 56.

A.23   Sterling, B., *The Hacker Crackdown: Law and Disorder on the Electronic
            Frontier*, Bantam, New York, New York, 1992.

A.24   Smith, J., "No Harm Intended: A Behavioral Analysis of Young Hackers",
            Proceedings of the 8th National Computer Security Conference,
            Gaithersburg, Maryland, October 1985, pp. 36-42.

A.25   Schwartau, W., *Infomation Warfare: Chaos on the Electronic
            Superhighway*, Thunder's Mouth Press, New York, New York, 1994.

A.26   Watts, J., "Computer-Related Fraud in the Banking and Insurance Industries",
            Proceedings of the 7th DOD/NBS Computer Security Conference,
            Gaithersburg, Maryland, September 1984, pp. 207-213.

INDEX

*-property 40, 41, 44
.rhosts file 163, 173, 235, 237

access control 32, 145, 147
Access Control Lists (ACLs) 79-81
access controls
    access control lists 79-81
    capabilities based 78
    file passwords 77
    protection bits 82
access modes 75
access monitors 232, 233
accountability 45
action based intrusion detection 97
administrative security 25, 26
AFFIRM 38
American National Standards Institute
    (ANSI) 57, 58
application layer 143
application level gateways 170
assurance 45
assurance rating 256, 258, 260, 262
assured usage 146
asymmetric cryptosystems 210
at 120
audit data 47
audit logs 118, 122-127
audit record 100
audit trails 4, 91, 124-128, 133
auditable events 92
auditable information 92
auditing 32
authentication 32, 145, 146
authentication system 53, 60

authorized use 3
availability 2

B-spline functions 64
bastion host 166
Bell and LaPadula Model 39, 42, 48
Berferd 267, 271-276
biff 135
biometric authentication 62, 65
biometric keys 54, 60
biometrics 60, 151
block ciphers 203
BPL 10-13, 16, 17, 19
broadcast 140
burden 15, 17
Burleson 284

Caesar Cipher 194
calculator authentication 59
Canadian Trusted Computer Product
    Evaluation Criteria (CTCPEC)
    251, 253, 257-263
capability list 78, 79
cascading problem 153
CC (see Common Criteria)
CERT (see Computer Emergency
    Response Team)
chipping 287
choke 170
chosen-plaintext 208
ciphertext 193
circuit level gateways 169
Clark-Wilson model 41, 42, 48

classes 254, 261, 262
cleartext 193
Clipper Chip 208
Common Criteria (CC) 251, 259-263
communications integrity 150
component connection view 153
compromise protection 150
Computer Emergency Response Team
    (CERT) 16, 109, 119, 120, 272,
    273
confidentiality 2, 145, 147, 152
confinement property 40
connection-oriented service 143
connectionless service 143
Constrained Data Items (CDIs) 43
continuity of operations 151
Cooperating Security Manager (CSM)
    107
countermeasure 17
countermeasures 9, 17, 18, 21
covert channels 32, 254
    storage channels 32
    timing channels 32
cron 120
cryptanalysis 193
cryptography 32, 193
cryptology 193
CSM (see Cooperating Security
    Manager)
CTCPEC (see Canadian Trusted
    Computer Product Evaluation
    Criteria)

damage assessment 118, 123, 124,
    139
damage control 117, 118, 123, 135
Data Encryption Standard (DES) 203
data integrity 145, 148

data link layer 143
decryption 193
delegation of authority 157
denial of service 3, 122, 150, 151,
    235, 238
DES (see Data Encryption Standard)
DIDS (see Distributed Intrusion
    Detection System)
Diffie-Hellman Algorithm 210
Digital Signature Algorithm (DSA)
    216
Digital Signature Standard (DSS) 216
digital signatures 215
digraphs 96
Discretionary Access Controls 46, 48,
    83, 84
Distributed Intrusion Detection
    System (DIDS) 105
distributed systems security 155
Dockmaster 100
documentation 45
Domain Name Service (DNS) 170
doorknob rattling 103
Drawbridge 172

Electromagnetic Pulse Transformer
    (EMPT) 287
emacs 125, 268
EMPT (see Electromagnetic Pulse
    Transformer)
EMPT Bombs 286
encryption 147, 193
end-to-end encryption 148, 202
Escrowed Encryption Initiative 208
Escrowed Encryption Standard 208
ESIGN 216
ethics 5
execution domains 30

facial profile authentication 66
facial profiles 54, 60
families 262
FC (see Federal Criteria)
feature extraction 63
Federal Criteria (FC) 253, 259-263
file passwords 77
File Transfer Protocol (FTP) 125,
    134, 164, 226, 271-273
finger 134, 135, 164, 271, 272, 276
fingerprint authentication 65, 67
fingerprint cleaning 63
fingerprints 53, 54, 60, 62-64
    ridge ends 63, 64
    ridge gaps 63
firewall gateway 165
firmware 27
forgery 62, 64, 70
forks 64
FTP (see File Transfer Protocol)
functional rating 261
functionality rating 256

gateways
    application level 170
    circuit level 169
    firewall 165
    packet filtering 165
    screened host 166
global connection view 153
Goguen-Meseguer model 44, 45, 48
Gypsy Verification Environment 38

hand geometry 54, 60, 67–69
Hannover Hackers 267
Haystack 101
HERF 287
HERF Guns 286

Hierarchical Development
    Methodology (HDM) 38
H_Clean 276, 277

IDEA 206
IDES 97
inetd.conf 273
information flow controls 76, 86
Information Technology Security
    Evaluation Criteria (ITSEC)
    251-253, 255-263
Information Warfare 281-285
    levels 283-285
    weapons 285-287
informational keys 54
initiator 147
insider threat 16
integrated circuits 58
integrity 2
integrity check value 149
Integrity Verification Procedures
    (IVPs) 43
interconnection rule 153
International Standards Organization
    (ISO) 57, 58, 142
Internet 275, 277
Internet Worm 267, 275, 285
intruder profiling 96
intrusion detection systems 91, 93
irreversible public-key cryptosystem
    210
ISO (see International Standards
    Organization)
ITSEC (see Information Technology
    Security Evaluation Criteria)

Kernelized Secure Operating System
    (KSOS) 41

key 194
key distribution 201
Key Escrow 208
keystroke analysis 96
Knapsack Algorithms 211

link 135
link encryption 148, 202
loss 15, 17

magnetic cards 54, 56, 64
malicious code 225, 231, 242, 247
  trojan horses 241-246
  viruses 225-234
  worms 235-240
malicious program 225, 247
malicious software 285, 286
Mandatory Access Controls 46–
  48, 83
masquerading 94
message authentication 3
MIDAS 100
military security structure 39
Mitnick, Kevin 283–285
Morris, Robert T. 285
multi-level security 46, 47
MULTICS 41, 80, 100
MX record 170

NADIR 107
netlog 172
netstat 135
network intrusion detection 103
network layer 143
network management 152
Network Security Monitor (NSM) 104

Network Trusted Computing Base
  (NTCB) 150
Network-user IDentification (NID) 106
NFS 135
NIS 135
"no read up" 39
"no write down" 40, 44
non-repudiation 3, 146, 151
NSM (see Network Security Monitor)

object reuse 29, 46
one time pads 200
Open Systems Interconnection (OSI)
  142
Orange Book (see TCSEC)
Originator Controlled (ORCON) 83
Owner/Group/World 82

packet filtering gateways 165
pass phrases 54
passwords 4, 53, 54, 151
patching 117, 120, 123, 133, 134
personnel security 25, 26
phone phreaks 271
phonemes 61
physical keys 53, 54, 60
physical layer 142
physical security 25
pirated software 242
plaintext 193
point-to-point 141
presentation layer 143
privacy 5
Propagation of Local Risk 155
protection bits 82
protection table 75
proxy gateway 170, 175

public key cryptography 210

questionnaires 54, 55, 123

reference monitor 31
remote execution 134
remote login 134
remote shell 134
retinal prints 54, 60
reversible public-key cryptosystem
     210
rexec 125, 134, 135, 166, 276
rhosts 163, 173, 235, 237
ridge ends 63, 64
ridge gaps 63
ridges 63, 64
risk 15, 16
risk analysis 9–11, 16, 17, 21
rlogin 125, 134, 135, 147, 164, 166,
     271–273
root 127, 131, 268, 272, 275
ROT13 195
router 165
RSA 213
rsh 125, 134, 135, 271, 272, 275,
     276

S-Boxes 206
safeguards 9, 15-19
sampling 61
Sandza 283
screened host gateway 166
screened subnet 168
Secure Ada Target 45
Secure Communications Processor
     (SCOMP) 41
security calculator 54, 59

security domains 30, 147
security kernel 30, 32
security levels 39
security models 32, 37, 38
     Bell and LaPadula 39, 42, 48
     Clark-Wilson 41, 42, 48
     Goguen-Meseguer 44, 45, 48
security policy 45
selective routing 147
sendmail 125, 268, 272, 276
sendmail DEBUG 272
sensitivity labels 47
separation of duty 41
session layer 143
shadow password files 123, 129, 132,
     133
shareware 242
signature analysis 60, 69
signature authentication 69, 70
simple security property. 39
single use password 55
Skipjack 208
smartcards 54, 56, 58, 59, 151
SMTP DEBUG 271
sniffers 286
specification 37
sprayd 135
Stoll, Clifford 284
stream ciphers 203
substitution ciphers 194
sunrpc 166
superincreasing sequence 211
superuser 119, 124, 125, 127, 131,
     275
susceptibility 15, 17, 21
symmetric cryptosystem 203
systat 135

talk 273

TAMUSC 117
target 147
TCP 134
TCP WRAPPER 164
tcpmux 135
TCSEC (see Trusted Computer
     System Evaluation Criteria)
telnet 125, 164, 271, 272
TEMPEST 286
Texas A&M University 117, 118, 172
TFTP (see Trivial File Transfer
     Protocol)
threat 9, 15-17, 21
tiger scripts 173
time bomb 286
timesharing 29
TIS Firewall Toolkit 173
traffic flow
     analysis 148, 202
     confidentiality 152
     integrity 146, 148
tranquillity principle 40
Transformation Procedures (TPs) 43
Transmission Control Protocol 134
transport layer 143
transposition ciphers 201
trigraphs 96
Trivial File Transfer Protocol (TFTP)
     134, 135, 166, 172
Trojan horse 84, 94, 120, 124, 225,
     241-247, 268, 286
Trusted Computer System Evaluation
     Criteria (TCSEC) 45, 47, 251–
     260, 262, 263
Trusted Computing Base (TCB) 46

Trusted Information Systems (TIS)
     173
Trusted Network Interpretation (TNI)
     149
trusted subjects 41
tunnel 172
TYMNET 270
typing signature 96
UDP 134
Unconstrained Data Items (UDIs) 43
UNIX 82, 126, 132, 134, 147, 163,
     164, 174, 235, 237, 275, 276
user authentication 53
user profiling 95
uucp 135

valleys 63
van Eck phreaking 286
VAX 276
verification 35
vi 125
Vigenere Ciphers 197
Vigenere Table 197
virus 95, 225-236, 242-247, 282, 286
virus identifier 230, 231, 234
VMS 80
voice print 54, 60-64
vulnerabilities 9
vulnerability 15, 17

well-formed transactions 41
World Wide Web (WWW) 30
worm 225, 235-242, 244, 247, 275-
     277, 286